OUTLAWS with BADGES

Written by Laurence J. Yadon and Robert Barr Smith

PELICAN PUBLISHING COMPANY
Gretna 2013

The word "Pelican" and the depiction of a pelican are
trademarks of Pelican Publishing Company, Inc., and are
registered in the U.S. Patent and Trademark Office.

Library of Congress Cataloging-in-Publication Data

Yadon, Laurence J., 1948-
  Outlaws with badges / by Laurence J. Yadon and Robert Barr Smith.
  pages cm
Includes bibliographical references and index.
  ISBN 978-1-4556-1658-9 (paperback : alkaline paper)—ISBN 978-1-4556-1659-6 (e-book) 1. Outlaws—West (U.S.)—Biography. 2. Peace officers—West (U.S.)—Biography. 3. Frontier and pioneer life—West (U.S.) 4. West (U.S.)—History—1860-1890. 5. West (U.S.)—Biography. I. Smith, Robert B. (Robert Barr), 1933- II. Title.
  F594.Y33 2013
  364.15'52092278—dc23
                                      2012029882

Printed in the United States of America

Published by Pelican Publishing Company, Inc.
1000 Burmaster Street, Gretna, Louisiana 70053

OUTLAWS with BADGES

Contents

Preface

Our quartet—*100 Oklahoma Outlaws, Lawmen, and Gangsters; 200 Texas Outlaws and Lawmen; Ten Deadly Texans;* and *Arizona Gunfighters* coauthored by Dan Anderson—focused on the emergence of law and order in Oklahoma, Texas, eastern New Mexico, and Arizona. And *Old West Swindlers* examined fraud, graft, and corruption on the American frontier.

Outlaws with Badges was prompted by a single question posed in many ways during interviews, speeches, and book signings over the past six years. No, most Old West lawmen weren't criminals, but these pages present some former outlaws turned good, former lawmen gone bad, and some of the lawmen who moonlighted as robbers and rustlers. And we couldn't include all of them.

We have made every effort to provide the most accurate, historically accepted version of events, while providing credible, alternative versions or interpretations either in the text or footnotes. Names and places are spelled in accordance with common modern usage, with alternatives found in primary sources placed in parentheses or referenced in footnotes. Every effort has been made to reference the generally accepted dates of events described here, with alternatives referenced or footnoted as appropriate.

Robert Barr Smith (*Tough Towns, Outlaw Tales of Oklahoma*), who previously guided our efforts as a consulting editor, contributed the prologue and first eight chapters of this work.

Judgments made concerning the relative credibility of competing sources, dates, and any errors sifting fact from mythology have been our own.

Prologue

Bad Guys with Badges:
A Vast Amount of Trouble

Western outlaws were losers, by and large, as criminals are today. As a rule, they weren't very bright either, which helps account for them even being outlaws. But they were tough, ruthless men, and they rode in a largely trackless, sparsely populated, rugged land that gave them plenty of shelter from the law.

The other side of the coin was the lawmen. They were just as hardy and usually somewhat smarter than the men—and the occasional woman—they pursued. The trouble was that the lawmen were generally ill paid—U.S. Deputy Marshals were paid by the arrest, for instance, and bore their own expenses.

If they had to kill an outlaw who tried to kill them—except on a "dead or alive" warrant—they even ended up paying for the burial of the bad man's remains. Moreover, their lives were in danger every day. For instance, more than sixty lawmen were killed west of Arkansas riding for Judge Parker's court in Fort Smith.

Long hours on horseback in all kinds of weather, constant danger, and miserable pay made the outlaw life sometimes seem an attractive alternative to law enforcement. Every outlaw, or would-be outlaw, dreamed of the Big Strike, financing a secure life of leisure in Bolivia, Mexico, or some place else far away. It is little wonder, then, that some peace officers turned their coats. On the other hand, the outlaw who survived often longed for respectability, the comparative normalcy of a real town, and a real bed to which he could go home.

It took a tough man to catch a tough man, and there was no advantage in requiring a background check for honesty. There was always a market for peace officers, and as long as they did the job nobody cared much about their past. In fact, a certain reputation, a "rep," was often a handy attribute: the lawless were less likely to take a chance on tangling with a known fast gun.

Some of them managed to play both lawman and outlaw at once. Take Burt Alvord, who served as a deputy to tough John Slaughter, the man who cleaned up Cochise County in southern Arizona. Alvord was also a town constable and a train robber, sometimes simultaneously, until he decided being a bad man was a full-time job.

The same was true of Bill Stiles, who followed Alvord to the wild side and also served as a town constable, until both he and Alvord went bad as a full-time career. The wanted pair even ordered two coffins delivered in Tombstone for their "funerals." However, the law wasn't having any of the tales that both men had passed on, and the pursuit continued, eventually snapping up Alvord.

Stiles later changed his name and went back to being a lawman; ironically, he ate a bullet in 1908 while lawfully employed. About the same thing happened to Matt Burts, sometime deputy town constable and sometime train robber with Alvord and company. Burts spent some time in prison for robbery and then came in second in a gunfight in 1908 or 1925, depending on the source. Whatever the year, he was permanently dead—the usual fate of the western bad man.

All Wool and a Yard Wide

However, this was not the case for Christopher Columbus

Perry—who called himself Charles—a formidable lawman, a quick and accurate shot, and a cool hand in a crisis. Unlike most of the lawmen who went bad, he was also smart enough to realize that there wasn't much advantage in turning outlaw when the law would turn around and chase him.

Perry was city marshal of Roswell, New Mexico, and was famous for being a storied, phenomenal shot with his rifle—one head shot in darkness exterminated one of the criminal brothers Griffin at a measured 126 paces. That made it a clean sweep for the law, because Perry had already put an end to Griffin's brother a little earlier that same night.

Perry's reputation as an effective, fearless officer bloomed; he became county sheriff, then a deputy United States marshal, and the newspapers started comparing him to Pat Garrett. Perry was one of the officers who unsuccessfully worked on the mysterious disappearance and probable murder of prominent lawyer Albert Fountain and his eight-year-old son.

Perry was also the subject of the most astonishing claptrap ever written about the world of fast guns. It is well worth quoting:

> [he] carries his revolver in front of his belt instead of behind, so that by a quick muscular movement of the stomach he can toss the pistol into his hand before his adversary has time to draw on him.[1]

Anyone who believes this is sure to love the Tooth Fairy and the Easter Bunny, as well; however, this tale does not detract from the real lethality of Perry the lawman.

There was also a dark side to Perry. Dee Harkey, a very tough hombre in his own right, commented that Perry "was mean as hell and liked to kill fellers." Ultimately, Perry left law enforcement, not to stick up banks or stagecoaches, but to make money the easy way. He simply disappeared, and some $7,600 in county tax money disappeared with him. Also going with him was the inevitable mysterious woman who has never been identified. There is some reliable evidence that he showed up once in Capetown, South Africa. All that remained after that was rumor and surmise, including tales about his involvement in the Boer War. The mystery endures to this day.

A Matter of Business

Pussycat Nell was an enterprising businesswoman as the madam of a thriving brothel in Beer City, just across the Kansas line in "No Man's Land." This curious appellation was the nickname given to what is now the Oklahoma panhandle, for in those wild days it was literally lawless. Because of a surveyor's error in laying out state borders, no state or territory owned it. But it had one great advantage for the enterprising business man or woman: Kansas was dry in those days and No Man's Land wasn't. Carrie Nation's ax-wielding sorties at the head of her Anti-Saloon League had seriously crippled a man's chance to get an honest drink up in Kansas, and the thirsty men of Kansas sought an oasis at which they could have an honest drink.

This spelled opportunity for Beer City. Nearby Liberal, Kansas, was a railhead town, with the usual host of cowboys eager for booze and female companionship.

Beer City did not have a school or a church, but there was plenty of the sort of entertainment a tough young cowhand craved. Business was so good that some of the soiled doves in southern Kansas commuted to work in Beer City in a hack that made a convenient daily trip.

But there was one fly in Nell's ointment. His name was Lew Bush; he was the town marshal, who was apparently self-appointed. He called himself the law in Beer City, and, because he apparently was unpaid, he casually levied on all the businesses in town for his livelihood, which included not only his meals and his liquor but also his female entertainment.

Nell had her house on the second floor of the Yellowsnake Saloon, a convenient arrangement for cowboys putting away tarantula juice at the bar downstairs. All would have gone well had it not been for the intrusions of Bush. Nell was an astute businesswoman, and the time taken from her girls by Bush could have been rented to paying clients. Nell was not a retiring type and made her displeasure known. Apparently considerable friction followed, and Nell solved the Bush problem by poking her shotgun through a window of her establishment and giving Bush both barrels, of which he expired.

No punishment was ever handed out to Nell. Nobody much missed Bush, considering what he was. Furthermore, he was known to do some rustling on the side. The whole matter was a demonstration of the classic two-fold western attitude toward the sudden departure of well-known pains in the tuchus. First, "he had it coming," and second, "who cares?"

Sanctimonious Assassin

"Good riddance" was surely the consensus about the passing of Jim Miller, better known as "killin' Jim" or "Deacon Jim." He played lawman for a while, but his chief business was assassination—he was a killer for hire. What made him especially contemptible was his custom of faithfully attending church between expeditions to kill people. That habit, plus his customary sober, black, broadcloth suits and immaculate white shirts led to his nickname of "Deacon."

Miller started going wrong early. There is substantial evidence that at the tender age of eight he may have murdered his grandparents, and at seventeen he was convicted of the murder of his brother-in-law. He was lucky on appeal. The judgment was reversed, and he was never retried. But he learned nothing.

His associations were with the dregs of society: Mannen Clements, cousin to the deadly John Wesley Hardin; he even married Clements' sister. He hired on as a deputy sheriff in Pecos, Texas—it was wonderful cover for his rustling sideline until he was caught stealing mules and promptly fired by Sheriff Bud Frazer

In the summer of 1892, Miller opposed Frazer in the next election for sheriff and lost, but it had no effect on his reputation. He ran for city marshal, won, and began to surround himself with hardcases much like himself. Finally, in May of 1893, the gang went too far in pushing the locals around, and Sheriff Frazer, who was away at the time, hurried back to town. He came with Texas Rangers, too, warned by a citizen that Miller intended to kill him when he stepped off the train. Miller lost his chance and his job.

The quarrel went on simmering, until Frazer had enough and ambushed Miller, putting three slugs into his enemy's chest in a space no larger than a coffee cup. Miller should have been dead, but he wasn't. The rumor developed that he wore a steel plate under his omnipresent black frock coat. In spite of Miller's violence, theft, and the probability that one of his cronies had murdered the man who warned Frazer, many citizens of Pecos still supported Miller because of his sanctimonious behavior and a public "conversion" he staged.

Frazer lost the next election and left town. That should have been the end of the feud, but when Miller found out Frazer was visiting a nearby town, he stalked the ex-sheriff to a saloon where Frazer was playing cards and put both barrels of a shotgun into him. Miller was acquitted, partly it seems, because of his very public participation in his church.

At least by now, and probably earlier, Miller had begun his

career as a killer for hire. He was even beginning to "predict" the death of his next target. For instance, he forecast the death of a man who testified against him, thus:

> Joe Earp turned states evidence on me, and no man can do that and live. Watch the papers, boy and you'll see where Joe Earp died.

He seems to have somehow gotten arsenic into the prosecutor's food, too, although the initial diagnosis was "peritonitis."

Miller moved on to Fort Worth, opened a rooming house with his wife and, of course, joined the church. Meanwhile he was offering to kill sheepmen at the bargain price of $150 a head. He expanded his line of work to include farmers—those troublesome fences—and even murdered a lawyer who had successfully represented several farms against big cattle interests.

He hired on to kill a U.S. deputy marshal at the behest of a couple of real dirtbags, the Pruitt boys. Again it was a shotgun in the night. Miller survived this one, too, although he spent some time in the calabozo prior to trial. Once that inconvenience passed, he hired on to kill really big game out in New Mexico: Pat Garrett, the lawman who had rid the world of Billy the Kid. This was a big payday: $1,500 for the job.

His next job was an even bigger prize: $2,000 to kill a rancher from Ada, Oklahoma, a man named Gus Bobbit, as the result of a long-standing feud with a couple of unscrupulous saloon owners. Miller held up his end, blowing Bobbitt into eternity with his favorite weapon. But this time he left enough of a trail for the law to follow.

The trail first led them to a nephew of Miller, a youngster named Williamson. He admitted that he had sheltered Miller before and after the killing and had loaned him a horse; but, Williamson said, "he said he'd kill me if I talked"—quite believable, knowing Miller. Williamson was duly arrested, along with a go-between, and his two employers were lured back out of Texas with a simple telegram, ostensibly sent by Miller: "come to Ada at once. Need $10,000. Miller."

They came from their safe haven south of the Red River and ended up in jail also. But, before a trial could be held, the good citizens of Ada had already had enough of Miller. Jailed, he was putting on the dog in a most irritating way by having steak sent to him twice a day, having his cell floor carpeted, and regularly having the barber call on him, figuratively thumbing his nose at the citizenry. This did not sit well with them.

The finale came when the town learned that Miller had retained the great Moman Pruiett to defend him. Pruiett was a legend in the southwest. He had never had a client executed, and before Pruiett was through he would compile an astonishing record of 304 acquittals in 342 murder cases. This was the last straw; the citizens were almost certain that this mass murderer would go free again. The town of Ada wasn't having any.

And so a large band of good citizens went down to the jail one night, overpowered the guards, and extracted Miller, his two employers, and the go-between who had seen to the payoff. All four were dragged to a nearby stable and strung up from the rafters with little ceremony and nothing much that passed for due process of law. Before he died, Miller actually boasted of his crimes: "Let the record reflect," he is said to have bragged, "That I've killed fifty-one men."

Officially, nobody ever learned who the hangmen were; nobody tried very hard. An Ada historian put it succinctly, and probably spoke for the whole town:

> The forty-odd men who took in the lynching were honorable men, for the most, who had patiently endured desperado rule until it could no longer be tolerated. . . . [I]t can be written down as the one mob action in America entirely justified in the eyes of God and man.

Miller and his three co-conspiritors hanging from a barn rafter in Ada

And if that pronouncement seems somewhat presumptuous when applied to God, it sure expressed the townspeople's sentiments that Ada was a cleaner place.

Four Sixes to Beat

There was not much to like about John Selman, whose early life in Arkansas and various Texas towns, including notorious Fort Griffin, was relatively peaceful, as far as is known. Fort Griffin was a wild town, and there Selman made a couple of dubious friends: a prostitute, intriguingly named Hurricane Minnie Martin, and John Larn, a thoroughly rotten type who specialized in rustling.

Minnie became Selman's lover, although he already had a wife and children. Larn gets a chapter of his own in this book, so suffice it to say here that as far as anybody could ever tell he had, as the judges sometimes say, no redeeming social value whatsoever.

Selman bought a saloon in wild Fort Griffin but made most of his living rustling with Larn. When Larn passed to his reward,

Selman and his brother—called Tom Cat—moved to New Mexico and went into the holdup business. This lasted until the Army got tired of it, at which point the Selman boys took up rustling out in west Texas.

Meanwhile, Larn went into the butcher business—one can easily guess where and how he got the raw material. For the next few years Selman was in and out of Mexico, and in and out of shady operations. Then Selman abruptly turned to the side of the angels as constable of El Paso. He enjoyed no peaceful term in office. He killed Bass Outlaw—a deputy U.S. marshal who turned savage when full of booze, which was as often as not.

Then, in 1895, he eliminated the deadly John Wesley Hardin. Hardin was a famous badman, starting at the age of eleven when he very nearly stabbed another boy to death. He had been leaving a trail of corpses across the southwest ever since, killing at least twelve men, probably more.

Selman took no chances—Hollywood gets it all wrong when it comes to old West gunfights: there wasn't any of this walking stiff-legged up to impossibly close range, saying something stupid like "this town ain't big enough for both of us," and then blazing away from the hip. Wyatt Earp is said to have commented that it was not the first shot that counted, as much as the first aimed shot, something entirely different. Earp himself has been portrayed in umpteenth movies and television shows, perhaps none capturing his story as well as *Tombstone,* or as poorly as *My Darling Clementine.* Selman saved himself a good deal of danger and trouble, and simply shot Hardin in the back while he was rolling dice in the Acme Saloon. Hardin had rolled four sixes, almost surely a winner, when Selman ushered him out of this world.

Hardin's departure was unlamented, and Selman was acquitted of murder, regardless of the fact that he had shot Hardin behind the ear and then pumped more rounds into him after he hit the

John Selman (Western History Collections, University of Oklahoma Libraries)

floor. It doesn't fit the Hollywood pattern, but the professional gunfighter was interested in only one thing as quickly and easily as possible—staying alive, and ensuring that the other guy didn't. Selman won a measure of renown for ridding the world of Hardin, but he had little time left to enjoy it; less than a year after Hardin was shot, Selman was shot down by lawman George Scarborough.

Never Bring a Cane to a Gunfight

Barney Riggs came by the vocation of gunman naturally. Two of his brothers stood trial for murder and were acquitted, and Riggs carried on, killing at least four men, maybe more. He settled, if one can call it that, in Cochise County, Arizona, and is rumored to have had a hand in killing two Mexican men and three women while returning from a horse-stealing expedition.

Riggs couldn't stay out of trouble for long, and trouble came not only in the form of stolen horses, but also in the form of a woman— his wife Vennie who, it appeared, had been playing unseemly games with a man named Hudson in her husband's absence. Riggs was apparently willing to forget that fact, but when Hudson bragged publicly about his conquest of Vennie, Hudson's reward was three bullets out of the darkness and a trip out of this world.

The law began their search for the shooter, and Riggs wasn't hard to find. The law simply watched Vennie and followed her when she rode out to bring supplies to her husband. Riggs' trial had its high moment when the prosecution, in one of the flowery orations common in the courts of the day, equated him with a renegade Indian. Riggs' response was typical of the man: "yes, you son-of-a-bitch, and I'll murder you!"—not the sort of thing you should say in front of a judge and jury. Riggs went to prison with a life sentence in the hellhole of Yuma, the end of the world even for free and honest men.

He would, however, be out more quickly than that, for in less than a year a major convict rebellion convulsed the prison. Riggs immediately put himself on the side of the angels, took a pistol away from one of the rebels, and killed him with it. In the process he saved the warden's life. Being the hero of the moment, Riggs was granted a pardon, on the condition that he depart Arizona Territory and never return.

Riggs did so. He headed off to California, but not for long. Texas beckoned, and in 1893 he became a deputy sheriff down in Pecos County, where he became famous, not only for his prowess with a Colt but also for his coolness in time of crisis. In his time he faced down some of the toughest badmen the country had to offer—and won.

Riggs married again, although it is unclear whether he and Vennie were ever divorced. The feud between Deacon Jim Miller and Sheriff Bud Frazer—his new father-in-law—was at its height, and when Miller murdered Frazer, Riggs sought revenge. Miller tried to beat him to it and sent a couple of hired guns to take out Riggs. Both men, like Miller, wore steel vests, but it didn't do them any good. After Riggs won that confrontation two-to-nothing with a pair of head-shots, he was again charged with murder, but the jury was only out about long enough on this one to roll and smoke a cigarette.

The verdict was not guilty. Riggs settled on his ranch in Pecos County, but this "wizard with the gun," as one cowboy called him, started hitting the bottle harder and more often. His wife left him, and understandably so, because one day, boozed to the eyelids, he poured coal oil on Mrs. Riggs and threatened to set fire to her.

The last act for Riggs came about when he again lost the foul, mercurial temper that had haunted him all his life. Ordered to pay child support, he took umbrage at the young trustee appointed by the court to receive the money. He abused the young man in public and struck him with the cane he carried. The last act came when Riggs again approached the young man with his cane. What happened then is not entirely clear. Whether Riggs reached toward one pocket or simply attacked the trustee again with his cane, the trustee's response was a bullet in the chest for Riggs. He staggered off down the street and died the next day.

It was a sad end for a man who had been a fearless lawman, unflappable in times of crisis. As one man said, "One may as well try to excite a hippopotamus as fluster Barney Riggs."[2] In spite of his violent temper, Riggs was admired by many for facing up a variety of hardcases and driving them out of the country. Ironically, his killer went on to a long, illustrious career as a peace officer.

Thus, this concludes some general observations on that tough breed who worked both sides of the law. The following chapters deal with some extra tough, extra mean, extra nasty men, and a good place to begin is the abiding tragedy that came to be known as the Lincoln County War.

OUTLAWS with BADGES

Chapter 1

Dirty Dave Rudabaugh:
The Scum of the Earth

Dave Rudabaugh was a murderous bully, and that was on his good days. He stole and killed and brutalized people. He turned state's evidence and sold out his friends. And, in an outlaw society not famous for painstaking personal hygiene, he was widely known for his permanent and penetrating odor.

Due to his antipathy toward honest soap and water, Rudabaugh's smell preceded him by a quarter of an hour. Not for nothing was he known as "Dirty Dave." He stank. He had also, as one writer put it, "the look of a man who enjoyed sleeping in his clothes,"[1] which was putting it mildly.

Altogether, Rudabaugh was entirely without redeeming social value—a possible sociopath with psychotic overtones. In addition to his other grossly unattractive attributes, he had a vile temper. He lost his head regularly, and one day his foul disposition would cause him to lose his head literally and permanently.

Rudabaugh's father had been killed in the Civil War, and his mother had no luck in raising him. When he grew up—as much as he ever would—Rudabaugh tried working as an express messenger, a bartender, a ranch manager, and a cowboy. One account says he pushed longhorns in the massive trail drives north from Texas to the Kansas railheads after the Civil War.

For a while, he worked for Charlie Rath, the frontier

entrepreneur of Dodge City, driving freight and hide wagons to and from the railhead. Along the way, he narrowly missed the ferocious Adobe Walls fight, having hauled a load of hides out of the buffalo-hunters' outpost only days before a large band of Kiowas, Cheyennes, and Comanches attacked the place. Driving wagons full of hides was not for Rudabaugh, even if he was working for popular Charlie Rath. Rudabaugh decided early that he liked money more than regular work, and in time he took up the outlaw business. He turned to rustling cattle and stealing horses and may have begun his graduate work in larceny by sticking up stages in the Black Hills. Some accounts say he also rode with an outlaw gang in Texas. Considering Rudabaugh's nasty temperament, most of the tales of his lawless nature are probably true. However, he first appeared as a known, wanted criminal in the summer of 1877.

In that year, the Santa Fe railroad—or maybe it was Dodge City mayor Dog Kelley—offered a Dodge lawman ten dollars a day to run down Rudabaugh and bring him in. Wyatt Earp never did find Rudabaugh on that trip, but he made a friend. Following Rudabaugh's trail south into wild and woolly Fort Griffin, Texas, Earp met up with a consumptive, cold-eyed gambling man called Doc Holliday, sometimes dentist, most-times gambler, and shootist extraordinaire.

As the story goes, Doc told Earp that Rudabaugh had headed for west Texas. Earp followed Rudabaugh there and elsewhere, finally returning to Fort Griffin early in 1878. There Earp discovered Rudabaugh had headed back to Kansas. So had Holliday. He and his long-time companion, Big-Nose Kate Elder—a lady who rented by the hour—had reportedly departed Fort Griffin at the high lope just ahead of a mob, after Holliday eviscerated a local hoodlum.

Early in 1878, Rudabaugh reappeared in Kansas with a bang.

Before daylight on Sunday, January 27, he and four other thugs held up a train at Kinsley in one of the worst-bungled hold-ups of all time. Rudabaugh, a hoodlum called Roarke, and several others, decided that holding up a train might make a fine payday. At first they contemplated hitting the Santa Fe train and its express car in Dodge City itself, but Roarke demurred. Tough Charlie Bassett was marshal in Dodge just then. Roarke sensibly wanted no part of Bassett's quick and accurate Colts.

After much quarreling, the gang settled on plan B: they would stick up the train at Kinsley, a wide spot in the road where they should meet no resistance. And so they plodded north in miserable winter weather, even abandoning the chuck wagon they had brought with them to serve the inner man. On January 26, 1878, the gang rode through light snow and piercing cold to snatch their bonanza from the railroad.

They obviously had not planned very well. In the dead of night, on the way into town, they stopped at a railroad worker's shack to inquire whether the train they wanted was on time. The railroad man was understandably suspicious, seeing that all his nocturnal visitors had their faces blackened. When Rudabaugh got out his revolver and began to fondle it, the railroad man got the hint. He told the gang what he could, wished them Godspeed, and went back to bed.

At the Kinsley depot, the gang stuck up the agent, one Kinkaid. Kinkaid, cool and tough, showed the gang an empty cash drawer, and convinced them that he couldn't open the safe, (in which rested 2,000 good American dollars). The plucky agent was stopped in the act of taking on the whole gang with a Derringer.

With no profit in the depot, that left the train as the next target. A citizen of Kinsley, understandably put off by the gang's black-face disguises, ran for a gun, pursued by a bullet from Rudabaugh's revolver. Kinkaid tried to warn the train's engineer, but that worthy, clad in earmuffs against the wintry blasts, could hear nothing and thought the agent was simply shouting a greeting.

The train was stopped, at least. But the gang was then frustrated by a tough, resolute express messenger who answered their demands to stand and deliver with pistol bullets. At the same time, Rudabaugh was spraying slugs about indiscriminately, in the theory that if he were hostile enough, nobody would interfere. He was right, at least until the gang forced the crew to move the train down the line, ready for looting. At about the same time, an angry crowd of Kinsleyites came galloping up out of the snow, banging away with everything they had. After a good deal of noisy shooting—and no casualties on either side—the gang scattered, departing into the snowy night with the posse hot on their heels. The snow covered their tracks, and they won clear. They had no loot, but at least they were free.

However, they were not free for long. Determined posses beat the bushes in all directions in spite of the wretched weather. An Army patrol from Fort Dodge got into the chase, as well. Worst of all, the gang attracted the enthusiastic attention of a formidable young lawman from Dodge City.

Kinsley was less than forty miles down the line from Dodge, out of which rode a posse led by Ford County sheriff Bat Masterson who promptly ran down Rudabaugh and one other man. Even then, at only twenty-three, Rudabaugh was said to be the veteran of "a wild career in crime," but he was taken without a fight. When Masterson closed in on Rudabaugh and his companion, Rudabaugh started to go for his own gun. He froze in mid-reach, though, hearing the ominous "click" of posse man John Joshua Webb cocking his own weapon. "I wouldn't do that if I was you," said Webb pleasantly, and Rudabaugh quickly decided that Webb was right.

During his preliminary hearing, Rudabaugh appeared "cool and collected," according to the *Ford County Globe*, as he should have been since he was about to become a witness against his former comrades. As the *Kinsley Graphic* put it,

> Rudabaugh . . . was promised entire immunity if he would "squeal," therefore he squole. Someone said there is a kind of honor among thieves; Rudabaugh don't think so.[2]

So, as the paper said, Rudabaugh "squole," and he "squole" so convincingly that his erstwhile comrades changed their pleas to guilty. Rudabaugh then hung around town long enough to convict Roarke, the last survivor of this inept mob. One other gang member had chosen to shoot it out with a lawman and came in second.

His ratting done, Rudabaugh sanctimoniously announced that he was going straight. He may even have taken semi-honest work as a deputy during the Santa Fe, Denver and Rio Grande Royal Gorge war. By late 1879, he did in fact go straight; he went straight to New Mexico where he robbed and pillaged around Las Vegas.

Rudabaugh would try anything as long as it was crooked. For a while, all went well, because Las Vegas at the time was run by as choice a collection of killers as ever walked the West. They were called the Dodge City Gang, and they mostly ran the town, at least until one of their number—the selfsame John Joshua Webb who had stopped Rudabaugh's abortive holdup of the train—killed a rancher. Webb was arrested and jailed for murder. Rudabaugh, obviously considering Webb a valuable colleague, tried to break him out of jail, but succeeded only in killing a deputy, a solid citizen named Lino Valdez.

With things heating up around Las Vegas, Rudabaugh headed for safer climes, though not for honest work. He headed for a hotbed of trouble, Lincoln County, New Mexico. And there, at Whiskey Jim Greathouse's stage depot near Anton Chico, he met

"Billy the Kid" McCarty, who was surely his kind of desperado. Rudabaugh quickly joined up with the Kid and the hardcases who made up the McSween army in the bloody Lincoln County War.

Rudabaugh fit right in. If the Kid, Charlie Bowdre, and Tom O'Folliard were tough and mean, Rudabaugh was tougher and meaner in spades, or at least meaner. According to an old friend of the Kid's, "If ever there was a living man the kid was afraid of, it was Rudabaugh." Other old-timers said the same thing. The Kid, said one, "never dared talk to him as he did to Charles Bowdre" and the rest of his gang, thus suggesting that Rudabaugh was as dangerous as he was odoriferous, even to his friends of the moment.

Nevertheless, Rudabaugh joined the Kid and his followers in a variety of criminal enterprises, such as running stolen horses, robbing stages, and on one occasion holding up an Army paymaster. At the end of November 1880, however, Rudabaugh, the Kid, and others were trapped by a posse at Greathouse's stage depot, about forty miles from White Oaks, New Mexico.

Capturing the ranch cook while he was out cutting some early-morning firewood, the posse men sent that frightened minion inside with a note for the Kid telling him to surrender because they had him surrounded. Greathouse himself came out within a few moments, bringing the scribbled reply: "Go to hell," or words to that effect. Diplomacy obviously wasn't working.

Then, posse member Jim Carlyle, with more courage than good sense, volunteered to go inside and parley with the gang. This was not a good idea. Approachable at first—even giving Carlyle a drink—the Kid's attitude changed when he saw Carlyle carrying a pair of his own gloves, captured earlier in the chase. The Kid turned sullen and ugly, sneering at Carlyle:

> Jim, you haven't finished your drink. Drink up, you won't be able to later on . . . your type should not be permitted the benefit of drawing even if you had a gun.[3]

This all sounds somewhat high-falutin' for the Kid, but whatever he said made Carlyle understandably nervous. At two o'clock in the afternoon the time for parley expired, and one of the posse men fired a single shot to signal the end of the truce. Carlyle, perhaps expecting a general battle, bailed out of the ranch house through a window and was killed in a burst of firing. Much more shooting followed, with nobody else hit on either side; that night the outlaws got away clean.

To this day nobody knows who really killed Carlyle. The Kid, of course, later said that neither he nor his comrades were responsible; the posse members said the same thing. Understandably, nearly everybody blamed the outlaws. Greathouse's building was burned down along with another ranch, and a lot of angry lawmen hit the trail, pushing hard after the Kid and his cohorts.

On December 19, Rudabaugh, the Kid, and some kindred spirits visited Fort Sumner seeking newspapers and refreshment of various kinds. Maybe they wanted current news of the posse's actions, or maybe they just liked to see their names in print. In any case, a Pat Garrett posse ambushed the gang, killing Tom O'Folliard. Rudabaugh, his horse mortally wounded in the melee, scrambled up behind another gang member and escaped.

Garrett stayed close behind the gang, tracking his quarry through the snow in bitterly cold weather. Two days before Christmas, Garrett surrounded the remaining gang members in a small, rock building at Stinking Springs. The posse shivered through the night and at dawn permanently ventilated Charlie Bowdre when he emerged to feed his horse. Then the gang's horses were either killed or driven off by Garrett's men. With no food, no escape, and a dead horse jammed into the doorway of their shelter, the remaining gangmembers surrendered, returning to Las Vegas ignominiously in a guarded wagon.

Rudabaugh was about as popular as the flu in Las Vegas. Lino

Valdez had been well-liked. A number of citizens believed that a tall tree and a short piece of rope were about all the due process Rudabaugh had coming. Accordingly, as a precaution, he was jailed in Santa Fe, on both the Las Vegas murder charges and a federal stage-robbing indictment. Rudabaugh was duly convicted of stage-robbing and sentenced to a term of years; he must have hoped that he'd spend the next few years in a federal prison, while the state murder charges were forgotten.

However, it was not to be. Rudabaugh was forthwith tried for the death of Lino Valdez. Predictably, Rudabaugh passed the buck—it never stopped with him, anyway. "Little Allen did the killing," he said and, of course, he claimed to be sinless. As he'd done before, Rudabaugh tried to dump the blame on a comrade. He claimed that he had heard a shot and turned around to see poor Valdez, down and dying. "I said to Little Allen, 'what did you do that for?'"

This time, however, the jury wasn't having any and neither was the judge. The penalty was death by hanging and "May God have mercy on your soul." The sentence would be carried out in Las Vegas. Rudabaugh's return to his old stomping ground was not a happy one. Not only was he facing a short walk to the scaffold and a long step down, but the townspeople cordially loathed him, and he knew it. As one reporter wrote, Rudabaugh showed a restless, uneasy condition of mind:

> [He] retained a stolid, hangdog demeanor and showed no disposition to recognize any of his old acquaintances . . . now the chained culprit, doomed to the decree of justice or possibly Judge Lynche's mandate, for we hear the grumblings of men who have revenge in their hearts.[4]

No wonder. The *Las Vegas Optic* added that Rudabaugh looked and dressed about the same as he did in Las Vegas, "apparently not having made a raid upon clothing stores."[5]

So, willy-nilly, shabby, stinking Rudabaugh had his reunion with John Joshua Webb, again as a resident in the San Miguel County lock-up in Las Vegas. Rudabaugh spent most of 1881 there until, in September, Rudabaugh, Webb, and three others somehow got hold of a revolver and tried to break free. They changed their minds abruptly, however, after jailer Herculano Chavez dispatched one of their number, Tom Duffy, to his reward—heavenly or otherwise.

By early December, however, Rudabaugh was free. He, Webb, and three others managed to acquire a knife, a poker, and a pick and dug their way out, disappearing between the darkness and the dawn. Considering that the noise of somebody hammering away with a pick is a little loud even for a small-town jailer to miss, one can't help wondering whether somebody got paid to go deaf temporarily.

Rudabaugh left the Las Vegas area in some haste, but to this day nobody is sure exactly where he went. The last months of his life, much like the early years, are forever shrouded in the shadows of time. There is, however, some evidence that he turned up in Tombstone, Arizona, drawn to trouble as usual, like iron filings to a magnet.

Down in Cochise County Rudabaugh chose the wrong side again, allying himself with the "cowboy faction": the party of the Clantons, the McLaurys, Curly Bill Brocius, and John Ringo. By the time Rudabaugh joined up with the cowboys, the "OK Corral" fight was history and Billy Clanton and the McLaury boys were extinct, but there was still plenty of shooting to do.

It may be that Rudabaugh was part of the savage night-time ambush of Virgil Earp. Five men attacked Virgil, and four of the attackers were identified by various witnesses. One of these witnesses was gang member Indian Joe, who gave his information just before Wyatt Earp shot him full of holes. But nobody seemed to know who the fifth attacker was. He was "new around the mining camp," and nobody could, or would, give him a name. Virgil Earp was shot down on December 28, 1881. Rudabaugh had broken out of jail in Las Vegas twenty-five days earlier, so he would have had plenty of time to ride south and look for more trouble.

On the other hand, many years later Wells Fargo agent Fred Dodge said cowboy adherent Johnny Barnes confessed that he had been the fifth man in the group who gunned down Virgil Earp in the dark. Barnes, a more likely choice to have been in the band that attacked Virgil Earp, had been a member of the Clanton bunch for quite some time. Rudabaugh would have been a newcomer. Still, Barnes would not have been "new around the mining camp." If the other witnesses are to be believed, the fifth attacker could not have been Barnes.

Whether he was involved in the attack on Virgil Earp or not, Rudabaugh may well have been a cowboy gunman by the following spring. In the famous fight at Iron Springs, Wyatt Earp reportedly recognized Rudabaugh as one of the ambushers. In May 1882, the *Ford County Globe* told of the Iron Springs fight:

> Wyatt and Warren Earp arrived some days ago and will remain awhile. . . . Wyatt says after the first shock he could distinguish David Rudabaugh and Curly Bill, the latter's body showing well among the bushes.[6]

Wyatt Earp would surely have recognized Rudabaugh from the Dodge City days, and there is no reason for him to allege falsely that Rudabaugh was at Iron Springs if he was not.

However, in Stuart Lake's biography of Wyatt Earp, the only biography for which Wyatt Earp actually provided information, Rudabaugh is not mentioned as a cowboy partisan. Describing the Iron Springs fight all those decades before, Wyatt Earp was very clear and very specific, at least as Lake quoted him:

From the instant I laid eyes on Curly Bill, I was seeing and thinking clearly. Nothing that went on in that gully escaped me, although what happened in a very few seconds takes much longer to tell. . . . I recognized Pony Deal, and as seven others broke for the cottonwoods, I named each one as he ran, saying to myself, "I've got a warrant for him."[7]

Earp named all of the seven to Lake, but Rudabaugh was not among them.

There is no way to determine which account is accurate—the tale as related by Lake, or the quote from the *Globe*—or for that matter, whether either one of them is. If one assumes Earp actually gave both versions, the *Globe's* story is more probable because it was written when Earp was in his prime and had no motive to embroider a story of the fight. Lake's interviews with Earp were conducted more than forty years later, when the old lawman was coming to the end of the trail, and when, perhaps, he thought he might turn a dollar on the story of his life.

Regardless of who ambushed Earp, Doc Holliday, and the others at Iron Springs, Curly Bill all but certainly died there, chock full of shot from Earp's shotgun. Rudabaugh, if he was part of the fight, escaped. After Curly Bill went down, and after Earp and his friends killed several more of the cowboy gang, the survivors—presumably including Rudabaugh—lost a good deal of their interest in Arizona generally and Tombstone specifically.

Mexico looked far more promising—and a whole lot healthier. Rudabaugh made his way south of the border and stayed there. At this point the mist gets thicker. Nobody is really sure how Rudabaugh finished his earthly course. One story has him marrying and settling down. He may have turned up, a broken man, more than thirty years later in Deer Lodge, Montana. A man named Dave Rudabaugh did indeed appear in Deer Lodge—at least that's who he said he was. The trail ends there, unconfirmed.

But the most common story about Rudabaugh's last days puts

him in Mexico, south of the Arizona line in Chihuahua. It is a very good tale indeed, and almost certainly true—hopefully, if only for the poetic justice of its ending. Here's how it goes.

What Rudabaugh was doing in Chihuahua is not entirely clear. Maybe he had moved his robbing business south of the border; maybe he was simply hiding from the American law; maybe the living was just easier in Old Mexico; or maybe, according to one entertaining tale, Rudabaugh was actually working.

This story recounts that Rudabaugh had repeatedly robbed payrolls belonging to the local cattle-king, Terrazas (sometimes Terrasas), governor of Chihuahua. Terrazas was a big operator, big enough that during the Spanish-American War, Chicago meat packers wired him to ask whether he could supply them with 50,000 head of cattle. Terrazas is said to have wired back only, "what color?"

Maybe. Whether the story of the telegram is true or not, Terrazas was certainly an important man. He may have employed Rudabaugh to protect his herds on the reasonable thesis that it's better to hire the fox to guard the hen house than to worry about where the varmint is and what he's up to. Perhaps, as another version of the story has it, after being hired to run one of Terrazas' ranches, Rudabaugh stole from his boss and was fired as a result. Rudabaugh, of course, resented being fired, which didn't improve his naturally ugly disposition.

Whatever the reason, Rudabaugh hung out in the town of Parral, taking out his resentment on the inhabitants by making life generally miserable for them. To Rudabaugh, the local citizens were all "greasers," a sort of subhuman helot or serf who could be shot, beaten, and shoved out of the way at will. The locals didn't like Rudabaugh much either.

Things came to a head—literally—on February 18, 1886. Nobody knows precisely what happened in Parral, but this much is reasonably certain: Rudabaugh was being his customary, ugly self in a local cantina. According to one account, he pushed aside several Mexican patrons, ordered a bottle of tequila, and spat part of it on the floor.[8] After this warm-up, Rudabaugh proceeded to play poker with some of the locals. Upset at losing and screaming that he'd been cheated, Rudabaugh quickly sought to change his luck by killing two of the players and wounding another. He then, after spraying enough bullets around to clear the cantina, took his leave. One story says that he couldn't find his horse and, therefore, went back inside the cantina.

This was no ordinary night in Parral. The citizenry had had enough of this blustering bully, and a bunch of them ambushed Rudabaugh in the street outside the cantina—or possibly inside the place when Rudabaugh re-entered. This time there were no other hoodlums to help him, no excuses to make, no lies to tell, nobody to rat on, and no place to run.

Thus was the end of Dirty Dave Rudabaugh, full of holes in a town that hated his guts, mourned by absolutely nobody. Well known and generally detested throughout the southwest, Rudabaugh's demise was widely reported in Arizona and New Mexico newspapers, such as the *Las Vegas Optic*. There was no hint of regret for his passing.

Like the Bard's Thane of Cawdor, nothing in Rudabaugh's life became him like the leaving of it—for he gave the good citizens of Parral reason to celebrate. And they did so, exuberantly. "The natives of Parral got a procession in honor of the event," as the *Tombstone Democrat* put it.

They declared a fiesta and commemorated their tormentor's demise by cutting off Rudabaugh's ugly head—scruffy mustache, hat, and all—impaling it on a pole, and parading it in celebration around and about the plaza of the town. An American photographer

Dave Rudabaugh's head after his death (Western History Collections, University of Oklahoma Libraries)

even captured a picture of a citizen solemnly holding Rudabaugh's head on a platter—still complete with hat—a little reminiscent of Salome, but with a droopy mustache, holding the head of John the Baptist.

The *Las Vegas Optic* summed up Rudabaugh's repulsive nature pretty well:

> Dave Rudabaugh, who was recently killed at Parral, in the state of Chihuahua, Mexico, was what might be called an "all around desperado." He was equally proficient in holding up a railroad train or a stage coach or, as occasion offered, robbing a bank, "shooting up" a frontier settlement, or running off stock. He indulged in these little peculiarities for a year or two in Arizona.[9]

Had anybody put up a headstone for Rudabaugh, which nobody did, it might have read something like this: "Good riddance."

Chapter 2

Hoodoo Brown and Company: The Thugs of Las Vegas

Out in Las Vegas, New Mexico, another set of hoodlums set up in the law enforcement business. Las Vegas was as wild a place as there was back in the 1880s, and a bunch of uglies called the Dodge City Gang was about all the law there was. It wasn't much. Their idea of law enforcement consisted mostly of intimidating anybody who disagreed or interfered with the rackets of the group, who pretty much ran Las Vegas to suit themselves. Some evidence suggests that they also turned their hands to matters much more serious than shaking down residents and visitors, namely holdups, larceny, and even murder.

They were, in short, a law unto themselves. The gang, or some of its members, even sat as a tame "coroner's jury" from time to time, which meant that the gang members had virtual immunity from prosecution, especially considering that the top judicial officer in town was not only in cahoots with the gangsters, but their leader.

The boss of this coterie of felons rejoiced in the name of Hoodoo Brown—although he began life as Hyman Neill—and he called himself "justice of the peace and acting coroner." For a while Brown did indeed have his own way around Las Vegas, until the summer of 1881 when even the citizens of rough Las Vegas had had enough and ran him out of town. He allegedly departed in the company of the widow of one of his deputies.

Brown was lucky, for by his exodus he escaped trial for murder and robbery. Furthermore, it was rumored that seduction and adultery were an incidental part of the background of his crimes. Maybe so, for a Chicago paper reported that Brown and the deputy's widow had been "skylarking through some of the interior towns of Kansas ever since."[1] Brown is said to have died in Mexico, leaving a common-law wife. Whether it was the deputy's widow is not recorded, although in later years a woman in Leadville asserted that she had been married to a Hoodoo Brown who was killed in a gunfight.

This part of the history of the West is further complicated by the fact that there were at least two Hoodoo Browns, as unlikely as that seems. One was a crooked bum masquerading as a pillar of the law. The other Hoodoo Brown, by contrast, was an upstanding community leader, a tough and resourceful man who successfully ran a series of commercial enterprises, hunted buffalo, scouted for the Army, and finally settled down to become a pillar of the community in Meade County, Kansas.

Maybe one Brown borrowed the name from the other, but "hoodoo" was a common slang word of the day, meaning bad luck or something that brings bad luck—probably a corruption of "voodoo." In any case, it was more commonly used in those days than it is today.

The Las Vegas Hoodoo Brown held court, such as it was, in a saloon. He is said to have hammered for order with the butt of a Winchester in lieu of a gavel. The justice he handed down, if one can call it justice, was whatever suited his "business" operations and, of course, whatever fines could fatten the city treasury. He even made Judge Roy Bean look like a pillar of the law.

While the good times lasted, the crooked Brown was supported by equally corrupt gunman-turned-city-marshal John Joshua Webb and a rich collection of worthless drifters. Among Webb's deputies were the deadly Mysterious Dave Mather and that veritable prince of thugs, Dirty Dave Rudabaugh.

Mysterious Dave Mather (Western History Collections, University of Oklahoma Libraries)

Brown's boys not only pushed the locals around but branched out into rustling and, it was said, even murder. With the law on their side, they must have figured they had, as the saying went, the world by the tail. And, for a while, they did. However, the halcyon days of undisturbed graft and criminality in Las Vegas were not to last. What finally tore it, even for the tough citizens of the town, was the murder of the stockman Mike Kelliher, shot down in a Las Vegas saloon. One version of the story describes Kelliher as a wealthy rancher, carrying a sizable roll of money from the sale of a herd. Maybe so. Perhaps the gang had eyes on his poke from the beginning, or maybe they just picked a fight. Nobody knows anymore.

Regardless, city lawman Webb shot him down. This killing was the beginning of the end for Brown's little cabal. Badge or no badge, Webb ended up in the slammer. He had pushed the citizens too far, too often.

Webb had some prior law enforcement experience. In fact, he had been among the Bat Masterson posse that ran Rudabaugh down after a botched train holdup in Kansas. When the posse caught Rudabaugh, he had at first shown a predilection to shoot it out, until Webb pulled a gun on him, offering him a choice between surrender and a gut full of lead. Rudabaugh was a scumbag, but not a stupid one. He surrendered.

Now, however, Rudabaugh and Webb were jolly crooks together, comrades in the fragrant Las Vegas cabal. When that gang broke up, Rudabaugh killed a lawman in an attempted jailbreak to free a comrade—the jailbird was none other than Webb, in the slammer for murder.

Jailed himself for the murder of a popular local deputy, Rudabaugh escaped with Webb and made his way to New Mexico, where he became one of Billy the Kid's cohorts in the Lincoln County War.

Mysterious Dave Mather went on being sullen, nasty, and belligerent, drifting from town to town, apparently unable or unwilling to settle down, and leaving trouble in his wake wherever he chanced to land. He is said to have killed a man down in Mobeetie in the Texas panhandle and was later accused of robbing a train, a rap he beat.

He distinguished himself in Dodge City when he pulled a gun—in church—on a preacher who, allegedly egged on by Masterson, was determined to cheat the devil of Mather's soul. The preacher's efforts, delivered right in Mather's face, produced intense amusement for Masterson and some of the gamblin' fraternity scattered throughout the church, but not for Mather.

Mather never could take a joke, especially if it was on him, and despite all the preacher could do, the devil won this one. Mather suddenly sprang to his feet shouting "hallelujah!" and blasting away at the church lights with his revolver. That put an abrupt end to his conversion. As the story goes the preacher and his assistants vanished unceremoniously through the church windows without wasting the time to open them.

Fêted in a saloon that night surrounded by much laughter, Mather, sullen as usual, finally looked up from his poker game and addressed the jolly multitude: "I'm willing to answer for anything I ever done, and nobody can say I cheated 'em in words or cards." He then added a cautionary word—vintage Mather—"and if anybody wants to say otherwise, I'll kill him right now."[2] This pretty much put an end to the conversation and a damper on the merriment.

Not much is known about Mather's early career, except that he came from New England. He spent about four years in Dodge City, where he managed to get seriously knifed in 1874. Then, in about 1878, he showed up in Arkansas, rustling cattle and eventually graduating to buffalo hunting. That is, when he wasn't carousing in the mushroom towns along the railroad as it drove west.

After that, Mather apparently got the law-and-order bug and became active in vigilante doings—lynchings and such—and as a part-time police officer. He fell from grace when, in the summer of 1878, he showed up in Mobeetie, Texas, with Wyatt Earp of all people. Apparently the purpose of the expedition was an attempt to peddle fake gold bricks to gullible cowboys. It ended when the town marshal discovered the scam and told them both to take a hike. Earp went back to being a lawman in Dodge, but Mather went to try some new country.

Mather got a fresh start in Las Vegas, a town full of bad hats— killers, robbers, and other scum. Mather fit right in and became part of Brown's party of goons led by none other than John Joshua Webb. In addition to Webb, Mather, and the odoriferous Rudabaugh, there was Tom Pickett, said to be a psychopath, and acting like one.

Pickett had not been much use to mankind all his life. Late in life he served as a deputy marshal, but prior to that his history was one long career of professional lawbreaking. In trouble for stock theft at the age of seventeen, his family—a good one—mortgaged their home to buy him his freedom. His response was to leave his family and hook up with the Las Vegas gang. He wore a badge for a while and then moved on to Fort Sumner to go rustling with Rudabaugh, Tom O'Folliard, Billy the Kid, and the rest of that lawless bunch of punks.

Pickett had enough after Pat Garrett got into the chase. He left for Arizona where he became a hired gunman in the Graham-Tewksbury feud. Wounded, he gave that one up, married briefly, and then passed his remaining years punching cattle, gambling, tending bar, and prospecting. He made it to seventy-six, however, an unusual feat for a saddle tramp who for many years' time made his living with a gun.

Hoodoo Brown and his cohorts actually did some good along

the way. There was the matter of a gang of hoodlums led by one Tom Henry, the same sort of bullies Brown collected around himself. Inevitably there would be a clash, and it happened when Henry and his boys were howling it up in a local saloon—and wearing their guns. Going around armed was verboten in Las Vegas, as it was in many other western towns. For someone as crooked as Brown and his boys, it would interfere with one's high-handed business to let anybody else walk around carrying a weapon. Mather and a deputy named Joe Carson, sought out the Henry gang and demanded that they give up their guns. Henry and his crew decided they wouldn't.

A wild gunfight followed, and Carson was shot down before he had a chance to fire. But Mather, apparently bulletproof, killed two of Henry's gunmen. Helped by his last man, Henry got away, leaving a blood trail. The whole incident made the unwounded Mather the hero—or at least the sensation—of the moment.

Just a few days later, Mather broke up a potential shootout between a couple of railroad men and their foreman by abruptly ushering the foreman into the hereafter. The story goes that the railroad man had his pistol in his hand and Mather did not, but when their confrontation came, it was Mather who managed to open his coat, draw, cock his revolver, and get off a fatal shot into the railroad man's gut.

One would think that Henry would have had enough of any place close to Las Vegas and would have given the town and its general vicinity a wide berth. Instead, he was captured and dragged before the only law there was in the city, Hoodoo Brown. Brown set a trial date, but that seems to have been an inconvenient wait in Mather's eyes. Mather appointed himself leader of a lynch mob. They got a couple of ropes, dragged Henry and his cohort—both wounded—out to a windmill on the edge of town, and saw to it that Carson was avenged.

Whether it was the *ad hoc* execution that moved him or not, Mather now drifted away from Law Vegas. Always on the move and frequently in the midst of trouble, he descended to a new low in his career. After a stint in the slammer for possession of counterfeit money and a short-lived employment as a peace officer—again—he ended up in Dallas and became, of all things, a pimp. Even that less-than-dignified employment came to an end when he blew town for Fort Worth with a pocketful of jewelry belonging to the madam for whom he had worked.

There were consequences. The madam, a doughty lady called Georgia Morgan, followed Mather, accosted him, and proceeded to bash him about the head with her .45. She added further injury by having him arrested and returned to Dallas, charged with theft. The charges were dropped, but Mather had had enough of Texas and went back to Dodge.

For a while, all went well. He was appointed a lawman again and bought a piece of a dive called the Opera House Saloon. That brought him into direct competition with another deputy, Tom Nixon, who owned a rival establishment. Worse still, Mather was suspected of harboring more than friendly feelings toward Mrs. Nixon. At least Nixon thought so.

The upshot of it all was that Nixon took a shot at Mather and thought he'd killed him. But he hadn't, which was a shame, for when Mather settled the matter he didn't miss. Shot in the back, Nixon fell, and Mather put three more bullets into him as he lay helpless. Even for Mather this was pretty ugly. But a jury brought in an inexplicable verdict of not guilty—presumably on grounds of self-defense. Mather turned his hand to farming, of all things, but then drifted away again.

Mather is said to have killed a man in Ashland, Kansas, and then to have been the law briefly in New Kiowa, Kansas. Then he moved on to Lone Pine, Nebraska. There, ever the recluse, he lived alone outside the town until he simply disappeared one day. There are stories, or legends, about what Mather did thereafter, including serving in the Royal Canadian Mounted Police. But there is nothing provable, and that service is, in any case, unlikely. The Mounties were a tough but honest lot, distinctly not Mather's cup of tea, and highly unlikely to welcome a thoroughgoing dirtbag like him.

And so Mysterious Dave Mather was simply gone. No records exist of anybody missing him.

As for the rest of the gang, Webb—who late in his short life called himself Samuel King to cover his lurid past—fled to Mexico with Rudabaugh. After Rudabaugh's death, Webb returned to Kansas and worked as a teamster for a couple of years. He died of smallpox in 1882.

Henry Newton Brown, killed after attempting bank robbery, Medicine Lodge, Kan., 1884 (Western History Collections, University of Oklahoma Libraries)

Chapter 3

Henry Newton Brown:
It Was All for You

Prominent among the deadly, colorful cast of characters who fought for the bitter antagonists in the Lincoln County War was one of history's deadliest gunmen, a reluctant outlaw named Henry Newton Brown.

Brown was a Missouri boy who left home at seventeen like so many restless young men of the day. He drifted from job to job— farmer, cowpuncher, buffalo hunter—until he finally found his natural calling as a law officer. He was something of an odd duck, uncommon among lawmen and outlaws in that tumultuous time, for he neither drank, smoked, nor chewed; legend says he didn't gamble either, in a day when gambling abounded.

On one hand, Brown was the perfect example of a man with all the qualities required of a peace officer in those wild days, a man who'd take on the Herculean task of taming the mushroom towns that sprouted in the wake of Manifest Destiny's drive to the West. He was aggressive to a fault, one of those rare men who were not only pugnacious but were not afraid of much of anything either.

He found it convenient to change his stomping ground after he killed a man out in the Texas panhandle; therefore, he drifted over into New Mexico. There he signed on to punch cattle for Major Lawrence Murphy, one of the chief antagonists in the fabled Lincoln County War. Murphy and his partner James Dolan were determined to be the economic power of Lincoln County.

They did not much care how they did it and collected a group of hoodlums-for-hire to eliminate any opposition.

When he first came to the Seven Rivers country Brown worked for Murphy for eighteen months, but then some sort of dispute over wages poisoned the relationship. Brown was disappointed enough—or angry enough—to ride over the hill and hire on with fabulous cattle baron John Chisum, founder of the major trail north from Texas to the Kansas railheads. Brown then joined the array of hired guns known as the Regulators, an unpleasant collection of Murphy opponents under the leadership of English rancher John Tunstall and his lawyer business partner, Alexander McSween, which included Billy the Kid, John Middleton, Tom O'Folliard, Jim French, John Joshua Webb (aka Sam King), and an assortment of other hardcases.

Brown was in the thick of it. On the morning of the first of April 1878, as Sheriff William Brady—a Murphy partisan—strolled down a Lincoln street past Tunstall's store with his deputy George Hindman and three other men, Brown, the Kid, and two others rose from behind the store's adobe wall and opened fire without warning.

Brady was killed and Hindman was mortally wounded. Another man was also wounded slightly, but the return fire from the other Murphy gunhands sent the Kid and his sidekicks into precipitate retreat, the Kid with a minor leg wound.

It was only the first skirmish.

Three days later came the fight at Blazer's Mill, when Brown and other Regulators were taking a breather in their search for more Murphy supporters. Then a single Murphy partisan, one aptly-named Buckshot Roberts, entered and immediately demonstrated enormous courage and a marked lack of good sense.

Brown and others pulled their weapons and summoned Roberts to surrender, surely not expecting his reply. "Not much,

Mary Ann," said Roberts, and opened fire at close range with his Winchester. Roberts got a bullet in the gut from Regulator Charlie Bowdre, but that did not stop him. Roberts kept on firing and managed to reach cover in the mill building.

Roberts was dying from his stomach wound, but he died game, as the western saying went. He wounded Regulators George Coe and John Middleton and killed the leader of the band, Dick Brewer. That was enough for the surviving Regulators, who departed forthwith without trying to finish the mortally hurt Roberts.

A little more than a month later, Brown and a few others struck a camp on the Pecos River; a fight followed, in which two of the opposition were shot and another killed, supposedly a man nicknamed "Indian." The prize was a herd of horses Indian and the other men had been guarding, with which Brown and his companions departed.

Then came the battle of Lincoln that summer—the attack on the Tunstall store by Murphy partisans. Though McSween and some of his men died near his blazing home in an inferno set by the Murphy men, Brown and two or three others found cover on the roof of a small building nearby. From there they sniped at the much larger besieging force without noticeable result, except for Bob Beckwith who was shot and, in the quaint language of the day, expired.

Regardless of who killed Beckwith—his death is commonly attributed to Billy the Kid—the rest of the action was a disaster for the Regulators, including the tragic and needless killing of McSween.

The lawyer died as he fled the flaming ruins of his house, shot down in spite of the pleas of his wife who ran from the burning building to beg for safe conduct from the besiegers. The Kid and some of his companions escaped, shooting wildly into the night, as did Brown and two others, who scaled an eight-foot wall and disappeared into the darkness.

For a while after that, Brown turned to stealing stock with the Kid and others, without justification, legitimate or not. The Murphy-McSween war was long over with by then, but stock rustling was profitable and, in the eyes of the Kid and his companions, sure beat working.

But in the autumn of 1878, as they pushed a stolen herd in the panhandle near Tascosa, the gang started to crumble. The Kid and O'Folliard began to get a hankering for their old haunts in New Mexico, Webb and Middleton decided they would go home, and Brown—for whatever reason, now lost to history—decided to stay in Tascosa. Perhaps it was the local attractions that kept him there.

Tascosa in its day was a considerable metropolis. Its Exchange Hotel, a sort of Mecca for anybody with a few dollars and a hankering for something like respectability, had honest-to-pete wood floors, the height of grandeur for that place and time.

And for those who did not care all that much about respectability, Tascosa had some less reputable watering holes like the Equity Bar and Captain Jenks' Saloon. Booze there was in quantity—if not quality—and soiled doves to fulfill the cowboy's only other serious need were abundant.

The "sporting ladies" of the town—gals who rented by the hour—gloried in intriguing handles like Gizzard Lip, Frog Lip Sadie, Homely Ann, Slippery Sue, and Boxcar Jane, who was presumably designed for heavy duty.

Brown first found honest work there as a cowhand. He then worked for a while as a county sheriff's deputy and was good at what he did. On one occasion he forced a belligerent cowboy to back down by placing his own revolver on a table equidistant between them and challenging the trouble-maker to beat him to it. The cowboy left town.

But in time Brown's belligerence got him fired from being a

deputy, and fired again after he went back to being a cowpuncher. After that Brown drifted to present day Oklahoma, and then to Caldwell, Kansas, one of the wild railhead towns of the day.

In Caldwell, Brown wangled a job as deputy city marshal to Marshal Bat Carr, a very tough cob himself, so efficient that the city fathers had presented him with a solid gold badge in appreciation of his house-cleaning efforts.

The two cleaned up Caldwell in short order, and Brown became the marshal in 1882. He hired as his deputy a Texas gunman named Ben Wheeler—who had at least a couple of aliases. He was apparently a kindred spirit, and the two men kept Caldwell quiet and orderly. So grateful were the city fathers that on the first day of 1883 they gave Brown a brand new Winchester with a silver plate suitably engraved with their thanks.

The citizens thought a lot of Brown, who was bringing in more to the city treasury in fines than the city was paying Brown and Wheeler put together. The *Caldwell Commercial* presumably spoke for the great majority of the citizens:

> Few men could have filled the position he has so acceptably occupied . . . cool, courageous and gentlemanly, and free from the vices supposed to be proper adjuncts to a man occupying his position.[1]

Along the way Brown killed more men, local bad hats whom nobody missed very much, further enhancing his formidable reputation. One of them expired during the pursuit of Ross, an entrepreneur engaged in management of the family business, horse stealing. In a wild gun battle in April of 1883, Brown, Wheeler, and three other lawmen fought the patriarch of the clan, his wife, two sons, daughter, and daughter-in-law. When the smoke blew away, one son was dead, the second badly wounded, and the rest of the group under arrest.

Brown seems to have been quiet and polite as a usual thing, but in his pursuit of those who disturbed the peace of Caldwell he was remorseless—a little like tough John Slaughter of Cochise County, who famously told his deputies, "I say, I say, shoot first and shout 'throw up your hands' after." That saved a lot of expense to the county, not to mention hung juries, acquittals, appeals, and that sort of bother.

The month after the Ross fight, Spotted Horse, a Pawnee, caused a ruckus in a Caldwell grocery, waving a pistol about after entering at least two places in town—including a private home—rudely and without invitation, demanding to be fed. The call went out for Brown.

On this occasion Brown showed uncharacteristic restraint, ordering Spotted Horse to come with him and drawing his gun only when the Pawnee fumbled for his. Even then, Brown held his fire until his adversary drew. He then shot Spotted Horse four times. Spotted Horse lasted about two hours, and then the *Caldwell Journal* could proclaim solemnly, "Spotted Horse is No More."[2] And he no longer was.

The same year, Brown got crossways with the gambler Newt Boyce whom he arrested and jailed for slashing two men in a saloon one Friday night. Boyce got out the next morning, but he bitterly resented his arrest and spent the Saturday drinking and sulking. He finished by threatening Wheeler with a pistol.

That brought in Brown, carrying his Winchester, and in the ensuing confrontation Boyce reached for his own gun. Brown shot him in the right arm, a slug that not only broke a bone but tore into his side. Boyce was dead before daylight.

Brown had it all: respect, decent pay, and domestic bliss. For in March of 1884, Brown married schoolteacher Alice Maude Levagood, apparently a real love match.

Some say it was love that finally, paradoxically, destroyed

Brown, for he bought his bride a house and all the fixin's. That cost money, though, and got Brown into serious debt. Some accounts suggest that maybe that was what moved him to depart from his new respectability and ride off with Wheeler and two Texas cowboys, Billy Smith and John Wesley.

Both cowboys were top hands on a spread called the T5, although Wesley was described by a Medicine Lodge, Kanasas, paper as having an "evil, reckless expression of countenance," and Smith as having a "hardened expression"—whatever that may mean.[3] It is only fair to record that the paper wrote these descriptions after the four were in custody for murder with a whole town baying for their blood.

Brown's announced purpose in leaving town with his little posse was to pursue outlaws down in Oklahoma, but what they really had in mind was money that was quick, easy, and wholly illegal. In fact, the four did not go to Oklahoma, but rode off to Medicine Lodge, Kansas, some seventy miles away. Two more cowhands were supposed to fill out the gang, but one of them killed the other over a gambling game and departed for the High Lonesome.

The objective of Brown and his three companions, the Medicine Valley Bank, proved to be no pushover. The bank's president, E. W. Payne, unwisely went for his gun, and the gang shot him down. Then they wantonly killed cashier George Geppert as he stood helplessly with his hands raised. Resourceful to the end, Geppert managed to stagger to the vault and lock it before he died.

By now the citizenry of the town were aroused, and the four would-be robbers took to their heels. By what would be for Brown a terrible coincidence, one of the pursuers was a man for whom Brown had once worked. The gang got away temporarily, galloping through a driving rain, but now their leader had been identified.

If their luck had started out bad, it now got worse, aided by the usual stupidity of the western outlaw. They had had the foresight to stash fresh horses in a canyon of the Gyp Hills. Now pursued, they headed for their fresh mounts, on which they could easily lose their pursuers and their tired horses.

They got the wrong canyon.

They had remembered a landmark for the proper canyon, a farmer's fence—trouble was, while they were off robbing and killing, the farmer had improved his fence, eliminating the landmark, and causing the outlaws to take the wrong turn. Now there was no way out from the box canyon with no fresh horses and an angry, determined posse of citizens bottling up the only exit.

A ferocious firefight followed, but the posse was not going to go anywhere. It dawned on Brown and his boys that their opponents not only had determination, but more importantly, had access to those things the outlaws did not, such as reinforcements and the ability to resupply ammunition and food. Furthermore, the canyon was starting to flood as the rain continued to fall. The flood waters rose to at least two feet, and the outlaws knew their botched expedition into crime was all over.

And so Brown and his bedraggled gang called it quits. The populace of Medicine Lodge was profoundly angry over the murder of two of the town's leading citizens. The *Medicine Lodge Cresset* reported that the outlaws' appearance was greeted with ominous shouts of "hang them, hang them."[4] Brown and the others were quickly jailed, and guards posted to protect them.

Whatever else he was, Brown was no fool, and he read the temper of the town, quickly foresaw the danger, and managed to slip out of his handcuffs. Perhaps he knew that banker Payne lived long enough to name Brown as his killer.

However, the guards posted to protect Brown were to no avail, for during the evening a large mob slowly gathered, overpowered the guards, and pulled the prisoners from their cells. One has to wonder how hard the guards tried to protect men who had killed fellow citizens from a posse of their friends and neighbors.

And so, when the mob burst in Brown ran, sprinting through the mob and dashing for an alley. He almost made it, but he could not outrun both barrels of a citizen's shotgun. Wheeler also ran and made it about a hundred yards before he fell, wounded, but he still joined the other two survivors in a noose under a nearby tree.

Brown's wife was left with only a letter from her husband of a few weeks, a weepy farewell that included the words, "it was all for you, sweet wife, and for the love I have for you."[5] No doubt those tender thoughts were a great comfort to a new widow.

Some careful researchers have questioned whether the writer of the letter was really Brown, because an earlier writing was apparently signed by Brown with only an "X", indicating he was probably illiterate. But there is evidence that, illiterate or not, he was the same Brown who ran with the Kid and ended up as marshal of Caldwell. The most probable explanation is simply that some decent soul wrote the letter for him, a common thing in a day when many men had little or no schooling.

You don't have to know how to read or write to punch—or rustle—cattle and horses. Or kill men.

Chapter 4

John Larn:
The Evil Genius of Fort Griffin

In its time Fort Griffin, Texas, was as wild a place as North America could boast, the kind of settlement Hollywood film-makers would invent, but Fort Griffin was very real and very dangerous. It was the hub of what was called the Clear Fork Country of West Texas, named for the Clear Fork of the Brazos, the region's chief river. There was a military post there, and the town—such as it was—commonly was called "the Flat" to distinguish it from the real fort. For a while, the troopers were the law around the fort, but once that changed to civilian control, chaos followed, for there wasn't any civilian law worthy of the name.

So Fort Griffin drew characters like flies to honey, and a lot of them were not the sort to invite home to dinner. Doc Holliday spent some time in Fort Griffin. It is there that Holliday first met Wyatt Earp, the story goes, while Earp was in pursuit of another sometime-resident of the town, Dirty Dave Rudabaugh. With Holliday was his mistress Big-Nose Kate Elder and other residents and visitors including storied gambling lady Lottie Deno, killer John Selman, and Pat Garrett.

Lottie Deno—worth a word or two—was not only an accomplished poker player, but also a remarkably attractive redhead who stood out from the general ruck of frontier women in looks, temperament, and behavior. She never seemed to lose her pleasant manners and engaging ways even in times of crisis.

She is said to have come from a fine southern family that was ruined in the Civil War and to have learned the gambling trade from her ne'er-do-well husband who deserted her after he knifed a man to death.

One story about her tells of a poker game in Fort Griffin where Deno was playing at a table that included a couple of belligerent characters called Smoky Joe and Monte Bill. Well, somewhere during the game Bill and Joe had a falling out, and both went for their guns. This produced, as usual, an abrupt exodus of the other patrons—except for Deno.

When the smoke blew away and the law appeared, nobody was around the saloon except Smoky Joe and Monte Bill, both deader than pork, having exterminated each other, and Deno, quiet and composed, counting her chips. The sheriff, a man named Cruger, said he was surprised she had not sought refuge like the other patrons. "Perhaps," said Deno, "but then you are not a desperate woman."[1]

Deno is said to have watched Doc Holliday break the faro bank in a dive called the Bee Hive, which advertised its pleasures thusly:

Within the Hive, we are alive,
Good Whiskey makes us funny.
Get your horse tied, come inside,
And taste the flavor of our honey.[2]

Holliday won a lot of that honey, something in the neighborhood of $3,000, a considerable chunk of money in those days. The story goes that Deno took over the busted bank, continued the play, and won back all three grand. The Flat was so colorful that there was seldom a dull moment. It was also a very dangerous place indeed.

One estimate of the casualty rate around the Flat came to about fifty-five in eight years, mostly wooly folks who killed each other with a variety of deadly weapons, sometimes over nothing more than a hard look or a refusal to have a drink. Plus of course, there were the usual arguments over cards, some lady who rented by the hour, or simply big-mouthed braggadocio. There were also some casualties produced by vigilante efforts to cleanse the area a mite.

There were lots of bad men around Fort Griffin and Shackleford County generally, but the worst of the lot, and maybe the most dangerous, was a murderous gentleman called John Larn. A gentleman he surely was, by the standards of the day, courteous to the ladies—he never swore, drank, or smoked in a woman's presence—and generally quite likeable. He made friends easily and mostly kept them, unless, of course, they got crossways with him, which wasn't hard to do.

Paradoxically, Larn was also a powerful force for law and order in the Fort Griffin country. A Shackleford County justice of the peace called him a "veritable Dr. Jekyll and Mr. Hyde,[3]" and that he was.

John Larn

Nobody knows a great deal about Larn's antecedents save that he came from Alabama. He did a lot of wandering early on, as a lot of footloose youngsters did in the West. Just what happened during his early travels is not entirely clear. There is evidence that he killed a man up in Colorado in some sort of argument over a horse. Apparently Larn stole his boss's horse—he said it was in lieu of the pay the man refused to give him—and, when his boss gave chase, Larn spun around and ventilated him.

Leaving Colorado—probably a healthy idea—he made his way down into New Mexico where he got crossways somehow with a peace officer and killed him, too. Larn kept moving and finally found some sort of settled life outside Fort Griffin working as a trail boss for a local rancher named Bill Hayes. He was still only a youngster, but his boss trusted him enough to send him off to Colorado with some 1,700 head of cattle, bound for market.

The trip was difficult, with one stretch of it through the terrible Llano Estacado, which was largely waterless for about a hundred miles. It was a rough trip at the best of times, until the herd won through to the Pecos River, where cattle and horses indulged in an orgy of drinking. The men did some killing, for they shot two Mexican horsemen at their halt along the river, apparently just because they were Mexicans. The remains were tossed into the river, but the violence was not over.

One of Larn's men—a very tough sort named Bill Bush—killed a fellow cowboy. A little later both Larn and Bush murdered a Mexican shepherd, for no perceptible reason because the man's flock was not disturbed. Maybe his offense was simply being Mexican. The shepherd joined the two other nameless riders killed on the Pecos and a lawman murdered in Trinidad, Colorado.

In early 1872, John Hittson, a prominent Clear Fork cattleman, began to organize a small volunteer army to deal with the Comancheros who had been decimating his and other ranchers' herds. Larn joined, of course, as did the brothers John and Tom Selman, and a host of others, including professional gun hands Chunk Colbert and the storied killer Clay Allison.

The Hittson Raid, as it was called, was a success; thousands of animals were recovered and a couple of suspected rustlers summarily killed. Sadly, not all the hired guns scattered very far. Frank Freeman, for example, stayed in New Mexico and amused himself by shooting down three men—again Mexican—and wounding a black soldier. Law and order had enough of him after that, and he found himself at the dirty end of a posseman's bullet. And then, in early 1874, Allison and Colbert got upset at one another and went for their guns. Colbert came in second. Allison lasted another few years until, in 1887, he managed to fall out of a wagon he was driving and died when a wheel ran over him. The world was a much cleaner place.

In spite of all this, or perhaps in part because of it—no shrinking violets are trail bosses—Hayes trusted Larn enough to give him a power of attorney and let him manage the home ranch while Hayes was away. It was a terrible mistake.

Larn paid his benefactor back by rustling his boss's stock and building up his own herd with the help of the power of attorney his boss had given him. It was a terrible financial blow to the Hayes boys. When Hayes and his brother discovered the rustling, a one-time trusting association turned ugly. Larn solved it by swearing out his own warrant charging the Hayes brothers with rustling and chasing them with a posse composed of the acting sheriff and a detachment of troops from the fort.

When they caught up with the Hayes brothers at a place called Bush Knob, what should have been a peaceful arrest turned into a massacre. Both of the Hayes boys died, along with Bush, the cowboy gunman who had been a close friend of Larn, and two more hands. To cap off the whole gruesome affair, the four surviving prisoners "attempted to escape" on the way back and were forthwith dispatched to join the rest of the Hayes outfit. They were either shot or hanged, depending on the version of the story. One cowboy thought they had been shot in their sleep, since their saddles, which they would have used as pillows, had been burned, presumably to cover bullet holes.

Eight men died in what is now known as the Bushy Knob Massacre, and a substantial herd was "recovered," as many as a thousand cattle and some forty horses. The impression around the Clear Fork country was generally that the "fight" and subsequent killing of the "escapers" was just plain murder.

There is some mystery to this that is hard to explain to this day. The soldiers had a lieutenant in command, and there was the acting sheriff, to boot. Either or both of them should have kept the violence to a minimum; heaven only knows what Larn told them that produced so violent a bloodbath. In any event, Larn was well on his way to building his own herd.

There still wasn't much law around Fort Griffin, and much of what existed was provided for years by a vigilante organization curiously called the Old Law Mob. It was supplanted later by a secret society known even more curiously as the Tin Hat Band Brigade, of which Larn was undoubtedly one of the organizers. Then, in February of 1876, Larn got himself elected sheriff of Shackleford County.

In that year things were so bad for the stockmen of the county that a paper in a nearby town summed the crisis up this way:

> The stealing of horses has become so frequent that the losers could not purchase fresh stock fast enough to satisfy the demand of the horse thief.[4]

That, along with his prominence with the Brigade, made Larn the major player in cleaning up the county. Now that he had his own spread, however ill-gotten, he became a force for law and order and for the eradication of rustling, as long as it applied to other people.

Larn landed a contract in the autumn of 1877 to supply the fort with cattle, anywhere from one to three a day. That quickly added up to a lot of beef, but as one noted historian put it, "the peculiar thing was that his own herd did not seem to get any smaller. But other people's herds did."[5]

Increasingly, Larn depended on John Selman as his chief assistant; he added a few other problem children, including Selman's brother, called Tomcat. They gathered regularly at a place called the Stone Ranch, where they seemed to be planning more devilries because Larn's herds still gradually expanded in size while surrounding spreads lost stock. Selman, who features more in this book later, does not seem to have been a known bad man before his association with the younger Larn. But afterward, he turned into a memorable killer.

Rustling soon resumed for Larn and others, and murder was fairly commonplace, such as the killing of a lawyer who was representing the wife of a local rancher in a divorce case. Apparently his offense was simply doing his duty to his client, but that was the way of things in early Fort Griffin.

For a while violence in the Flat subsided a little because the commander of the fort apparently had a gutful of the lawlessness and alleged that his jurisdiction extended to cover the Flat. The officer ordered the gamblers, whores, booze peddlers, and other undesirables to take a hike. Some of the lowlifes departed the Flat, but others simply moved across the Clear Fork out of the army's jurisdiction and continued whatever nefarious business kept them in booze and beans. Still, the Flat was a lot quieter for a couple of years, at least until 1874, when it returned to civilian jurisdiction and chaos resumed.

Then in 1876, Larn became sheriff of the county, which included not only Shackleford but a vast territory all around it. Now the fox was indeed watching the hen house, but at least he could be counted on to keep the rest of the foxes under some sort of control. At about the same time the Tin Hat Band Brigade came into being. Like so many vigilante organizations of the time, the Brigade was composed of "substantial" men, including, for example, the justice of the peace-*cum*-county-coroner.

And they were active. In April 1876, a Tin Hat Band Brigade posse ran down Charles McBride and Calvin Sharp, whose profession was horse stealing. Both of the wastrels were wounded in a running fight with the posse. Sharp died of his wounds, but apparently McBride was not sufficiently moribund for the posse. He ended up dangling from a convenient pecan tree. The local paper commented: "by inadvertence, perhaps, one end of the rope encircled his neck." As a final thoughtful touch, the posse left a pick and shovel beneath the tree, to accommodate anybody who chose to waste time planting the remains. The posse left a note with the body: "He said his name was McBride, but he was a liar as well as a thief."[6]

Meanwhile, another bunch of horse-lovers appropriated some horses that didn't belong to them, and Larn gave chase with a formidable posse and a detachment of cavalry that included some Tonkawa scouts. When the fleeing thieves split up, Larn's formidable force ran down the slower group of malefactors and made short work of them.

Joe Watson, Larapie Dan, and Red McCluskie, wounded in the fight that followed, were forthwith strung up and departed, as the paper said, "to a land where horses are not required."[7] The Brigade spared a buffalo-hunter named Burr, whose involvement in the rustling business was not clear, and a soiled dove called Mrs. Wolf who presumably returned to her horizontal profession in the Flat.

Along the way the population was reduced by a man named Faught, who was shot and wounded by City Marshal Big Bill Gilson. Vigilantes—presumably Tin Hat Band Brigade members—called on Faught shortly thereafter, removed him from his bed of pain, and attached him to a tree by his neck as well. They left a note, too, identifying him as "Horse thief No. 5" and adding that he had murdered a boy and scalped him to make the murder appear as if it had been the work of Indians.

The "No. 5" had an ominous ring to it if you were in the rustling business, implying that there was a death list of those who purloined other people's stock. There probably was. Significantly, the note added that Faught "would have company soon." He would.

Larn went off to Dodge City, where tough marshal Charlie Bassett had nabbed two more bad hats named Henderson and Floyd. While Larn was retrieving them, the Tin Hat Band- Brigade collected a man named Reddy, and he too ended up swinging from a tree outside Fort Griffin. The *Jacksboro Frontier Echo* captured the moment with its headline:

> One by One the Roses Fall. Court Proceedings on the Clear Fork, Judge Lynch Presiding.[8]

Larn, returning with his prisoners, promptly lost them to the Tin Hat Band boys, who "overpowered" two guards at the jail, extracted the rustlers, and promptly hung them—it is likely that the sheriff himself was one of the invaders.

There seems to have been substantial approval of the way the Tin Hats disposed of the rustler cases. One source estimated that more than 100,000 horses were stolen in Texas in just three years; the number of cattle must have been astronomical. But the Tin Hat boys were making an impression, and the papers generally supported their campaign. One paper wrote:

> Within the past two months five or six men have been found hanging from trees. . . . No one seems to know how they got there, nor are they sufficiently interested in the matter to inquire . . . the public verdict is suicide under the influence of remorse, caused by the larceny of a horse.[9]

Larn's fall from grace may date from another ferocious gunfight in the Bee Hive, one of those pointless, all-too-common episodes that started over some sarcastic language and ended with three men dead and several wounded. One of the dead was a big cowman named Bland who had been engaged in shooting out the saloon's lights when the scrap started. Larn's deputy, Cruger, was involved.

The trouble was that Larn believed that Bland, a friend of Larn's, had been cut down without warning, as related by another participant in the fight. He became estranged from Cruger and even from the gentlemen of the Tin Hat Band Brigade. He now spent a lot of time at the Old Stone Ranch with John Selman, his closest confidant.

Between them, Larn and Selman killed several more men and put the rest of their energy into ranching. Their methods were sometimes underhanded, even murderous. Take the case of the 1877 tragedy at Bottomless Wells, two sinkholes on the edge of a creek, where Larn and Selman met a pair of young men with a herd to sell.

It was a sweet deal for Larn. He and Selman rode off with the cattle and the two young men ended up weighted down and tossed into the Bottomless Wells. The same year Larn is alleged to have saved some more money by paying two stonemasons to do a great deal of work around his home—and then finishing their pay with bullets.

At least that was the common suspicion, and Larn's reputation declined further. Two bodies showed up in the river later; and although nobody could positively say that they were the remains of the masons, suspicion fell on Larn.

Larn didn't learn. Rather, he stepped up his rustling operations. His particular targets were small ranchers—"Grangers" to the bigger cattlemen—and in time a few of them had the tremendous courage to call on the law in the form of Deputy Cruger. Cruger knew the dangers of going out to Larn's domain. So when it came time to serve a warrant charging Larn with theft, Cruger took along a posse of his own and a couple of Texas Rangers.

Sure enough, there was a confrontation, but the law men did succeed in dragging the river on Larn's property—there were a good many hides weighted down out there, but none of the brands were Larn's or Selman's.

The Rangers were now in this one to stay, and they got some help when they captured Hurricane Bill Martin, already wanted for murder. Martin knew a lot about the doings of the Tin Hat boys, and he sang beautifully. Among other things, he told the Rangers about the murder of "English Jack" by a buffalo hunter, a killing immediately answered by a lynching. This time the vigilantes called themselves the Hunter's Protective Union. Most importantly, Martin was prepared to testify, and he knew a lot.

That was a serious threat to the peace and comfort of a lot of locals, many of them prominent men who had been members of the Tin Hat Band Brigade and just maybe the Old Law Mob before it. Very few of the county aristocracy wanted to dig up old bones—or old bodies, should it come to that. And so resistance to the use of the evidence was fierce.

Things went from bad to worse for the Grangers, what with night riders, shots in the dark, and the wanton killing of stock, including milk cows and calves. There were allegations that Larn had openly tried to kill one Granger. Some of the small ranchers gave up and moved on, but many did not. And by now the Tin Hat Band Brigade had turned on Larn as well.

At last a writ was issued for Larn, Selman, and several others, and a large posse went out to serve it. Cruger led them, and he had taken the precaution of first speaking to the heads of two powerful local families and securing their approval. The men sent to arrest Selman found he had been warned and fled, but Larn had not.

Knowing Larn's reputation and gun fighting ability, the posse went expecting a fight, but the affair ended, as T. S. Eliot put it, "not with a bang but a whimper." Larn emerged from his house early in the day to do his chores. He was not armed and was taken easily.

"Boys," he is reputed to have said, "it is the first time you have ever caught me without my gun," and he offered $500 to the posse to let him call his wife to bring him his weapon, an unlikely notion unless he intended suicide by posse. Larn would fight the whole bunch; he said they were cowards, et cetera. There were no takers, and Larn went off to jail in Albany, the county seat.

The building was not much, but it was an escape-proof jail if there ever was one. The local law said nobody had ever escaped from it, an unusual record for frontier hoosegows. During the day the prisoners were only shackled, but at night they were chained to the floor of the building with a long chain running through their leg shackles. There were guards, too, never fewer than two, and on this fateful night, Sunday the twenty-third of June, there were four.

They were dependable men: new Sheriff Cruger's brother, a one-time buffalo hunter named Poe, a saloon owner, and one other deputy. There was a story that Larn offered one guard $1,500 to let him escape, but it is probably legend because any escape attempt would have to get around the other three guards, as well. The night went on, peacefully at first; two guards turned in, and the other two stayed on watch. Until that is, there arose a "noise like the tramping of men's feet." And so it was. The guards estimated the mob's number at anywhere from twenty to thirty-five.

The guards were quickly disarmed, and an impromptu firing squad of six or eight masked men lined up in front of Larn. One of them asked Larn if he had anything to say. One source attributed Larn with this speech:

> Not to you cowardly murderers. But if you'll turn me loose and give me a forty-five, I'll fight your whole outfit. Go ahead; I'll take my medicine.[10]

They either didn't care about hanging Larn—the usual means of disposing of bad men—or didn't realize somebody in the jail must have the keys to the various locks. They simply blazed away at point-blank range and filled Larn full of holes. A witness said later that Larn died game, simply looking his executioners in the eye and dying in silence.

None of the guards recognized anybody, of course, and so testified at the coroner's inquest. The other prisoners were not even called, and the jury predictably found that Larn had left this mortal coil as a result of nine pistol bullets, fired by men who were, of course, unknown.

Officially, that is, for everybody in the county could at least guess who had rid the world of Larn, and there is reason to believe that some of the vigilantes were Larn's in-laws. Larn's loyal wife mourned him, but very few other people did.

Larn had started as a likeable, talented man, but he brought his ending upon himself. One resident pronounced his epitaph: "He was the meanest man I ever knew."[11]

Larn's death marked the end of an era in Shackleford County, or at least the beginning of a new one. It marked the last hurrah of the Tin Hat Band as well, and the advent of real, official law and order.

Chapter 5

Bob and Grat Dalton: Disaster at Coffeyville

Arguably no band of outlaws has been more famous in the popular history of the American west than the brothers Bob and Grat Dalton. In fact, in terms of loot collected, they were poor outlaws. They should have stuck to being lawmen, at which they were at least marginally successful.

Their brother Frank had been the genuine article, a respected deputy U.S. Marshal, killed by outlaws down in the brakes of the Arkansas River. A good deal of twaddle has been written about how Bob and Grat joined the side of the angels to avenge his death. One story claims Bob Dalton pursed a killer across several states before finally killing him in a wild shootout.

In another version of the tale, Bob was not only present when Frank was killed but also killed both the murderer and his wife on the spot. The story in fact was that another federal officer with Frank killed three of the remaining outlaws and still another deputy marshal got the last one later.

But Bob and Grat Dalton did indeed ride on the right side of the law, for a while anyhow, and their younger brother Emmett Dalton joined them as a posse man. It was not attractive work, at least to them, because a marshal's pay was small and slow in coming and the dangers were significant. When the brothers joined the marshals, fifteen Fort Smith deputies had been killed in just two years.

The Daltons' reputations as lawmen were not unblemished. As one pioneer woman put it, "when the Dalton boys were United States marshals they were cold and cruel." And there are all sorts of stories about them shooting too fast or shooting the wrong people; in one tale, told about both Grat and Bob, a Dalton brother shot an apple off a child's head William-Tell-style.

Furthermore, there were allegations of a protection racket, turning a blind eye to whiskey-runners—sale of alcohol in Indian Territory was a federal crime—in return for an appropriate payoff. A variation on that theme claims that the brothers planted booze in wagons full of pilgrims bound for the Promised Land in Oklahoma Territory. When the wagons would be stopped and the booze found, a "fine" would be imposed on the spot. Other crooked lawmen had practiced this dodge, and, given the Dalton boys' flexible morals, it is quite likely that they tried it too.

Whatever the Dalton boys' list of transgressions really amounted to, the United States marshal at Fort Smith decided he could dispense with the services of the brothers. At this point, at least in theory, outlawry looked easier than riding about in the Territory, taking chances, living rough and earning miserable wages. The brothers must have thought lawbreaking had to pay better than honesty.

One wonderful fable surrounds their time as lawmen and is often cited as a reason Bob and Grat Dalton were finally fired by the marshal. It is an engaging tale of lust, betrayal, revenge, and a delectable lass named Minnie. The story is partly apochryphal, but it is far too good to pass up the chance to include it here. It goes like this:

Bob Dalton didn't take kindly to anybody fooling around with his girlfriend Minnie, a delicious young thing, as the story goes. And that, says one of the west's durable fables, was why Charlie Montgomery ended up dead.

The tale tells that Minnie was Bob's girlfriend but that she might have been his first cousin or even his mother Adeline Dalton's "adopted niece." In any case, kin or not, Minnie and Bob Dalton were indulging in an occasional roll in the hay. Minnie is described in one fanciful book on the Daltons as "a little heartless coquette of a country lass . . . sprightly, saucy, thoughtless."[1]

Enter Montgomery, who was engaging in some horizontal gymnastics on Minnie's couch, or maybe Minnie was gracing Montgomery's bed. Legend tells us that Minnie had become intrigued with "the massive figure and engaging manners of Charley Montgomery."[2]

In time, according to one version of the story, Bob Dalton began to wonder what Minnie might be doing while he was away in his role as marshal. And so Bob and Grat searched Montgomery's quarters and there found a "lady's red-silk handkerchief" that Bob had given to his light-o'-love. Bob concluded that Montgomery had stolen not only Minnie's heart but the rest of her as well.[3]

Minnie, becoming aware of Bob's budding anger, lost no time departing Coffeyville with Montgomery by train. According to one fanciful account of the affair, Bob shot holes in their passenger car as it rolled out of town. Sometime later, Montgomery unwisely returned to Coffeyville to retrieve some belongings; this turned out to be a terminal mistake, for Bob promptly ventilated him.

Bob announced that he had killed Montgomery in the line of duty, claiming that his rival was nothing more than a lowdown horse thief, and Bob said he was a posseman for his brother Grat, then serving as a United States Deputy Marshal.

Sadly, this whole charming story is pure moonshine; the seductive Minnie is most likely a juicy invention, and she was surely not a cousin of any kind. Nor is there any evidence that she knew Bob Dalton from Adam, if, for that matter, she existed at all.

Montgomery was real, however, and he was a posturing lout

and penny-ante criminal, "a bootlegger . . . road agent and pimp."[4] And that was on his good days.

Jake Bartles, founder of the tiny hamlet called Bartlesville, was a tough, resourceful man who rightly suspected Montgomery of stealing merchandise from his store. As Bartles testified before a federal magistrate, Montgomery had approached Jim Long, a Bartles employee, with a proposition to "steal two mares and rob my store." According to Long, Montgomery proposed:

> that we could go into stealing and robbing and we could go into Mr. Bartles store here and then we can go out here and go to stealing some of these horses that were running in Mr. Bartles' pasture . . . and we can down Jake Bartles for his money.[5]

As the *Coffeyville Journal* pithily put it later:

> [Montgomery] had been playing some unwarranted games since his advent there . . . about a month ago he came to Coffeyville and represented himself as a U.S. Marshal, and had to be arrested and disarmed. He was suspected of . . . running off horses . . . and various petty crimes. . . . Lately he had appropriated two revolvers that did not belong to him, and had secured a horse that was not his own.[6]

Bartles summoned the law, which appeared in the form of Bob Dalton and several posse men. Dalton got word that his quarry would be at the house of Juno—or Junius—Brown, and, with posse men Jeff Gregg (Griggs) and Al Landers, he rode out to the Brown place.

Bob and his men wisely approached on foot. Bob tells the tale in the summary record of the hearing on Montgomery's death:

> I went to [the] south side of [the] house and Griggs and Landers went to [the] northwest corner. . . . Just as I stepped over the yard fence, the dog barked and I seen Landers dodge down behind the fence and just immediately I heard a gun fire.[7]

Montgomery shot at Landers and Gregg, and ran around the side of the house. Dalton heard Landers shout, "Stop! Throw up your hands!" and then another shot rang out. Dalton ran around his side of the house and met Montgomery head-on. According to Dalton, he challenged Montgomery but got no further than, "Stop, Charley!" when his quarry fired point-blank—about eight feet—into his face.

Miraculously, Montgomery missed, although the range was so short that the muzzle blast from his pistol scorched Bob Dalton's cheek. A round from Dalton's shotgun knocked the outlaw down on his hands and knees. Shot in the gut, Montgomery departed this life and did not return. Dalton told the magistrate that he went after Montgomery as "posse for my brother, who was a Deputy U.S. Marshal of this District." He admitted that neither he nor Grat Dalton had a warrant for Montgomery but were after him for "stealing the pistols and stealing a horse. When we heard he was going to leave the country, we concluded it was best to arrest him before he would be gone."[8]

Posseman Gregg testified before the magistrate that Montgomery leaped to his feet as the lawmen approached, pulled his pistol, and blazed away. The first shot tore through Gregg's hat brim and knocked his hat from his head.

Gregg and Landers returned fire almost together, and then, Gregg testified:

> deceased turned around corner of house out of my sight. Just as he got out of my sight, there was a pistol and a shotgun fired. The pistol fired just a little before the shotgun.[9]

Landers confirmed the stories told by both Bob Dalton and Jeff Greggs. He also denied any agreement to murder Charlie Montgomery and said Montgomery had fired at him from about fifteen feet. Landers testified:

As he [Montgomery] raised up from chair he drew his revolver. Whirled on his heels and fired a shot at me. I heard him say "Damn you" or "God damn you."[10]

Montgomery fired on Landers and Gregg, and one of his bullets tore some skin from Landers's right ear.

Landers also heard Bob Dalton shout at Montgomery, "hold up Charley!" He confirmed that "two or three grains of powder" were sticking to Dalton's right cheekbone after the fight and that Dalton complained that his face burned.

Jake Bartles denied that he "ever offered any money to defendants to arrest or kill Deceased." This interesting testimony was in answer to somebody's allegation that he and the Dalton boys had conspired to murder Montgomery. Bob Dalton and his two posse men supported Bartles's testimony, denying any such agreement.

Two more witnesses confirmed that four chambers of Montgomery's pistol were empty. One added that just before Montgomery was killed, he said the Daltons were after him.
The last witness, A. P. Lyman, was the most interesting man to speak at the magistrate's hearing. Montgomery came to Lyman's home, he said, on August 11 and told Lyman that

he would kill the whole damned ring and in this connection he mentioned . . . Jake Bartles . . . the Dalton boys as the ones who were after him, the parties he would kill.[11]

Thus the real story of Charlie Montgomery and Bob Dalton is sadly far from the salacious tale of the luscious Minnie.

To most people, at least, Montgomery was an unmitigated nuisance and departed this life largely unlamented. In view of the unanimity of the lawmen's testimony about what happened at Brown's farm, and considering the disreputable nature of the dead man, it is not surprising that the case ended before the federal magistrate and went no further.

In the casual, common law of the west, Montgomery just needed killing.

But once the brothers had left the fold of the law-abiding for good, they made up for lost time. The boys drifted out into New Mexico where, in Santa Rosa, they are said to have held up a faro game (or, depending on which account you read, a monte game or a Chinese laundry). Whatever happened, the Daltons made tracks for California, where their brother Bill had a place near Paso Robles.

In California, the Dalton brothers had a somewhat murky encounter with the law, and allegations linked them to a train holdup. It happened in early 1891 at Alila, a water stop down in Tulare County. Somebody robbed a train, all right, but how the railroad and the law determined that the Daltons were the culprits has never been clear. Considering the brothers's later history, the odds are pretty fair that the Alila incident was the Daltons' maiden voyage into the train business.

Grat and Bill Dalton wound up in jail, and their brothers Bob and Emmett went on the run. Grat was even convicted, although a dozen witnesses testified that at the critical time he was elsewhere, sopping up whiskey and playing cards—two of his three favorite pastimes, besides beating on people. He and some others broke out of the jail, and Grat eventually made his way back to his home country, where Bob and Emmett were waiting. They had passed their time stealing horses; and in May of 1891, at a place called Twin Mounds, the brothers shot down a member of a posse chasing them.

Alila and the Twin Mounds murder did not convince the brothers that a life on the run was not a good thing; instead, they turned to train robbery and attracted a gang of criminals as tough as they were—and just about as inept. They included "Blackfaced" Charley Bryant, "Bitter Creek" Newcomb, Bill

Power, Dick Broadwell, "Cockeye" Charley Pierce, Bill Doolin, a man called "Six-shooter Jack," and others, including an odd ducknamed McIlhanie, who was called the "Narrow Gauge Kid."[12]

Now the boys got down to train robbery in earnest. They hit a Southern Pacific train near Wharton, a tiny town in eastern Indian Territory near present-day Perry, Oklahoma. The gang followed that up by robbing another train—"The Katy," a nickname for the Missouri, Kansas, and Texas line—at Leliatta, and again near Wagoner. However, none of these raids came close to being the big strike every outlaw dreamed about.

Now at last they would get rich, they thought, because the train they were stalking was supposed to be carrying the Sac and Fox tribal annuity, worth something in the neighborhood of $70,000, a great deal of money in those days. The men stopped the train at Red Rock only to discover that they had the wrong train. They got less than $3,000 and, rather spitefully, went on to steal the guard's watch, small change, and even the crew's lunchboxes.

The fog of mythology that surrounds the Daltons produced a story that Blackfaced Charley Bryant had wantonly murdered the station agent at Red Rock. The biggest problem with this horrifying tale was that Bryant had been dead for the greater part of a year, having eaten a lawman's bullet and found it indigestible.

The next raid was scheduled for Pryor Creek, but Bob Dalton smelled trouble there and announced, "We'll outfox them. They'll be expecting us at Pryor Creek, but we'll be robbing the train at Adair."[13]

So they did, but the gang found the place inhospitable, for the train carried a force of lawmen who promptly opened fire on them. The gang managed to escape that menace and they galloped out of town. But as they did, they fired a dozen or more rounds at two unarmed men standing on a store porch. Both men were doctors, and both went down with leg wounds. One lost part of his foot; the other, Dr. W. L. Goff, would die of his wound.

If a real "code" of the west existed, it included the command-ment not to harm doctors or clergymen. Both were saviors of people and would treat the wounds—body or soul—of anybody at all: criminal or saint or anything in between. Thus, as a result of the attack on the two doctors and the murder of Dr. Goff, every man's hand turned against the Daltons.

With no place to hide securely, and any citizen likely to inform on them, Bob Dalton realized that it was high time to leave Oklahoma. But he and his brothers wanted to replenish their finances before they ran, and Bob had an idea he thought would allow them to leave with their reputation as big dogs still intact.

The Dalton boys moved north across the Kansas line with the law, in the person of formidable U.S. Deputy Marshal Heck Thomas, only about a day behind them. They had chosen to hit quiet little Coffeyville, Kansas, and try to do what no outlaw gang had ever done successfully before: They were going to rob two banks at once. It was a point of pride with the leader of the pack, Bob Dalton, that in doing so they would eclipse the record of their cousins, the Younger boys, who had never managed that feat over many long years as career outlaws.

Maybe it didn't occur to Bob Dalton that his cousins were then in prison in Minnesota after their failed raid on a bank in Northfield. Three of the men who had ridden with them were quite dead of bullet disease and had long been engaged in second careers as professional cadavers in a medical school.

So, instead of getting out of the line of fire immediately, the Daltons were going to pull another job, the big one, as much out of braggadocio as real need. This last job would turn out to be one raid too many and would bring mother Dalton more sorrow and shame than befell ten women.

The Dalton boys' mother was Adeline Younger, who was an aunt to the notorious Younger boys. She was a decent Christian lady who, at sixteen, made the mistake of marrying Lewis Dalton, a lazy wastrel who did little but travel the territory following the horses. He did get home often enough, though, that Adeline had fifteen children. Most of them turned out well, like her lawman-son Frank, but Bob, Grat, Emmett, and Bill Dalton were shame enough. Bill would go bad later on and eventually be killed by the law. Now it was the turn of the other three.

And so, on a pleasant morning in October of 1892, the outlaw band rode into Coffeyville for what they thought would be their last hurrah, the profit of which would finance their flight to the good life far away from the Territory. The choice of target was the first of Bob Dalton's very bad ideas; for the Dalton family had lived for a time in the Coffeyville area, and the brothers' faces were familiar to many of the residents.

Coffeyville was a small, quiet town where nobody carried a gun, including the acting town marshal (in fact a school principal). The residents of this peaceful place concentrated on peaceful pursuits, family, business, schools, and church.

But that didn't change the fact that they were still frontier people, men and women who did not like being pushed around by a bunch of shiftless hoodlums and who were not about to stand for it. Though they were unarmed, they weren't afraid to fight, and weapons were easily available.

The next major mistake also belonged to Bob. Probably in an attempt to make the split of loot greater for each participant, he left some of his best gunmen behind, including cool hand Bill Doolin, who was destined for a further career as a notorious outlaw. This day, the gang would sorely miss the firepower they had left behind.

When the gang rode into town, they attracted some attention. Among other things, they were all carrying sidearms and poorly concealed rifles and were riding good saddle horses—this in a town where people went about their business unarmed and traveled mostly by wagon or buggy.

Because he thought he knew the town well, Bob did no reconnaissance at all, another major blunder. And so, when the gang left their temporary camp on Onion Creek to ride into town and terrorize the townsfolk and set their robbery record, they were surprised to find that all in Coffeyville was not as they remembered it.

In the interest of civilized civic improvement, sidewalks and gutters and such, the Coffeyville city fathers had taken down the very hitching-post to which the gang intended to tie their all-important horses. "I'll be damned," said Bob, stating the obvious, "look, the hitching rack is gone."[13]

What to do?

They rode around the busy streets until they found a spot to leave their horses. It was a pipe sticking up from the ground in the alley behind the police judge's house, but it was a full 350 feet from the bank, a very long way to run if people were shooting at them. If that had been the only place to tether a horse, the gang should have waited, even to the next day, until they could leave their horses closer to their target.

They didn't. They tied their horses to the pipe, pulled their rifles from the blanket rolls in which they had awkwardly tried to hide them, and walked down the alley and out into the plaza toward the banks. Inevitably, it was not long before a merchant saw and recognized them, and the word traveled quickly that the notorious Dalton gang was in town. Bob and Grat Dalton, at least, had made an attempt to disguise themselves with false mustaches and beards, which were obviously phony.

And so, almost instantly, much of the town was alerted to the gang's presence; two hardware merchants began handing out weapons and ammunition to anybody who wanted them. There were plenty of takers, including livery stable owner John Kloehr, considered the best shot in town.

To the lack of reconnaissance, Bob added another couple of monumental gaffes. First, he left nobody outside—in the alley mouth, say—to provide covering fire. Second, Bob took young Emmett with him to rob the First National Bank. However, that left Grat Dalton to lead Powers and Broadwell into the Condon. Grat was older than Bob and would ordinarily have led the gang, but he had a serious handicap. In a world full of unusually dense outlaws, Grat Dalton stood out. He was dumber than a rock.

The banks—the Condon and the First National—both fronted on a sizable plaza, into which ran several streets and an alley. Also fronting on the plaza were a number of businesses, including two hardware stores, a drug store, a dry goods store, and the Lang and Lape Furniture and Undertaking Emporium, which would do a land-office business this day.

A number of other businesses were nearby, including Cubine's Boot and Shoe shop, makers of the famed Coffeyville Boot, which was beloved by customers because it was actually made on separate lasts for each foot.

Now word spread quickly, especially when the bandits carried their rifles into the plaza and barged into the two banks. Inside the First National, Bob and Emmett Dalton—both wearing masks—did a fairly efficient job of raking in the cash, in spite of the bank staff's deliberate foot-dragging. At last, Bob Dalton went into the vault personally and came out with an additional $10,000 the bankers had hoped to conceal. This money went into the grain sack with the rest of the booty that Emmett Dalton was holding.

But over at the Condon, nothing whatsoever was happening other than the staff and customers standing about with their hands in the air. Grat Dalton and his men threw down on everybody and filled a sack with a little currency and an estimated 200 pounds of silver. Obviously, Grat had not worked out how he would get that load out of the bank, let alone on a horse. During these proceedings, a customer entered the bank through a side door, saw all those weapons, and vanished.

When Grat Dalton ordered bank personnel to open the vault, young cashier Charlie Ball looked him straight in the eye and solemnly explained that the vault was on a time lock and wouldn't open for about ten minutes. Another employee helpfully jiggled the vault handle—he was careful not to pull on it, for there was some $40,000 inside. Because it was a business day and the bank was open, the time lock had, of course, opened also. Only a real oaf would have believed Ball. That was Grat Dalton.

Years later Emmett Dalton, in an especially whiny passage from his autobiography, blamed Ball's "shifty falsehood" for the "deaths of eight men."[14] It didn't occur to him that his lawless greed, and his brothers', had something to do with what followed. Of course, with Emmett, nothing was ever his fault.

But Grat was the original oaf, so all he said was "we can wait,"[15] which ranks high among the most moronic things ever said by an outlaw—not a class notable for intellectual brilliance. He and Powers and Broadwell stood stupidly around in the Condon while the town armed itself outside. Even a glance out the bank's window would have revealed the gathering of the townsmen with rifles.

And at last, as even Grat began to wonder if he had been bamboozled, Bob and Emmett Dalton came out of the First National, and somebody took a shot at them.

The shot missed, although it scared a sign painter so badly that he fell off his scaffold. Other townspeople who didn't know about the trouble began to shoo children inside, seek shelter, and lock their doors.

Down at Cubine's, George Cubine—the only man in town who had a weapon in his place of business—grabbed his Winchester and went out to do battle. He took a crack at Bob and Emmett, who turned abruptly and ran back through into the First National. The bank men and customers they had herded in front of them as human shields kept moving out through the front. One bank officer, Tom Ayres, turned hard left and ran to Isham's Hardware to borrow a rifle.

Meanwhile, bullets poured through the windows of the Condon. Broadwell returned the fire, but his shooting was lousy, and one of the townsmen got a round into him. "I'm hit," he yelled, "I can't move my arm."

Bob Dalton had turned back to the door of the First National and now opened fire on the town's defenders. "You hold the loot," he told Emmett, "I'll do the fighting." He immediately wounded one of the defenders and hit another a little later. The second, Lou Dietz, was hit hard, but the bullet was deflected by an iron spanner in Dietz's pocket. The resulting wound was no more than a monstrous bruise.

Back at the Condon Bank, Powers was also hit before even leaving the building. He is said to have cried out, "I am shot. I can't use my arm. It's no use. I can't shoot anymore." Differing accounts attribute these words to Broadwell, but it is probable that both men were wounded long before they left the Condon building.[16]

Now Grat Dalton's stupidity came into play again. Even Grat could see that the Condon was drawing bullets like a carcass draws flies. It was high time to go. A customer who entered and hastily departed through a side door during the hold up had to have come from somewhere, but the significance of that did not penetrate what passed for Grat's brain.

So instead of fleeing out that door and putting a whole building between them and those deadly rifles over at the hardware stores, Grat led his men back out the way they had entered, across the plaza, which now became a huge shooting gallery. At first, he even told a couple of bank employees to bring along the monstrous grain sack full of silver, but they quickly gave up that notion. All three outlaws were quickly hit as they ran across the plaza heading for their horses, their lifeline so far away down the alley. Witnesses saw dust puff from their clothing from the impact of the bullets. But they managed to stay on their feet for at least a little way. Meanwhile, Bob Dalton killed one young townsman in the alley behind the First National. He then went to the end of the alley, turned into the street beyond it, and turned another corner, coming in behind George Cubine and another employee of Cubine's. He shot Cubine—a friend in other years—in the back, killing him. When the other man, a Civil War veteran, gallantly picked up Cubine's rifle, Bob killed him as well.

He then drilled Tom Ayres through the face, a wound that should have killed him but miraculously did not because a citizen rammed his thumb into the wound and managed to stop the bleeding. Bob and Emmett Dalton then kept going down back streets, sheltered from the citizens' fire.

Powers went down for good in the alley after trying to find shelter in a building. The door he tried was locked, and a bullet got him before he could reach his horse. Grat Dalton found refuge behind an oil tank wagon and killed town marshal Charlie Connolly. When the temporary lawman stepped out into the alley, he was tragically facing the wrong way. But now livery man Kloehr went into action, drilling badly-wounded Grat Dalton through his neck, breaking it, and putting him down for good. He turned on Broadwell and nailed him, and town barber Carey Seaman put a load of birdshot into the outlaw for good measure. Broadwell miraculously made it into the saddle and out of the alley, only to fall dead a short distance away.

This left Bob and Emmett Dalton, who were unscathed so far. Bob was still cocky. "I can whip the whole damn town," he yelled to Emmett, "I hit two. Now let's get to the horses."[17] But once they emerged into that deadly alley, everything changed. Bob went down hard, probably hit by a round from a shooter at one of the hardware stores.

Sitting in the alley, he kept on spasmodically working his Winchester, spraying bullets aimlessly. One of them went into Isham's Hardware and killed an inoffensive butter churn; another missed a case of dynamite stored at Isham's by an inch or two.

Now it takes more than a bullet to explode dynamite—despite what the movies portray—unless it has aged enough for TNT to form little drops on the exterior of the sticks. The condition of the dynamite at Isham's is not known, but, luckily for the citizenry, nothing happened.

Then Kloehr, or somebody at Isham's, nailed Bob Dalton again, and he fell over on his side in the dirt of the alley, finished.

Emmett Dalton had managed to mount his horse still carrying the grain sack full of money, but he was hit repeatedly: in the groin, torso, shoulder, and arm, which was broken. Still, young Emmett, short on brains and morals as he was, was not short on courage. He turned his horse back into the maelstrom of fire and reached down toward his brother. There's much mythology—created by Emmett, mostly—of a heroic final exchange between the two brothers, but the chances are that Bob was either already dead or too far gone to say anything at all.

But the day was over for Emmett, too, when barber Seaman put both barrels of his shotgun into him, blowing Emmett from his horse. The fight was finished, with a couple of hundred rounds fired in just a few moments. Four townsmen and four gang members were dead or dying, Emmett was a blasted wreck, and at least three citizens had been wounded. The alley—appropriately called "Death Alley" today—was a shambles of human corpses, puddles of blood, and dead horses.

Bob and Grat Dalton (Author's collection)

Emmett Dalton was moved to the second-floor office of Doctor Walter Wells and Wells began the almost Herculean effort of patching Emmett up. While he was so engaged, a group of very angry townspeople appeared in the doctor's office with a rope.

Their plan was simplicity itself: attach one end of their rope to Emmett and the other to a convenient pole just outside the good doctor's window. Step two was to propel Emmett through the window into space, thereby saving the taxpayers the expense of trial and execution and such inconveniences as hung juries and appeals.

"No need for this," said the doctor. "This man's going to die anyway." A voice from the crowd: "You sure, Doc?" Dr. Wells: "Hell yes, he'll die. Did you ever hear of a patient of mine getting well?" Somebody laughed, the tension broke, and Emmett would survive to spend long years in prison and write his self-serving book.[18]

Thus ended the Dalton gang. They weren't much as outlaws, either in planning or in execution. After the boys were finished by the citizens of Coffeyville, pompous brother Bill Dalton escorted his mother to the town and made an ass of himself, fulminating about revenge and how his brothers were justified in shooting people. He then turned outlaw on his own hook, if he wasn't one already. He wasn't even as good at it as his brothers had been, and he ended up on the dirty end of a lawman's bullet down in Oklahoma.

Bob and Grat Dalton took up permanent residence in Coffeyville. The only thing they got from that bunch of tough citizens was their headstone: the pipe to which they had hitched their horses in the deadly alley.

Chapter 6

Wyatt Earp: Down by the Creek, Walkin' on Water

Wyatt Earp couldn't quite walk on water, but some western history writers have canonized him to the point at which it's hard to tell who he really was. He is cast as a hero beyond reproach, the ultimate lawman, the veritable Spirit of the West.

But then there are the other writings that have downplayed anything approaching hero talk and cast Earp as a lowlife, one reference calling him and his brothers "the fighting pimps." This reference seems to stem from the Kansas days, in which Earp was supposed to have run a harlot or two, or a whole house, in addition to maintaining law and order. It also may have something to do with Earp's light o' love—possibly a soiled dove, as the cultivated saying went—whom he brought to Tombstone.

And depending on whose account one reads, the story worsens. One writer, for example, calls Earp a "saloon keeper, cardsharp, bigamist, church deacon, confidence man, and extrovert,"[1] and comments on his "stint of buffalo hunting (in violation of Indian treaty)," a violation no doubt indulged in by a thousand other men of his time. Another writer calls him, among other things, a "bunco artist and supreme confidence man."

Earp did indeed have a spotty past, starting, as far as history shows, in 1869 in Lamar, Missouri. He was town constable, as well as collector of license fees for the county. There was a wrangle in 1871 about whether he had turned in all the fees collected. A citizen filed a lawsuit against him, claiming that Earp had not turned in the full payment he had collected from the man.

Whatever happened in that controversy, Earp's next encounter with the law—more serious this time—was in the spring of 1871 when Earp, Edward Kennedy, and John Shown were jointly charged with the theft of two horses, each valued at $100. Kennedy was tried and acquitted, but Earp made his way through the roof of the jail, across the yard, and under the fence and departed in haste for, of all places, Peoria, Illinois.

In Peoria, he seems to have been arrested three times, all for the same earthshaking offense: "keeping and being found in a house of ill-fame." Earp appears to have lived in a brothel, but his function there is not known. Maybe he was only a lodger, but most likely he was something more—a bouncer, perhaps, or maybe even a pimp. Whatever his duties were, if any, the first arrest cost him $20; the subsequent arrests were more expensive.

In the spring of 1875, Wyatt Earp joined the city marshal's office in Wichita, dealing faro in his off-duty time. It was there that he apparently met future long-time friends Luke Short and Bat Masterson. The paper reported his service during that time as "unexceptionable," whatever that meant. In fact, his service appears to have been exemplary in a town where the local law regularly extracted fees from bars, whores, and pimps in the section of the town called Delano, across the rolling Arkansas River.

Dodge City was next, and it was there that Earp was fined a dollar for slapping Frankie Bell. According to a newspaper account, Bell, described as a brawny prostitute, "heaped epithets upon the unoffending head of Mr. Earp to such an extent as to provoke a slap from the ex-officer." Bell spent the night in jail and was fined a whole $20. Such was life among the demi-monde on the frontier.

This is some of the alleged criminal history of Earp. There

has also been some talk of the "confidence game," but record of that remains even more obscure than the allegations of pimping. Another legend claims that he was arrested down in Texas along with professional bully and shootist Mysterious Dave Mather; the offense was said to be selling gold bricks to cowboys. Maybe so, but it is worth remembering that very few cowboys had any money at all between paydays, let alone enough to make the gold-brick scam worthwhile.

Earp was not known to shy away from violence—he was handy with his fists, too—but there is no evidence that he was one of the swaggering shootists who went looking for trouble, like the men of the Clay Allison stamp.

The legion of anti-Earp writers included one man who supported his claims of Earp's villainy with letters "to the editor" from supposed "old timers." The trouble is, according to at least one source, the writer simply invented the sensational letters. Still another author, allegedly relying on material gleaned from Wyatt's widow, stated that Earp was a "conman, thief, robber and eventually murderer." The lady denied that she had said anything like what she was quoted as saying and threatened to shoot the author. His book was not published until well after her death.

Billy Breakenridge, Tombstone deputy to Sheriff John Behan, jail guard and janitor, census taker, and process server, did a thorough job of inflating himself in a book published in the twenties. In it, he weighed in on the debate by damning the Earp family, reflecting the views of his erstwhile boss, the ambitious Behan.[2]

The chorus of Earp critics, basing much of what they say on dubious sources, falls far too short of painting a true picture of the man. But then, nobody is neutral about the sort of man Earp was, which is consistent with his penchant for making loyal friends and bitter enemies.

Glenn Boyer, a highly respected Earp historian, put it pretty well:

> The writers who have sought to judge and convict the Earps probably never suspected (nor would have cared if they had known) that diligent research would reveal a different portrait of the Earps. . . . Logic, reason and facts make little impression.[3]

Even ranchers of the day tended to identify more with the so-called "Cowboy faction," who, like the ranchers, lived hard and worked outdoors with stock in all weather. Many of the ranchers weren't above lifting other people's horses and cattle themselves, an enterprise that was a regular industry with N. H. "Old Man" Clanton, his sons, and the rest of the Cowboys.

By contrast, the Earps and Doc Holliday were city folk, who wore fancy city duds, ate in real restaurants, dealt faro and other games for a living, and actually took baths from time to time. If a rancher took sides in the Tombstone feud, it was likely to be with the Earps' bitter enemies.

Leading Earp-hater Ike Clanton, testifying at the hearing into the so-called O.K. Corral fight, talked a lot—not always coherently—about the Earps "piping off" money from Wells Fargo and killing and robbing, as well. But then, Clanton—never an admirable character on his best days—had several motives to lie, such as hatred and self-protection. What is more difficult to understand is the verdict of a one-time Arizona state historian, who opined that:

> The Earps were professional gamblers. They were charged, first and last, with almost half the robberies that were of such frequent occurrence on the roads leading out of the camp.[4]

Wrong. None of the Earp brothers were ever charged with stagecoach robbery. Allegations, like the ranting of Clanton at the hearing into the O.K. Corral fight, don't count, but they sure don't help Earp's image in some histories either.

Of the ways in which Earp passed his days, not all qualified him as an angel, but he was hardly different from a thousand other men of his time and place. The cutting edges of the West were, as the saying went, no place for meek men.

This iconoclasm has not helped define Wyatt Earp or his brothers any better than the hero-worship that preceded it. There has been a lot of talk about Wyatt's involvement in robbery, bunco, larceny, and perjury, but in the end, there is very little factual evidence to support much of anything serious save the horse-stealing case and the subsequent jailbreak. That is a finding with which several veteran Tombstone historians concur, men who have given much time to painstaking research over many years.[5]

Worth noting is the fact that Wyatt's three periods of lawman service in Dodge City were regarded highly enough to produce a formal testimonial for him when he was accused of murder after the O.K. Corral fight. That generous gesture is not the sort of thing one would expect from citizens either hostile to or unimpressed with his service to them.

The Dodge City service was interrupted by a trip to Texas, probably in search of Dirty Dave Rudabaugh, one of the truly nasty men of the West. And the story goes that during that search, in wild Fort Griffin, Earp met Doc Holliday, who would shortly be leaving Fort Griffin in a hurry and under a cloud, leaving a very dead man behind. Although Earp did not catch Rudabaugh, he made a loyal and lasting friend in Holliday.

On Earp's arrival with his brothers in Tombstone, a wicked boomtown if ever there was one, he and his brothers did indeed gamble, and at least Wyatt Earp dealt faro in one of the multitude of saloons that graced Tombstone's rowdy Allen Street. The Allen Street dives never closed, day or night, and a man could take his pick of games: faro, poker, roulette, chuck-a-luck, and the like. Allen Street also provided music, stage plays, and horizontal ladies for the amusement of the miners.

The Cowboy headquarters, located in Galeyville, held the Clanton ranch, and from there the denizens rustled freely, mostly down in Mexico. For variation they robbed Mexican smugglers, stuck up the occasional stage, and shot anybody who objected. "Old Man" Clanton, the patriarch of the bunch, was arguably the biggest spider in the web, at least until he and some other rustlers came in second in a gunfight down along the border.

But now the stories of the criminal conduct of Earp and his brothers grew more serious. One evening in March of 1881, four bandits intercepted the stage between Tombstone and Benson. The robbery was a failure, thanks to the guts and quick thinking of Bob Paul, who was riding shotgun, but a volley of shots killed both the popular driver, Bud Philpot, and a passenger named Roerig. Paul, later a formidable and famous lawman in his own right, got off a round or two, wounding one of the robbers, and then grabbed the reins and urged the team on through the ambush.

Wyatt Earp—who almost certainly did not yet carry a deputy U.S. marshal's commission at this time—got a wire from Paul while he was dealing faro at the Oriental. Wyatt quickly assembled a small posse, which included his brothers Virgil and Morgan Earp, Masterson, and a Wells Fargo man named Marshall Williams, and the little group headed for Drew's Ranch on the Benson road. There they met Sheriff Behan and his own posse and got descriptions of the outlaws from the surviving passengers.

Suspicion quickly fell on four men—Bill Leonard, Harry Head, Luther King, and Jim Crane—who at least one writer says were Cowboy supporters. Earp learned that they had been camping for four days in an abandoned adobe along the Benson road. Most importantly, Crane and Leonard had been recognized by Paul and other passengers.

Predictably, Earp and Behan got crossways immediately, especially when Earp learned later that King had been stopped by Sheriff Behan, but had been allowed simply to ride away into Mexico. The other three suspects were later killed: two up in Hachita, New Mexico, the other in Guadalupe Canyon with Old Man Clanton and three other rustlers.

But now the story had spread that Holliday had been involved in the abortive stage holdup, although nobody could claim—then or later—to have seen him. However, his light o' love, Big Nose Kate Elder, either filed a complaint against him or furnished an incriminating statement. Earp partisans claimed she did so while she was drunk, a condition not uncommon for the lady.

Among the other holes in the evidence against Holliday was the time of the holdup. If the law's account is correct, Holliday couldn't have been present. He had been seen far away at a time that made it impossible to get to the holdup site unless his horse could fly like Pegasus.

Two more stories arose from the stage holdup. Earp claimed to have arranged with Ike Clanton after the holdup to set up the robbers so that he could get credit for the arrest; Wyatt was competing for the office of sheriff at the time. Clanton was to get the entire reward for all the robbers.

Clanton, on the other hand, claimed that Earp admitted to him that Holliday was the phantom murderer; Clanton said that Earp wanted to come up with the other three bandits and kill them before they could tell their story and implicate his friend.

Holliday was arrested and charged with murder, under the notion that he had been the rifleman who killed Philpot and Roerig. Somewhere the idea arose that he was, as one writer put it, somehow allied with the Earps in the crime. There is little evidence connecting Holliday with the murder even if the time problem is disregarded, and no evidence at all implicating Earp or his brothers. In time, the incident died a natural death for lack of credible evidence, but it left a county full of resentment.

Wyatt Earp, as he appeared 1886 (Author's collection)

Holliday, somewhat unwisely, stated that if he had been involved, the holdup would not have been bungled. Elder, no doubt regretting and certainly recanting her statement once she was sober, vamoosed, and Tombstone and Holliday—in both the geographic and biblical senses—knew her no more. The famous O.K. Corral fight—which actually took place near it in a lot next to Camillus Fly's boarding house—has produced so much mythology that nobody will ever know the precise details of what happened when and who did what in what order. What is certain is that trouble had been brewing between the Earps and some of the Cowboys for a long time.

Ike Clanton had spent the night before the fight drinking, and he extended his drinking into the morning, mouthing threats against the Earps throughout. He was also angry over an encounter with Doc Holliday the day before, muttering dark threats against the deadly dentist, as well.

In addition to Clanton's rantings there was the macho pride of everyone involved, which almost inevitably ended in bloodshed. Also, Wyatt Earp knew that two or three Cowboys had been seen in a Tombstone store buying cartridges, and there had been repeated warnings of the Cowboys' evil intentions circulated by Tombstone citizens.

Both Tom McLaury and Clanton had been "buffaloed" by the Earps—their skulls dented with a pistol barrel—shortly before the fight, which did not improve their tempers one bit. And there was, overall, the long-standing rivalry between the groups and the machismo of the frontier. There wasn't any question whether there would be trouble, only when, where, and how bad the trouble would be.

It turned out to be horribly bad.

In a matter of seconds, three men were dead or dying, three more were wounded, and two had run away rather than shoot it out. Who shot whom remains a mystery, although Wyatt Earp and others gave some specific details of the fight. Whether their details are entirely accurate remains open to question, if only because of the fact that the details of what happens in combat—in war or in an old West shootout—are not always remembered precisely by either side.

The McLaury brothers, Billy and Ike Clanton, and Billy the Kid Claiborne were in the lot next to Fly's with their horses when the Earps and Holliday walked up to face them. As with every other phase of the Tombstone epic, there are conflicting, irreconcilable accounts of what happened next.

As Wyatt Earp recounted the details in an 1896 *San Francisco Examiner* interview, the Cowboys had "sent us word that if we did not come down there they would waylay and kill us."[6] As Wyatt described the fight, he shot Frank McLaury after McLaury's first round missed. Morgan Earp, he said, exchanged shots with Billy Clanton and put him down. After that, Morgan Earp was shot by Tom McLaury, taking cover behind his horse and shooting from beneath its neck. Wyatt Earp shot at the horse, and when it cleared Tom McLaury, Holliday blew Tom McLaury away with his shotgun.

According to Wyatt Earp, although both Billy Clanton and Frank McLaury were down, they were sitting up in the dirt, still shooting. About this time Earp's brother Virgil was hit in the leg but shot Billy Clanton. And then Wyatt Earp related the strangest spectacle of the fight. Frank McLaury, almost certainly dying, struggled to his feet, staggered toward Holliday, and gasped out, "I've got ye now, Doc."

Holliday's reply, according to Earp, was classic Holliday style: "well, you're a good one if you have."[7] Or, in another version, "you're a daisy if you have."[8] Morgan Earp, down on his side, shot down Frank McLaury about the time McLaury hit Holliday in the hip.

Wyatt Earp's story has the poisonous Ike Clanton taking refuge in a nearby building and shooting from the windows, possibly at Morgan Earp, maybe at everybody. Ike Clanton didn't hit anything, but the distraction he caused could have made the difference in whether another of the Earp party was hit.

Virgil Earp's version of the fight is about the same. He told of repeated warnings by Tombstone citizens about the Cowboys hunting them. Some of those citizens, he said, offered help, not only their own but that of groups of men they would raise. Virgil Earp declined with thanks. He would put this fire out with the help of only his brothers and Holliday. He did, however, ask Sheriff John Behan to disarm the Cowboys, and Behan went ahead to talk to them.

Wyatt Earp was in a cold rage brought on by a brief court appearance by Ike Clanton. In addition to Clanton's big talk about killing the Earps, Clanton had been arrested for carrying a gun in violation of a town ordinance but had suffered only a light fine. Wyatt Earp was not pleased, and when he met Tom McLaury on the street he confronted him and exchanged words. Just what those words were is not certain, but the meeting ended when Earp struck McLaury with one hand and pistol-whipped him with the other.

And so, when Virgil Earp later confronted the Cowboys, Wyatt Earp may still have been angry. Virgil Earp approached the Cowboys, according to his account, still holding a cane in his right hand—his shooting hand. He obviously had no intention of immediately starting a fight. "Boys," he said, "throw up your hands, I want your guns" or "arms."[9] When Billy Clanton and Frank McLaury reacted by drawing their guns, Virgil Earp threw up his hand, "Hold on, I don't want that."[10]

This was the famous fight-at-the-O.K. Corral, which didn't happen there at all. There are all kinds of variations on what really happened in that deadly lot, ranging from the usual story—Wyatt Earp's version—to the massacre-of-poor-mostly-unarmed-men version told by Cowboy supporters and some revisionist historians.

According to the accounts, most or all of the Cowboy group had to be armed. Also, it is certain that they had access to two pistols and two rifles. Three members of the Earp party were wounded, and in terms of the number of casualties inflicted, although none of them died, the fight came out even. For another reason, it is highly unlikely that any one of the Cowboys was unarmed. Trouble was in the air beyond question, and nobody brings only a mouth to a gunfight.

One fact that persistently gets lost in the rhetoric about the famous fight is that Virgil Earp was the law in Tombstone, both city chief of police and deputy U.S. marshal. Tombstone had an ordinance prohibiting the wearing of firearms in town, unless one was entering or leaving, and Virgil Earp had every right to enforce that law. Wyatt and Morgan Earp were both "special police" under Virgil.

In the aftermath of the battle, accusations flew. Cowboy supporters called the killings murder, while Earp supporters mostly said "good riddance." Both town newspapers also got into the fray, consistent with their alliances to one side or the other, which did nothing to clear up the fog of opinion and partisanship that divided the county. John Clum's Republican-oriented *Epitaph* supported the Earps, as it had repeatedly before. The *Nugget* predictably took the other side, having long favored the Cowboy faction and Democrat Sheriff Behan.

A group of the town's leading citizens—Clum called them the Citizens' Safety Committee—showed up almost immediately after the shooting, in support of the Earps. Some of them may have been the men whom Virgil Earp said had offered him reinforcement prior to the gunfight. Behan also appeared, threatened to arrest the Earps, and was told he had better not try. Meanwhile, Ike Clanton and the Kid had found refuge at the jail, where they remained for a time.

Ike Clanton ran out on his companions, but he overflowed with righteous indignation after the event and filed no fewer than three murder charges against the Earps, two in Tombstone and the third in Contention City. The hearings that followed were replete with all manner of conflicting testimony. Like most other things surrounding the shootout, whether the McLaurys and the other Cowboys were getting ready to leave town or were preparing to go gunning for the Earp party is hotly disputed,

The witnesses could not agree on much of anything, except that three Cowboy partisans were deader than a nit, and the Kid and Ike Clanton had run for it. Bitterly debated questions abounded and remain to this day.

The Cowboys were all armed; no, they weren't. Virgil challenged, "You men are under arrest, throw up your hands" or something like that; no, he didn't. Somebody on the Cowboy side fired first; no, it was the Earps, or maybe it was somebody on each side simultaneously. Did Virgil Earp throw up one hand and shout "Hold on, we don't want that"? If he did, was he talking to his people, or to the Cowboys? Did the Cowboys have their hands raised? Did Tom McLaury open his coat to show he was unarmed? And so on.

Ike Clanton's notion was that the whole incident was staged by the Earps in order to kill him. That is the most manifest nonsense, as Judge Spicer pointed out, because logically, had Clanton been the target, he would have been the first to fall. Witnesses heard Clanton, his brother, the McLaury brothers, and the Kid talking loudly about how they would kill Virgil Earp on sight and kill all the Earps, "posturing" for the onlookers.[11]

The first hearing, in front of Judge Spicer, may have turned on a single very strong defense witness, a railroad man named Sills, who was just passing through Tombstone, and had no possible axe to grind. He not only heard the Cowboys' public threats against the Earps, but he also followed them and saw the gunfight next to Fly's. His account corroborated Wyatt Earp's.

And it seems certain that the Cowboy party, far from being unarmed, had at least two handguns and two rifles—the long guns in scabbards on their horses. Whether there were one or two more pistols remains disputed. Maybe one was picked up by a Cowboy sympathizer; maybe not.

Whether Tom McLaury was armed or not, as Judge Spicer said, was in fact wholly irrelevant, for he was "one of a party . . . making felonious resistance to an arrest."[12] Another source asserted that because of the nature of his wounds, when McLaury was shot he couldn't have had his hands up near his lapels to hold open his coat.

The gunfight left lasting hatreds, particularly among the so-called Cowboy element. In a letter to his father, another brother of the McLaurys stated that he had hired assassins to exact revenge for the brothers' deaths at the hands of the Earps. The intended victims were not only the Earps and Holliday, but also Judge Spicer, Mayor John Clum of Tombstone, and Wells Fargo man Marshall Williams.[13]

So, though the gunfight should have been the end of the continuing war between the Earps, Holliday, and the Cowboy faction, it was not over by half. The gunfight next to Fly's was followed by the ambush shooting of Morgan Earp and the crippling of Virgil Earp in a separate assassination attempt.

Wyatt Earp raised a sort of posse after that, with Holliday, Warren Earp, and some very tough friends, including Turkey Creek Jack Johnson and Sherm McMasters. When Earp and his men finished, Curly Bill Brocious, Indian Charlie, and Frank Stilwell were history.

The Cowboy to depart next was John Ringo, and his demise is a bit of a mystery. In July of 1882, Ringo was found in an isolated spot with his horse, coat, and boots gone, rags wrapped around his feet, and a hole in his head. That of course suggested suicide, but the Ringos of the West generally were not given to leaving the world that way.

Almost surely, somebody helped him on his way. Ringo was about as popular as the flu with a number of people. The killer could have been Buckskin Frank Leslie, according to one theory. Many people believed that a gambler called Johnny-Behind-The-Deuce, with whom Ringo had had serious trouble, was the prime suspect. Then there were Holliday and the Earps, who seldom relinquished a grudge against their enemies. In any case, nobody missed Ringo much.

In June of 1887, Ike Clanton and his brother Phin were run down fleeing a charge of rustling, far to the north in Apache County. Phin Clanton wisely gave up to the posse hunting them. He was tried and sentenced to ten years in Yuma. Ike Clanton either tried to run—his usual style—or fight. Whatever he had in mind, it was not a good idea, for the leader of the posse shot him down.

The rest of Wyatt Earp's fabled career is marked by the occasional tale of violence or crooked dealings. Most famously, he was accused of a crooked low-blow foul call when he refereed a heavyweight championship boxing match, a call he defended to his dying day. Allegations arose that he had deliberately disqualified one fighter for money, and he became the most detested man in California almost overnight.

Earp was involved in several killings, not only the shootout near the O.K. Corral, but the face-to-face extinction of Curly Bill Brocious at Iron Springs, also known as Mescal Springs. Even that incident is disputed, like nearly every other tale about the Earps in Tombstone. There are fables alleging that the man Earp blew away wasn't Brocious at all, although the identity of the dead man seemed all but certain.

Earp probably got some lead into another of the Iron Springs ambushers, Johnny Barnes. Although it was a serious wound, Barnes recovered partially and survived, until he was involved in another fracas someplace else and was wounded again. His first wound then became infected, and on his deathbed he confessed that it was he who crippled Virgil Earp from ambush.

Aside from his fight with the Cowboys in Tombstone, the fight with Brocious at Iron Springs was, at least as far as history is certain, Earp's only other man-to-man shootout, unless one considers his fight with Barnes as a third. He was, however, involved in some way in the deaths of various Cowboy partisans: Barnes, Indian Charlie, George Hoyt, Pete Spence, and maybe John Ringo as well.

Earp himself said he killed Frank Stilwell at the Tucson railroad station, when he and some others went there to cover the departure of crippled Virgil Earp for the west coast. According to Wyatt Earp, Spence grabbed the muzzle of his shotgun and imprudently pulled it, thus departing from this life unshriven.

The so-called "vendetta ride," the drive to kill or expel what remained of the Cowboy faction in the county, predictably drew applause from one side and condemnation from the other. For Holliday, the Earps, and the men with them, it also meant real trouble with the law, for this time there was no question about the deaths, except perhaps for Spence's.

The campaign against the Cowboys by Earp, Holliday, and a handful of followers was nothing short of a hunting expedition. Its aim was simple: revenge. Find 'em and kill 'em. Murder charges were the result, probably well-founded this time, although a lot of Arizona folks must have applied the ancient law of the West— "Who cares? They had it coming."

Earp and Holliday had made no bones about what they set out to do, and didn't stick around to fight the charges against them, which were much more dangerous than any before. They did the sensible thing and hurried off to diverse far-away places. Some attempt was made by the law to extradite Holliday from Colorado, but a helpful Colorado judge entertained a Colorado charge against him, which made him ineligible for extradition.

The controversy over the Earps and Tombstone will go on forever, and Earp surely helped perpetuate it. He was never shy about inflating his reputation, which was not only good for the ego, but helped a lot in a country full of bad men.

If he had a reputation as a formidable shootist, especially as a lawman, criminals were more reluctant to take him on. Lawmen did that, such as Bat Masterson, whose reputed score of twenty-six kills shrinks to maybe three, two of which were probably shot by his equally intimidating brother Ed.

Earp and his brothers were tough men in a tough land, who lived a life replete with multiple toils, snares, and temptations. A fair verdict would probably be that they were neither wholly good nor wholly bad, but men of their time. A saint Earp clearly was not. He has been called a cold-blooded murderer, but he does not seem to have been a professional shootist—certainly not in a class with Ben Thompson, Wes Hardin, John Selman, or any of the other big names in killing. Nor was any riding he did on the wrong side of the law to the magnitude of the big names like the Dalton, James, or Younger gangs. That's part of the fascination of the Tombstone story, and maybe it's enough to say it was the West in microcosm—a brave, brawny young nation coming of age, feeling its oats and bound for glory.

Respected Western historian Glenn Boyer, summed up Earp as follows:

> Wyatt Earp was a helluva good man to have around—provided you were not a crook or a phony. The same can be said of his brothers.[14]

Chapter 7

King Fisher and Ben Thompson: A Pair to Draw To

This is King Fisher's Road
Take the Other One

So the crude sign read, and most men did what it said. That was the way of it in the 1870s down in the Eagle Pass country of South Texas. The area was rife with rustlers from both sides of the border, hostile Indians of several tribes, and a choice collection of the trash of the border country.

Besides the detachments of the tiny frontier army, there was precious little law in the Eagle Pass country. What law there was was mostly the Frontier Battalion of the Texas Rangers. "Battalion" was a vast overstatement, for there weren't many rangers in the unit. From time to time, "special companies" were formed; one of these was commanded by a remarkable man, Capt. Lee McNelly.

McNelly's task was to bring some sort of peace to the "Nueces Strip," a section of South Texas continually plagued with robbery, murder, ranch-burning, and rustling. In April of 1875, when McNelly took command, five ranches had been burned by masked men in a single week.

McNelly had a hand in breaking up the Sutton-Taylor feud, the bitter series of killings between two families and their adherents, one of whom was the deadly Wes Hardin. It had all started over an argument between two stockmen over whether one of them had stolen horses in a herd and became a full-scale war for predominance in DeWitt and Clinton counties.

McNelly headed a tough, capable bunch of about forty Rangers. But things were about to change. Among other things, McNelly ordered that any prisoner captured was to be killed at once if an attempt were made to free him. It was obvious that McNelly meant business.

One particular group of offenders was a large band operating out of Mexico, and McNelly caught up with them before they could make it back across the border. The final score was Rangers sixteen, criminals one. But there was always more scum to track, and one of the Rangers' targets was John King Fisher, reputed— probably correctly—to be rustling cattle to bolster his own herds. He was a famous figure already, and he was destined to be infamous.

Even down in South Texas, where killings were regular and plentiful and hard men abounded, there was a scarcity of men who wanted to tangle with young Fisher. Nobody knew for sure how many men he had killed; nobody knows to this day. But every man knew he was greased lightning with a Colt, one of just a few truly ambidexterous shootists of all time. Nobody wanted to be the next statistic.

John King Fisher was born in Collin County, Texas, in 1854. His father, Jobe Fisher, moved west and supported himself by running cattle and working as a freight teamster at Lampasas and Goliad. King Fisher moved with him; but in 1869 Jobe Fisher sent his son to live in Florence with relatives, mostly to get him away from some "very questionable people," a family named Bruton.[1] Already a handsome lad, Fisher grew to be a top rider and a ferocious fist-fighter.

King Fisher was tough, but he was also a quiet, popular youngster who might have grown up to become a pillar of the community.

John King Fisher (Western History Collections, University of Oklahoma Libraries)

This changed the day he "borrowed" somebody else's stallion. He used it only a little while, the story goes, to chase his own stray horse; but, the stallion's owner was not pleased, and King was arrested. Eventually escaping from custody, King "lit a shuck," as the saying went, for Goliad and wisely did not return to Florence.

But trouble followed him. In the fall of 1870, Fisher and an older man were indicted for housebreaking in wild and woolly Goliad. As a measure of what Goliad was like in that far-off year, Fisher's indictment was only one of seventy-six returned for the same term of court. He was convicted, and at the tender age of sixteen he was shipped off to do two years in the tough state prison at Huntsville.

Fisher was pardoned after only four months, presumably because of his age, and left Goliad for greener pastures. His trail led south to the Nueces Strip, that lawless corner of hell between the Nueces and Rio Grande. In the 1870s, this area was crawling with scum of every description: rustlers, fugitives, and bandits from both sides of the border, as well as hostile Lipan Apaches, Kiowa, and Comanche.

In this same area were also a few honest people. Among these were tough Doc White, a Goliad man who was slowly building a cattle empire in this inhospitable war zone called Dimmit County. He and the other ranchers needed help just to hold on, and Fisher was exactly the man to give it to them. A man had to be his own law in Dimmit County, or he did not get much law at all. Other than the tiny U.S. Army, which was busy chasing Indians, the only law enforcement available to Dimmit County was the Texas Rangers. The Rangers, though, were stretched very thin indeed. In only three years, between 1875 and 1878, some 100,000 horses were stolen in the Eagle Pass area.

So the ranchers helped themselves, and Fisher helped the ranchers. He perfected his shooting with constant practice and rode as if he were part of the horse. He feared neither man nor devil, which was just as well, because a law-enforcer in the Strip needed a lion's courage, a lightning draw, and eyes in the back of his head. Ranger Captain L. H. McNelly put it plainly:

> [W]hen any man, Mexican or American, has made himself prominent in hunting these raiders down, or in organizing parties to pursue them when they are carrying off cattle, he has been either forced to move from the ranch and come into town or he has been killed.[2]

In spite of the odds, however, Fisher began to make an impression on the lawless element in the Strip, particularly on the rustlers who raided up out of Mexico. He shot quickly, he shot straight, and he was tireless on the trail of cattle or horse thieves. They began to fear him, those that continued living, as they feared nobody else.

Fisher had filled out now, a charming, pleasant six-footer who tipped the scales at about 185 pounds. He was a handsome man with dark hair, broad shoulders, and an odd combination of one brown and one black eye. He began to pay close attention to his appearance, too. When he really wanted to put on the dog, he was something to behold.

Around the crown of his huge sombrero he wore a solid-gold band, and the rest of his apparel was equally magnificent. A gold-embroidered Mexican jacket covered the finest of silk shirts, and the whole effect was finished off with silk scarves, spectacular leather chaps, and the finest of boots. One source says a pair of his chaparejos was made of tiger skin, a hide robbed from a circus by some of Fisher's less-than-law-abiding friends. Topping off all this finery were a pair of pearl-handled six-guns and silver spurs, replete with tinkling little bells.

He cut quite a figure in sleepy little Eagle Pass, the metropolis of the area. He was popular with all kinds of ladies, not just for his handsome face and his finery but for his unfailing courtesy and good nature. He danced gracefully with all the women at the area celebrations and was always, as a couple of them later said, "a perfect gentleman."[3] Still, Fisher owned part of an Eagle Pass wateringhole called the "Old Blue Saloon," a dive of distinctly evil reputation. It is also said that he held his liquor well, an unusual and welcome virtue in that hard-drinking time and place.

The whole area knew of Fisher's kindness to ordinary people who were victimized by the wild cowboys of the area, including his own hired men. Once, when two of his hands shot a poor man's oxen just to prove their marksmanship, Fisher extracted the price of the beasts from his cowboys and made sure the owner was paid. He had a legion of friends, including Porfirio Diaz, a future president of Mexico.

As Fisher's reputation grew, so did his ambitions. He started a little spread of his own down along Pendencia Creek. There was plenty of loose stock for the taking, some of it branded, some not, and he soon began to build a herd of his own. He also built a following. Fisher seemed to get along with nearly everybody (except the people he was chasing, of course), and all kinds of men enjoyed his company.

And so, a little at a time, he gathered around him a highly competent bunch of wild, violent *hombres* who would follow him anywhere without question. Fisher didn't much care where they came from or who they were as long as they obeyed him and kept their hands off his stock. He ended up with a virtual stronghold along the strip.

The only successful invaders of King Fisher country were the Texas Rangers; Fisher was arrested several times on warrants from various places for various crimes. But because he knew good lawyers, none of the charges stuck. King Fisher was indeed the virtual king of his own little empire.

Protective of his own stock, Fisher was reputed to be less particular about how other people's stock made its way to him. He welcomed stock from south of the border, paying his men to go get it and paying for the animals according to their worth. Along the way, his booming trade in purloined Mexican stock very nearly got him killed.

It seems that four of Fisher's *vaqueros,* disappointed in the price Fisher paid them for rustled Mexican stock, planned to kill him while they worked changing brands in one of his corrals. They had not reckoned on Fisher's instincts and blinding speed. As the vaqueros made their move, Fisher smashed one man's skull with a branding iron and then snapped up his six-gun and blew the other three from their perches on the corral fence.

Inevitably, cattle and horses with oddly smudged brands ended up among Fisher's herds. This was not unusual on the border; stock often wandered loose and half-wild, and cows do not much care whose brand they wear. But rumors persisted that Fisher's raffish cowboys were less-than scrupulous about the markings on the cattle they acquired.

For all the loyalty he inspired, for all his courtly nature, King Fisher was deadly as a rattler. He celebrated Christmas day of 1876, for example, down in Zavala County by blowing away a cowboy named William Donovan over some now-forgotten quarrel. On another occasion, after discovering four Mexicans stealing a horse from his corral, Fisher took a revolver from one of the thieves and shot the three others down.

As King Fisher established himself as one of the primary ranchers of the Nueces country, he began to take some interest in law enforcement. Three other men died at his hands on another day; their crime was the mortal sin of cattle-rustling.

According to most Texans' notion of right and wrong, Fisher was within his rights to summarily abolish cattle-rustlers and similar trash. Deputy sheriff Tom Sullivan, a former slave, summed up the popular view of Fisher (and Ben Thompson, the deadly Englishman) thus:

> [T]hey wasn't bad men; they just wouldn't stand for no foolishness, and they never killed any one unless they bothered them.[4]

Apparently, a good many people bothered King Fisher over the years, although nobody knows for sure how many. In later years some daring soul asked him how many men he had killed. "Seven," he said. "Seven, not counting Mexicans," shrugging off the untallied multitude of Mexican cattle-thieves who never made it back across the Rio Grande and maybe a few who objected to his rustling in Mexico.

One story, related by a dubious border character rejoicing in the curious handle of "Pest House Pete," claims that Fisher killed three rustlers on the south side of the Rio Grande and then ordered Pete to drag the bodies back across the river, esatablishing a false legitimacy for the killings. There is no confirmation for this tale, but it does sound like vintage King Fisher.

Fisher's later days on the border included more than his share of trouble. The Rangers, convinced that he was killing and rustling outside the law (they were probably right), managed to get a total of twenty-one indictments against him at one time or another. All of them ended in dismissals or acquittals, including a few cases tried outside "King Fisher country" in the counties close to Eagle Pass. The worst Fisher suffered was about five months in the "Bat Cave," San Antonio's notorious jail.

Captain McNelly, frustrated, tried to leave Fisher at least a little good advice: "Make sure you stay law-abiding, King. You've got a nice wife. You could make a good citizen. You'd also make a nice corpse. All outlaws look good dead."[5]

He should have listened.

Fisher seemed to mellow a bit as the years went by. For one thing, he was happily married and was the father of three daughters. By now he had moved into Uvalde and at last was officially back on the side of the law, this time as a deputy sheriff for Uvalde County. With a badge, he proved to be just as much of a terror to criminals as he had ever been without one.

Take the Hannehan boys, sons of Mary, a venomous harridan of the same name. In 1883, Jim and Tom Hannehan successfully stuck up the San Antonio-El Paso stage, but Fisher tracked them to their Leona River ranch. There, when the boys made the mistake of resisting arrest, King put an abrupt end to Tom, arrested Jim, and recovered the loot. Fisher's reputation was high among the good citizens; already acting sheriff, he declared he would stand for election as sheriff in 1884.

Indirectly, it was barbed wire that got King Fisher killed. Some seven thousand tons of the stuff had been sold in Texas by 1877, and early in 1884 the Texas Legislature produced laws to deal with the endemic crime of fence-cutting. The laws were complex, and Fisher traveled to the capital at Austin, ostensibly to learn more about it. While there, he chanced to meet Ben Thompson, the deadly Englishman.

Ben Thompson: The Deadly Englishman

Bat Masterson, who should surely know, said of Ben Thompson: "It is doubtful whether, in his time, there was another man who equaled him with a pistol in a life and death struggle."[6]

Ben Thompson was even in those days famous as a shootist, a gambler, and a lawman. He had been a soldier, too; after spending a few relatively peaceful years in Austin and New Orleans as, of all things, a printer and bookbinder, he joined the Army of the Confederate States. After the war, there was a shooting scrape in Austin, and Thompson bribed his guards and headed south to Mexico, which was then involved in civil war against French puppet emperor Maximilian.

Thompson survived that one—Maximilian did not—and returned to Texas only to embark upon a sea of troubles. His misadventures culminated in a threat to the life of a municipal official, probably a justice of the peace. For this, Thompson was sentenced to four years in prision, of which he served two. Then, in 1871, he betook himself to greener pastures, in this case wild and booming Abilene, Kansas. There he opened the Bull's Head Saloon with a partner, Phil Coe, and brought his family up from Texas.

Sadly, a buggy accident badly injured Thompson's wife and son. When they had recovered, Thompson sold out and returned to Texas, but he came back north in 1873 to the booming railhead town of Ellsworth, Kansas. This time, he also brought his drunken punk of a brother, Billy, who would be a perpetual burr under Thompson's saddle.

"Texas Billy," as he was known, worked as a dealer in the Bull's Head until Ben Thompson moved on to Ellsworth. Billy was given to wooing the wrong women, starting with Emma Williams. When she took up with Wild Bill Hickok, however, even Billy was smart enough not to compete. Next up was Molly Brennan, who later became part of history when she was a casualty of Bat Masterson's gunfight with Sergeant King. But Billy Thompson's chief amusements seem to have been booze and blustering, and he indulged in quite of lot of both.

In August, 1873, Billy got into big trouble when he killed Sheriff C. B. Whitney of Ellsworth. "Drunker than a hootie owl," as the saying went, Billy Thompson shot the sheriff, who was trying to keep the peace in a quarrel between the Thompson brothers and others over a card game. Apparently, everybody involved was highly intoxicated, and the argument spilled out into the street.

Ben Thompson (Rose Collection, Western History Collections, University of Oklahoma Libraries)

At least one shot was fired: Ben Thompson fired a round at Happy Jack Morco, a multiple murderer who was then a member of what passed for local police. The round missed, and quarrelsome Happy Jack lived on briefly only to die at the hands of another Ellsworth police officer.

Whitney, unarmed, tried to stop the fight, but Billy Thompson cut him down with a shotgun in spite of his pleas not to shoot. "For God's sake, leave town!" yelled his brother. "You have shot Whitney, our best friend!" Billy, true to form, replied that he would have shot even "if it had been Jesus Christ," which gives an insight into the vile character of the man.[7]

Ben Thompson was not prosecuted for anything to do with the killing, for the "street was full of armed men ready to defend Thompson."[8] Billy, after a further career of abusing people, was reportedly killed years later in Laredo.

Wandering to Leadville, Pueblo, and Dodge City, Ben Thompson added to his reputation for trouble and extricated his embarrassing brother from some shooting trouble up in Nebraska. At length, Ben returned to Texas, the home of his youth and the place where his formidable reputation began.

Along the way, he fought Indians and shot both a thief who invaded the bookbindery where Thompson was apprenticed and a Mexican soldier upset after losing to Ben at Monte. More serious were a shootout with "occupation" soldiers in Texas (in which there were several deaths) and the shooting of a Mexican officer down in Matamoros.

Then, in the early 1880s, Thompson joined the forces of law and order. He ran twice for the office of city marshal of Austin; the second time he was elected, probably on the old, solid basis that the streets are safer if the toughest man around is wearing a badge. He is said to have been an outstanding officer, proud of his office and the military-style uniform that went with it.

He resigned, however, after killing Jack Harris, a partner in the Vaudeville Variety Theater, a gambling house and bawdy theater in San Antonio.

Vaudeville Theater Shooting

Almost two years after the killing, Ben Thompson met King Fisher while both were in Austin on business. The two men were friends, although how they first met is not clear. They chose to visit the Vaudeville toward the end of a night on the town. Now Thompson may have shoved the killing of Harris into the back of his mind, but Harris's partners, Joe Foster and Billy Simms, had neither forgotten nor forgiven. And so, on March 11, 1884, when Thompson and Fisher strolled into the Vaudeville, the stage was set for real-life tragedy.

Both men had been drinking on the train into town; both continued to drink after they hit San Antonio. They visited a saloon or two, saw a play at the Turner Opera House, and ended up at the Vaudeville. Fisher may well have been ignorant of what happened on Thompson's last visit there, but Thompson himself had to know that a return visit was chancy. It may be that he told Fisher nothing about what had happened there two years before.

As usual with tales of violence in the Old West, there are several versions about what happened next. What really occurred sometimes blurs into fable, or is embellished upon (to be kind) by writers less-than-scrupulous about fact and more interested in readership.

Thompson and Fisher were joined in their box by Foster, Simms, and a local deputy-*cum*-bouncer named Jake Coy. Fisher apparently tried to help heal the long-standing bitterness between Thompson and the others and seemed to be succeeding with Simms. Foster, however, refused to shake hands with Thompson.

Exactly what happened after that is lost in a cloud of gun smoke and a fog of legend.

The Foster-Simms version of the affair was that Thompson drew a pistol, shoved the muzzle into Foster's mouth, and cocked the weapon. Coy grabbed it by the cylinder, and suddenly the night exploded in gunfire. When the melee was over, Foster was wounded in the leg (the wound proved fatal) and Coy was grazed, but both Fisher and Thompson lay dead in a puddle of blood on the theater floor.

The story of a quarrel gone too far sounds like it might even be true, except that Fisher, the master shootist, never got his pearl-handled revolvers clear of the holsters and went down with thirteen bullets in his body. Thompson, an equally formidable gunman, was shot nine times. A San Antonio reporter put it graphically:

> There they lay, weltering in their own blood, with their heads and faces carmined with their own life fluid. The stairs leading up to this place of horror were as slippery as ice, the walls were stained, and the floor was tracked with bloody footprints, while dissolute women with blanched faces, crowded around with exclamations, and amid broken sobs demanded to know, "Which is Ben" "Show me Ben" "Is that Ben?" so that even in death the grim reputation of the man stood forth as strong as ever.[9]

Flowery, no doubt, but accurate.

Other patrons said Thompson and Fisher were ambushed, cut down by concealed rifles and shotguns from a nearby box without a chance to fight. Foster, they said, shot himself. This version is far more logical than the Foster-Simms version. If the quarrel erupted into a fight in the usual way, it is unlikely that neither King Fisher nor Ben Thompson would have gotten their guns into action. Assassination or not, in the end, nothing came of the shooting except a handful of legends.

So passed Ben Thompson, officer and gunfighter *par excellence*, and King Fisher, top dog of the Eagle Pass country; both left behind a grieving family and many loyal friends. Fisher's tombstone could have said he died trying to play the peacemaker. Instead, for some years after Fisher was buried, vengeful Mary Hannehan visited his grave on the anniversary of her son's death, built a fire on it, and danced around it in terrible glee.

The King deserved better.

Chapter 8

The County Seat Wars: When the Good Guys Fought the Good Guys

These days, nobody cares much about where county government has its headquarters. But near the end of the nineteenth century, whether a town became the seat of county government was quite literally a matter of life and death to a lot of western communities. At one time in Hamilton County, Kansas, for instance, the settlements of Kendall, Syracuse, and Coolidge each proclaimed that they were the county seat, and no other.

Each town had its own county officers, offices, courts, and files. The citizen who had to pay taxes or sue somebody just had to hope he had paid or filed in the right place. If he hadn't, he had to do it all over again and possibly wait a long time before recovering his money.

If a new town could win the competition to become the seat of government, it also would win the business of the county officials and the courts and could compete for consideration as a stop on the all-important railroads, which were then pushing their iron tendrils everywhere. A place on the railroad line meant burgeoning commerce, trade, and growth—towns that were left behind by the iron horse withered and died on the vine.

And so the fortunes—and futures—of struggling western towns depended on whether they could secure for themselves the coveted title of "county seat." Some young, proud towns were willing to do almost anything to stay alive. Nowhere was the struggle fiercer than in southwestern Kansas in the 1880s.

Depending on which side one favored in the county seat debate, it was often hard to tell the law-enforcers from the law-breakers. In both towns—or even in three—the residents would passionately declare that the other city fathers were deputies of Satan himself and that their town's citizens were the only righteous people in the county.

Western Kansas seemed like the Promised Land to immigrant farmers and to many native-born Americans, as well. Many of these ambitious, hard-working people believed that increased cultivation somehow pushed the edge of the semi-arid belt farther west—"the rain follows the plow," men said. Nobody listened to the stockmen who warned that the idea was nonsense, and even some sensible ideas for irrigation were disparaged as discouraging immigration.

To hopeful, proud, ambitious citizens, it seemed a county seat was the sure path to prosperity for their small town. Speculators abounded. Eager profiteers were ready to back a raw, young community, staking their futures on the result. According to reports, otherwise honest, upstanding citizens were willing to lay aside:

> [every conscientious] scruple and to countenance if not to indulge in, bribery, intimidation, ballot-box stuffing, subornation of perjury, and kindred offenses in support of the prospects of the town of their choice . . . every villainy resorted to was merely [they said] an offset to the unconscionable devices of the opposition.[1]

And that odd view of what was right was true, in spades, of the towns' "lawmen," generally a marshal or sheriff. Some towns even platted new lots and gave them away to men from other places who thus became residents, at least until after the election. Bonds for every conceivable kind of civic improvement provided the money to finance these schemes.

Towns also issued warrants to pay for various expenses; the

warrants were apparently lawful on their face but in fact were used to create funds to underwrite the fight for the crown of county government. In this way a number of towns ended up with a substantial public debt, but without much in the way of public improvements to show for it.

All of this hanky-panky generated a good deal of heated litigation. In the case of *State v. Commissioners of Seward County*, for example, the court commendably decided:

> a secret canvass of the vote cast at a county-seat election, made by two members of the board of commissioners without notice to the third, or to anyone else, held on the open prairie at three o'clock in the morning by the light of the moon, without poll books, ballots or tally sheets, and without any record being made at the time, was not only irregular, but invalid.[2]

Some competing Kansas towns imported hardcase toughs to strut about and look threatening. The mere presence of such thugs was supposed to intimidate the opposition. Though these people were generically known as "killers," their bark was generally a good deal worse than their bite. One murder by a "killer" was recorded, but it appears that the gunman was simply trying to shoot the hat off an inoffensive citizen and aimed a little too low.

Still, there could have been really big trouble at about any time, for the partisans of competing towns had their weapons at hand and were ready to rally round and defend the vital interests of their homes. In fact, at least one such battle took place in Wichita County in February 1887 when a band of men from Leoti went to rival Coronado, and a gunfight ensued. When the smoke blew away, three Leoti men lay dead, and others had been seriously wounded.

Coronado folks said the Leoti people showed up drunk and looking for trouble, shoving innocent citizens around and firing indiscriminately. At least one of the Leoti crowd—a man named

Jack Coulter—seems to have been a very bad hat indeed. He was among the fallen, and local legend says his trigger finger went on jerking for half an hour after he passed to his reward—whatever that might have been.

The worst of the county feuds erupted in July of 1888, with the violent competition for command of Stevens County, Kansas. The towns of Hugoton and Woodsdale were going head to head for the honor, glory, and profit of being the county seat. Hugoton's point-man was C. E. Cook, a postmaster of McPherson, Kansas, who had left that place to become town manager of Hugoton.

His nemesis was Samuel Newitt Wood, a native of Mount Gilead, Missouri, who had come to Kansas at the age of twenty-nine to make his fortune. He had been a power in the free-soil party in Lawrence, Kansas, and was four times a Kansas legislator. He was also, in a small way, a minor newspaper mogul. He had founded the *Council Grove Press* and the *Kansas Greenbacker* at Emporia and had been editor-in-chief of Topeka's *Kansas State Journal.* At Woodsdale, which was named for him, he also ran two newspapers.

Hugoton was already the recognized county seat, but such minor details didn't worry Wood. Because recognition as a county seat required a showing that the county had at least 2,500 inhabitants, Wood attacked the census, alleging that some 1,200 names were fictitious, which might have been true given the ferocious competition of those days. In fact, one source asserts that the Hugoton census more than doubled the actual number of people in the county and included no fewer than two hundred sets of twins, on the face of it an unlikely circumstance.[3]

Riding to Topeka with the evidence, however, Wood was intercepted by Hugoton men who confiscated and destroyed it. Undaunted, Wood filed a lawsuit in the Kansas Supreme Court to annul the county organization. Before the matter could be heard, however, the state legislature confirmed the political status quo of the moment, in effect endorsing Hugoton as the county seat.

Still undaunted, Wood developed a plan to invite a railroad company to build across the county. The scheme called for the tracks to run through Woodsdale to the north and the town of Voorhees to the south. Such an arrangement would leave Hugoton, which was located in between the two, without a railroad. With any luck, Hugoton would eventually die on the vine and wither away, leaving the way open for Woodsdale to become the county seat.

Thus, Wood continued to be an irritating thorn in the flesh of the Hugoton leaders. He worried them so much, in fact, that they kidnapped him and spirited him across the Kansas line into No Man's Land. No Man's Land was the far western panhandle of what later became Oklahoma, and nobody from Woodsdale or anyplace else in Kansas had the slightest jurisdiction down there. The excuse for seizing Wood was a dubious warrant charging him with libel, and the men who whisked him away spread a story that

Beer City, No Man's Land

Wood had been paid off and left on a hunting trip. This fooled no one, and a rescue party rode south. Finding a note from Wood lying on the trail, they pursued harder. At last, they surrounded Wood's kidnappers and rescued him.

Wood and his supporters called a public meeting in Voorhees in May of 1888 to discuss bonds for their coveted railroad. In the course of the meeting Sam Robinson, the Hugoton town marshal, got crossways with the under-sheriff and slugged him with his revolver. Though nothing was badly hurt except some feelings, Ed Short, the Woodsdale marshal, later showed up in Hugoton, intent on dealing with Robinson.

"Short's reasoning," wrote one commentator, "was to ride into town, shoot Robinson and ask questions later, which he did."[4] But although Short looked about for his quarry, he did not find him. Then Robinson, apparently warned of Short's intent, appeared from the county attorney's office and sat down outside, "pistol in hand." Short lost no time in opening fire.

Now Kentucky Sam Robinson did not take kindly to any attempt either to curtail his liberty or to shoot him, for, in the words of one historian, he was a hardcase who:

> had already made a record for himself as a six shooter artist in Pratt and Barber Counties and who was probably about as cold-blooded a murderer as ever drew a gun.[5]

Short and Robinson emptied their pistols at each other, hitting nothing. During the fight Short's horse wisely bolted, and because local men were quickly gathering to support Robinson, the horse's panic was probably the best thing that could have happened to Short. Pursued by hostile Hugoton men, Short retreated, in some confusion, without his quarry. The people of Hugoton rejoiced.

All of this simply exacerbated the hard feelings between the two towns and built a fire under the already boiling enmity between

Short and Robinson. If hostilities were over for the moment, the peace would not last. Defeated and embarrassed, the Woodsdale men nursed their anger and waited for a chance to recover their dignity by striking out at the infuriating Robinson. And on Saturday, July 21, they got their chance.

On that day, Short heard that Robinson and other Hugoton men—A. M. Donald and the brothers Charles and Orrin Cook— had taken their families down into the No Man's Land on an excursion, either to go fishing, gather wild plums, or both, depending on the account.

Despite the fact that he had no authority in No Man's Land, Short was not deterred by a little legal disability, and he headed south with a two-man posse, carrying the warrant he had tried to serve in Hugoton. About half a mile out of the fishing camp he halted and sent in a local settler with a note demanding that Robinson surrender. One source tells that Short and his men came very close to the camp and opened fire when Robinson refused to give in.

Robinson took counsel with his friends, who wisely advised him to flee, reasoning that if he stood and fought he would endanger the women and children in the camp. Robinson saw the reason in this and left the camp forthwith. Although Short and his men pursued, and at one point had Robinson surrounded in a settler's dugout, their quarry got away clean in the end. Frustrated, Short sent a message to Stevens County sheriff John Cross at Woodsdale asking for help.

Cross was happy to assist. Not only was he a loyal Woodsdale man, but there had been bad blood between him and Robinson dating back to the last election for the office of sheriff in which Cross had beaten Robinson for the office. So Cross headed south, taking with him four men: Cyrus W., or Theodosius, Eaton; Robert Hubbard; Roland, or Rolla or Rollo, Wilcox; and a youngster called

Herbert Tonney or Toney or maybe Tooney. They rode hard to help out their fellow townsmen but found nobody at the fishing camp any longer.

The remaining fishermen and their families had sensibly packed up and headed for home. Once there, the fishermen spread the alarm, and a posse from Hugoton began riding south to bail Robinson out of the trouble they thought he must be in. Instead of finding Robinson, however, they ran head-on into Short and his men, and everybody began blazing away. By the time the shooting died away—around nightfall on July 25—a lot of ammunition had been expended, but nobody had been hurt.

Short's party, outnumbered, broke off the action and headed back north, up toward the Kansas border and Stevens County, having achieved nothing at all. They had ignominiously fled before the Hugoton party and had lost all hope of catching the hated Robinson. In fact, Short and his men were pushed clear across the Kansas border and a long way further toward the town of Springfield, far away from the tragedy which was about to unfold south of the state line.

Sheriff Cross and his men were also on their way back to Stevens County, tired men on tired horses. As night fell it was obvious that they needed to rest and water their mounts. They headed for a place called Wild Horse Lake, a shallow, grassy depression in the prairie that filled with water in times of heavy rain, hoping to find forage, rest, and water.

At about nine o'clock they came to a haymakers' camp at the lake where they stopped for the night—or maybe, according to one source, only for an hour or so.[6] The camp was only some eight miles south of the Stevens County line—today it lies in Texas County, Oklahoma. Already at the lake was a haying crew consisting of a man named Haas, his two sons, and a fourth hand, with their teams and wagons.

Cross and his men were tired and, perhaps because of their fatigue, they were also careless. While their horses grazed nearby, Cross and two of the others bedded down at the edge of some haystacks, a little way from the camp of the haymakers. The other men went to sleep in a wagon nearby. None of them thought to keep their weapons by them. The guns remained on their saddles, a little distance away—too far.

The Hugoton posse was on the way, with twelve men, some on saddle horses and some in buggies. Earlier that same evening, as they camped for their evening meal, Robinson rode into the camp, safe and sound. Happy to see their friend in one piece, the posse sent a message home to reassure Robinson's wife of his safety and decided to move on to camp for the night at Wild Horse Lake. The mounted men, including Robinson, rode on ahead. The buggies followed, perhaps two hundred yards behind them. After moonrise, between ten o'clock and ten thirty, they approached the hay camp at the lake.

Asleep in the moonlight, Cross and his people didn't hear them coming, according to the only survivor, and awoke to find themselves looking down the barrels of Hugoton rifles. "Surrender!" yelled Robinson, adding a little redundantly, "We have you surrounded on all sides and you cannot escape." The Woodsdale men would have had to run the gauntlet of Hugoton bullets at very short range to reach their weapons, and so they surrendered. As it turned out, they would have been better advised to fight, whatever the odds.

Whatever happened after that, the Hugoton men said it was "a running fight." It is better known to history, however, as the Hay Meadow Massacre. Robinson would not believe that none of his enemies had a weapon within reach until the Hugoton men searched their captives and made certain they were unarmed. Robinson then turned on Cross. "Sheriff Cross, you are my first man,"[7] he said, and coldly shot Cross down with his Winchester. He turned to Hubbard then. "I want you too," said Robinson, and he drove a slug into Hubbard, as well.

At first, Wilcox and Eaton, asleep in a wagon, escaped the notice of the Hugoton invaders. But once the shooting began Eaton, now wide awake, climbed out of the wagon where he had slept and ran. Robinson and a couple of others gave chase, there was a shot in the night, and the pursuers returned without Eaton. "I have," Robinson declared, "shot the man who drew the gun on me," apparently referring to the incident at Vorhees.[8]

A posseman named J. B. Chamberlain then shot Tonney with the boy's own revolver. He didn't shoot very well, and Tonney twisted his body to minimize Chamberlain's target. Tonney, who only got a shoulder wound, threw himself on the ground and played dead, trying not to breathe visibly. He lay there frozen and terrified, listening to Robinson and some of the others hunting for Wilcox.

Wilcox was soon found, and Tonney lay still while Wilcox was brought back to where his friends lay dead. The killers asked who he was. Wilcox said that he was only a settler, but Robinson did not believe him and casually shot him down.

The killers carefully lit matches and examined the faces of their enemies, making certain they had left nobody alive. According to some sources they also fired a second round into each of the bodies. Then it was Tonney's turn and once more, unintentionally, Chamberlain saved the young man's life. "He doesn't need a second bullet," Chamberlain bragged. "I took careful aim."

The petrified haymakers must have thought they would be next, but Robinson and his posse left them alone, unaware that Haas had already sent one of his sons to Voorhees to give the alarm. Robinson and his men rode off toward home satisfied, leaving the grassy depression soaked with blood. A lot of it was

Tonney's. The youngster was alive, but he knew he needed help quickly. He dragged himself onto his horse and pushed on north, running into a rescue party from Voorhees the following morning.

Young Haas's report of the killings had already spread, and men were on their way south to bring in the dead from Wild Horse Lake. A Voorhees peace officer, fearing for Tonney's safety, wanted to move him on to Liberal, Kansas, where the boy would surely be safe from the furies of Hugoton, but Tonney was too weak to travel. And so the officer stashed him in a cornfield, where he was left to survive as best he could until a posse arrived from Woodsdale to bring him home.

Both Woodsdale and Hugoton were now on full alert, with everybody carrying weapons and watching the roads for the approach of their mortal enemies. Had the two sides tangled the result might have been an all-out bloody war, but before either side moved the governor sent his attorney general and a couple of militia officers down to investigate.

The governor's party found Hugoton defended by a crowd of citizens armed with "weapons of every description and as many as they could conveniently handle."[9] The visitors did some investigating, and then went on to Woodsdale, where, in the words of one party member, "we were confronted with the presence of rifles, revolvers and various kinds of shooting-irons. Every man we saw was carrying some kind of a weapon."[10]

In Woodsdale the investigators spoke with the men who had recovered the dead from Wild Horse Lake, and with Tonney, the sole survivor. They also spoke with Haas, the haymaker, who corroborated Tonney's tale—although one source asserts that the haymaking team disagreed about who opened fire on whom at Wild Horse Lake.[11]

As a result of their findings, the governor's investigators recommended dispatch of military peace-keepers, and the governor sent in a truly formidable force. No less than a whole regiment of the militia marched into Stevens County, eight companies of soldiers complete with the regimental band and a battery of Gattling guns. The troops separated the warring parties and disarmed everybody, searching houses and controlling traffic in and out of both towns.

And then the legal maneuvering began, a byzantine process that dragged on and on for more than a year.

Wood struck the first blow, getting federal arrest warrants for roughly twenty citizens of Hugoton on charges of conspiracy to commit murder. The conspiracy had been formed in Kansas, Wood argued, even though the killings had taken place south of the state line. The federal court in Kansas disagreed, however, and ruled that it had no jurisdiction over anything that happened down in No Man's Land.

And so Wood hied himself off to the Northern District of Texas, but that court also refused to take jurisdiction. Wood, now greatly wroth, angrily wrote the United States Attorney General:

> It had been over a year since these cold-blooded murders were committed in No Man's Land, and the law of last winter in cases of felony gave the court of Paris, Texas, jurisdiction. . . . Is it possible that these cold-blooded murders are to go unpunished?[12]

Wood then followed his own advice and tried the Eastern District in Paris, Texas; this time he got results. The judge ruled that the court did indeed have jurisdiction, and the grand jury returned a true bill. Twelve Hugoton men were arrested, including the contingent that traveled to the murder site by buggy.

The defendants' attempt to obtain a writ of *habeas corpus* from the Circuit Court of Appeals failed. However, Robinson, the chief culprit, was not among the defendants, for he had wisely fled. He ended up in Florissant, Colorado, in May of 1889, where he tried to hold up a store-*cum*-post office.

Robinson served hard time for this crime, left prison in 1898, and then disappeared from history. The rest of the horseback murderers had run also. Four simply disappeared, while the fifth man fetched up in Belgium, with which the United States had no extradition treaty at the time.

The charge on which the defendants were arraigned was not murder, curiously, but conspiracy to commit murder. This odd charge may have been Wood's idea originally, the theory being that while the killing was done in No Man's Land, the decision to kill had been made way up in Kansas. It might also have been an attempt to avoid the defense offered by the buggy contingent, who said—probably truthfully—that they had not even reached the lake when the firing began.[13]

Twelve defendants stood trial. Tonney had recovered and became the prosecution's star witness. He seems to have convinced the jury, even though he placed among the culprits a number of Hugoton men who were demonstrably far away at the time of the murder. Two haymakers also testified. Both seem to have told the jury that something like a pitched battle had taken place at the lake, but otherwise they disagreed. One said the Hugoton men had done all the shooting; the other thought Cross and his men had fired first.[14]

Wood was in the midst of things as usual, doing all he could to whip up anger against the defendants. He obtained subpoenas for some three hundred witnesses, some of whom knew absolutely nothing about the killings. He was a vengeful fury and nemesis to the defendants, but he may also have had a somewhat baser motive in his pursuit of the Hugoton murderers. As one writer put it:

> In the preparation and trial of the case, he was the real prosecutor, the district attorney having been a mere figurehead. Wood had freedom to subpoena whomsoever he saw fit . . . a coachload of this class of witnesses reached Paris at six o'clock one evening, registered the following morning, were then excused by the

prosecuting attorney, received their certificates of attendance, averaging perhaps a hundred dollars each, and started home the same day.[15]

Wood, also commissioned as a deputy marshal at the time, is said to have bought up some of the certificates at a discounted rate, and made money on them.

Despite Wood's remorseless pursuit and his eight-hour oration to the jury, six of the defendants successfully pleaded alibi, and were duly acquitted. The other six, however, were convicted and sentenced to hang on December 19, 1890. One defendant, John Jackson, actually made a speech justifying the murders, an oration which one writer piously said "aroused general sympathy for the condemned." Cook, the posse's leader, made a "brave and stirring speech," which also touched the hearts of many of his listeners.[16]

Four of the accused men had served with the Union army, which naturally aroused the sympathy of many Kansas men who had also served. In that age of lodges and clubs, Cook turned out to be a member of the Kansas Traveling Men's Association and all of the defendants were either Knights of Pythias or Knights of Honor. The brothers of both organizations sent contributions to the defense fund from all over the nation. Nashua, New Hampshire, where the Cook family had lived, raised $2,200, a goodly sum for the time.

The judgment was appealed, of course, and the case wended its way all the way to the Supreme Court of the United States, which reversed the conviction after the state attorney general confessed error.

Among other things, the former state attorney general had been permitted to testify, over defense objection, that he had investigated the killings and concluded that they were deliberate murders. The attorney general sent a judge to investigate the conduct of the trial. As a result, the trial judge was reprimanded and the prosecuting attorney was fired.

The Kansas Legislature now got into the act, and passed a resolution demanding that the charges be dismissed. Thirty-eight of the forty legislators concurred with the resolution, and the state's leading executive officers joined in. Kansas was Republican, and so was President Harrison. Therefore, he referred the whole vexing question to his attorney general, who gave it to his first assistant, who sat on it, thus following the ancient bureaucratic maxim that if one does nothing about a vexing problem and does so long enough, it will often go away.

It did. For by now the indefatigable Wood had left the stage. One day in June of 1891, he went to look at some records in a Hugoton church used as a courthouse. As he left the building, he passed Jim Brennan, a defense witness in the Wild Horse Lake case whose testimony Wood had attacked in his final argument to the jury.

Once Wood had his back to Brennan, Brennan shot him. As Wood tried to run to safety, Brennan shot him again. Wood was carried into the church and soon died. The sparkplug of the prosecution was gone. Brennan was never prosecuted, perhaps because the few hundred men in the county were all partisans of either Wood or the faction—including the county judge—who opposed him.

Wood's partner committed suicide, and three other leaders pushing the prosecution also died, violently or otherwise. And so, in the fall of 1895, the case was at last dismissed.

Short left Woodsdale in 1889, going off to Colorado apparently to recruit "boomers" to occupy Oklahoma lands not yet open to settlement. As a deputy U.S. marshal, he left this life in a blaze of glory in August of 1891 in Garfield County, Oklahoma Territory. While taking Dalton gang member Blackfaced Charley Bryant to jail on a Rock Island train, Short was shot by his prisoner with a purloined pistol. Before he went down, however, tough Ed Short filled Bryant with Winchester bullets, taking the outlaw with him.

If nothing else, the whole sorry affair had helped get No Man's Land some law of its own. The federal government at least recognized that so far the people there had been coping with outlaws and hoodlums on their own, without regular law enforcement or courts.

And the treasured title of county seat? Woodsdale simply disappeared, gone with the wind—only one house remained by 1897.[17] Long-suffering Stevens County finally got its county seat: Hugoton.

Chapter 9

Henry Plummer:
Into a World Unknown

Two hooded men in the middle of the road waived big shotguns at the stagecoach driver, forcing him to slowly grind to a halt that Monday morning, October 26, 1863, in present-day Montana.

The gunmen immediately focused on "Bummer Dan" McFadden. Despite his disheveled, lazy appearance, he was filthy rich. Not long before, Dan had stirred himself into action just long enough to strike a rich lode he called the Dakota; he turned that money into even more cash by running "Bummer Dan's Bar" in Alder Gulch. Now he was returning East with his winnings on the Peabody-Caldwell stagecoach from Virginia City, California, to Bannack, Montana. That day, he was carrying as much as $2,500 in gold dust, worth some $43,000 today.

Somehow, the highwaymen knew all about his boodle. They even knew that he was hiding a third pouch chock full of gold dust in his pants.

This was very suspicious, as was the offer of a fellow passenger named Bill Bunton to take McFadden's gold out of his pockets for the robbers. Some of the other passengers, whom Bunton had hosted the previous evening at his Rattlesnake Ranch, even sensed that Bunton was *acting* when he begged the robbers not to kill him.[1]

Bummer Dan probably didn't consider himself all that lucky, but he was. Earlier that very month, Lloyd Magruder, who made a big pile selling dry goods in booming Virginia City, left with about $12,000 in gold dust and simply disappeared—forever.

More holdups came after Bummer Dan was picked clean, bringing the total number of robberies from October to early December to five; rumors in area brothels, mines, saloons, and stores often attributed these robberies to Henry Plummer, the affable sheriff of the Bannack mining district. He was pleasant enough—Plummer was just never around when the robberies occurred. Or was he?

Most historians now agree that the sheriff was born William Henry Handy Plumer in Maine some 2,700 miles due east of Virginia City in 1832.[2] The Plumer family had been Puritan stalwarts in New England as early as 1770. His father, Moses Plumer, died when Henry was about fifteen, and soon, perhaps four years later, young Henry headed west to California in the gold rush.[3] When he was twenty, Plumer sailed to Panama; after a sweltering interlude there, he boarded the S.S. *Golden Gate* and arrived in San Francisco on May 12, 1852. During the next year, he ranched and mined in Nevada City, California, with a partner known only as "Robinson." [4]

April 1854 found Plumer in a new business with a new partner; the future gunfighter and supposed stage robber had become a baker, of all things. In one advertisement, he offered "The best assortment of bread, cake and pastry to be found" in Nevada City, California.[5] In November 1855, when Plumer was twenty-three, he sold his house there to a business partner. Due to a clerical error in the deed of sale, he then became "Plummer" for the first time.[6]

Plummer intended to depart San Francisco for Maine, but he returned to Virginia City instead. He was elected city marshal there as a Democrat in early 1856. The election was close, but this did not stop him from promptly becoming involved in several difficulties.

The first was a barroom gunfight in which Plummer's friend George Jordan was shot and killed before the city marshal could intervene. Jordan had just been arrested by a deputy for breaking a man's jaw with a piece of lumber and was released on a $500 bond.

This was followed by a massive town fire which some grousers blamed on Plummer, because he did not force merchants to keep full water buckets on hand as was required by law.

These were difficult times. Sheriff Wright and a deputy were killed by their own posse on November 3, 1856, as Wright and Plummer tried to recapture Tom Bell Gang stalwart Jim Webster. The culprit had escaped from Plummer's "escape-proof" city jail, and Webster escaped again in the confusion of the gunfight.[7]

A coroner's jury found these deaths accidental. However, in the aftermath, Plummer exchanged some bitter correspondence with posse member Wallace Williams, which was published in the *Nevada Journal.* Of course, Williams might have killed Sheriff Wright himself during the wild exchange of shots.

Plummer now turned his attention elsewhere. He focused on bringing in fugitives and polishing his credentials for a September 1857 race for the California State Assembly. He apparently lost only because a significant number of Democratic miners voted for the anti-Catholic American Party.

At midnight fifteen days after the election, Plummer killed John Vedder in front of Vedder's wife Lucy at the Vedders' Spring Street home. Traditionally, this killing has been thought to be romantically motivated. Historian Bill O'Neal concluded, for example, that "Plummer killed a man whose wife he was having an affair with."[8]

Although Plummer was convicted twice of murdering Vedder, there was very little evidence to prove he was having an affair with Vedder's wife. There was, on the other hand, substantial evidence that Vedder was an abusive husband. On August 15, 1857, within six months of his imprisonment, Plummer walked out of San Quentin with a pardon in his pocket; this was partially justified by medical assessments predicting his imminent death from tuberculosis.

Some historians have suggested that Plummer somehow faked the illness, perhaps by spattering a pillowcase with blood after cutting himself. However he received the pardon, he soon became a constable on the Nevada City, California, police force. Plummer secured his tenure in that position by collaring his fellow San Quentin alumnus "Ten Year" Smith. Yet Plummer's boss, City Marshal Tompkins, was soon defeated, and Plummer was out of a job.

In the late spring of 1860, Plummer was prospecting ninety-six miles to the east at Carson City, Nevada, but before long he was back in Nevada City. Though he was supposedly mining, Plummer spent most of his time carousing in bordellos, notably Irish Maggie's, not far from where he once toiled as a respectable, if somewhat bored, baker.

On the evening of Wednesday, February 13, 1861, W. J. Muldoon became tired of waiting for Plummer to finish his business in one of the upstairs rooms. When Muldoon complained about the delay, Plummer promptly pistol-whipped him for his trouble. Muldoon seemed to recover quickly, but he died unexpectedly several weeks later.[9]

Henry Plummer (Author's collection)

A Most Useless if not Dangerous Man

On Sunday, October 26, 1861, Plummer killed again in Nevada City, this time at the Ashmore brothel in an argument with William Riley, an ardent secessionist, over politics. The debate began in the bordello foyer after Plummer had visited his paramour, "Mrs. Plummer." A local newspaper account reported:

> [T]hey had both been drinking pretty freely and got to quarreling in the entry room when Riley struck Plumer on the head with a knife, cutting through his hat and inflicting a deep wound in his scalp. Plumer at the same time drew his revolver and fired at Riley. The ball took effect in his left side and killed him instantly . . . Riley was a . . . young man about 21 years of age and was formerly from Huntsville, Missouri. He had been living within the vicinity of Nevada for a year or two and we are informed was quarrelsome and dissipative.[10]

Plummer was jailed, treated for his wounds, and apparently allowed to escape when the hoosegow door was opened for "Mrs. Plummer." Having killed one Confederate sympathizer, Plummer sought refuge with another. He returned to the Carson City, Nevada, cabin of his friend Billy Mayfield.

Back in Nevada City, his one-time ally, *Nevada Democrat* editor Tallman Rolph, opined that Plummer's retreat was prudent because a trial for murder would probably leave him "a most useless if not dangerous man."[11]

A short time later, Carson City Sheriff John Blackburn began questioning Mayfield about Plummer's whereabouts. The fugitive was lounging on a mattress in the rafters of a nearby cabin above a false ceiling, with enough food and water for several days. Still, Blackburn was suspicious enough that he questioned Mayfield again several times. And perhaps there was more at work here than just a police investigation; Blackburn was as ardent a Unionist as Mayfield was a secessionist.

By the evening of Monday, November 18, 1861, Mayfield had irritated Sheriff Blackburn enough during a saloon encounter that Blackburn tried to make an arrest—his last ever. Instead, Mayfield fatally stabbed Blackburn for asking too many questions about Plummer—the one who had killed the outspoken secessionist William Riley back in Nevada City. Mayfield was convicted of killing Blackburn but escaped prison. He led a Confederate raid on Florence, Idaho, the next October before disappearing from history.[12]

Plummer's whereabouts during the winter of 1862 are simply a mystery, despite an erroneous newspaper report that he was hanged. On July 24, 1862, he surfaced at Lewiston, Idaho, with San Quentin escapees William Ridgley and Charles Reeves in the midst of yet another gold rush. Plummer even checked into the Luna House hotel using his real name. One story—and perhaps it is just that—claims Plummer stood down a lynch mob intent on hanging another man in Lewiston that summer.[13]

Plummer killed a fourth man on August 23. The victim was Pat Ford, one of many itinerant dance hall owners who followed the gold strikes of that era. Ford invited Plummer, Ridgley, and Reeves to his place in a gold camp near Lewiston called Oro Fino and soon wished he hadn't. After the trio destroyed his saloon tent, Ford tried to stop Plummer from escaping by killing his horse—just before the trio filled Ford with lead.[14] Plummer wasn't finished.

Dry-Gulched at the Goodrich

"You won't shoot me when I'm down?" Jack Cleveland whimpered from the floor of the Goodrich Hotel in Bannack as he held his bloody stomach wound. "Get up!" Plummer demanded. When Cleveland obeyed, Plummer shot him again in the head and in the chest. Cleveland was gone within three hours; when he died, he probably took a secret or two with him.

That winter day, Wednesday, January 14, 1863, had started like many others in Bannack: cold and clear. Three days earlier, Gen. John McClernand and Adm. David Dixon Porter captured Arkansas Post some 1,800 miles to the east, thus assuming *de facto* control of the Arkansas River for the Union.

This was probably of little interest to Plummer and Cleveland, who had arrived in Bannack as fugitives. Earlier, Plummer had traveled into this part of present-day western Montana, then still a part of Idaho Territory, with his one-time crony Charles Reeves. They stayed with early Missoula County luminaries and brothers Granville and James Stuart in the fall of 1862.

Generally, the Stuarts were good at sniffing out a bad man. That past August, they helped lynch a suspected horse thief without much evidence beyond the bad first impression he made. In memoirs published some fifty-three years later, Granville Stuart remembered Plummer and Reeves as "two fine-looking young men" inquiring about gold discoveries across the Rocky Mountains in the Beaverhead Valley of present day southwestern Montana.[15]

Plummer and Reeves took separate paths from there. Early October found Plummer and a new companion named Jack Cleveland at Fort Benton, a trading post started by the American Fur Company on the Missouri River about seventeen years earlier. How Plummer and Cleveland met is unknown.

Fort Benton was already shut in for the winter when Plummer and Cleveland arrived. Because no boats would venture east until the following spring, they found temporary work at a government-run Indian farm James Vail operated about sixty miles to the west.[16]

Plummer met the love of his life there. Vail and his family came from Ohio to convert the stubborn Blackfeet to Christianity, commerce, and agriculture, perhaps even in that order. The warriors were having none of it—and called their new government directed occupations women's work.

Vail's staff included his sister-in-law Electa Bryan, a pert twenty-year-old who came west to escape a bad relationship with her widowed stepmother back in Ohio. Plummer did small chores around the Vail farm while courting Electa in his spare time. Despite his checkered past, she soon accepted his marriage proposal and even agreed to wait for his return in the spring.[17]

Cleveland and Plummer left the Vail farm in early October 1862 and headed south to Bannack, where the duo parted company under less-than-amicable circumstances. When the Stuart brothers arrived at Bannack on November 22, Cleveland had become overtly antagonistic towards Plummer for reasons that remain unexplained.

Soon, Cleveland was boasting "Plummer is my meat," a nineteenth century way of saying that he could kill the man any time he wanted to. Initially, Plummer tolerated Cleveland as one would a child, although this would soon change.[18]

Christmas in Bannack was far from merry. Anyone with any mining experience could see by then that Bannack was nothing more than a small placer strike. The term "placer" was derived from "plassers," a corrupted Spanish word for shoal. Yes, there was some gold, notably along the meandering shoals of little Grasshopper Creek. Because the district lacked any major deposits, there was a real danger Bannack might become a ghost town.

And because of this, despite the mild, atypical winter conditions, there was very little to occupy the Bannackians that winter except to ponder the fate of George Edwards, who had ventured into the nearby countryside to care for his livestock and never returned. Many suspected that Cleveland, already known as one of the roughest men in a tough mining crowd, had killed Edwards in early January. Edwards's bloody clothing had been found near a creek.[19]

Cleveland had certainly made an impression. One local luminary described him as "a desperado of the vilest character"; yet the same observer considered Plummer, whose dark past was known or at least rumored, to be a man "intending to reform and live an honest and useful life."[20]

This was just not Cleveland's month. First, an old neighbor from Galena, Illinois, wandered into Bannack and asked Cleveland if his real name was John Farnsworth, a robber who had escaped from Plummer's city jail along with Jim Webster in the incident that led to the death of Sheriff Wright. Cleveland threatened to kill the man if he told anyone about their past acquaintance.[21] And then, on the morning of January 14, 1863, Plummer shot Cleveland for simply talking too much.

The Goodrich Hotel might have been the best in Bannack then, although the building was scarcely wider than twenty feet with four flimsy colonnades and a second story balcony of sorts. Cleveland had staggered into the Goodrich late that morning. Several locals, including Plummer and Jeff Perkins, were sitting around a corner stove in the hotel "saloon," perhaps talking about the recent return of seasonally icy conditions. Cleveland was looking for Perkins, who, he claimed, owed him money. Both Plummer and Perkins insisted the debt had been repaid; when Cleveland persisted, Plummer plugged the ceiling and then Cleveland.

Cleveland was, at least, a realist. Three hours later, he whimpered "Jack has got no friends" and then quietly crossed over. There was no wake—those Bannackians who knew Cleveland best liked him least.[22] Thus it was no surprise that Plummer remained free for the time being; no one volunteered to alert the authorities in far-away Yankton, the Dakota Territory Capitol, which was a long, bone-jarring 950 miles away.

At about the same time, Plummer's only surviving friend in the area was stirring up problems with the local Bannack tribe. Charles Reeves had married a Bannackian woman but abused her and left for the nearby hills. Soon he returned, first with Charley Moore and later with William Mitchell; they tried to abduct her after killing three Bannack tribesmen and a French fur trapper unlucky enough to be in the village.[23]

Reeves, like Plummer, was an easterner, born in western Pennsylvania. He spent several years in Texas before moving on to California, where he was convicted of theft but escaped twice from San Quentin prison. After Reeves, Plummer, and another man killed dance hall owner Pat Ford in early September 1862 at the Oro Fino mining camp near Lewiston, Idaho, after breaking up his place, Plummer and Reeves rode separately back into Bannack, just before Plummer partnered up with poor, friendless Jack Cleveland.

Eight days after Plummer killed Cleveland, he left Bannack with Reeves, Charley Moore, and William Mitchell. Their destination was a hideout some sixteen miles north of Bannack on Rattlesnake Creek.

A four-man posse began following their tracks in the snow at first light on January 23 and found them at about noon. Plummer negotiated a "guaranteed" trial by jury for each desperado and was himself cleared of any charges in Cleveland's death within hours of their return to Bannack.[24]

However, the Bannackians were inclined to give Reeves, Moore, and Mitchell typical mining camp justice. This often consisted of a town meeting where a howling mob, temporarily sanctified as a "jury of the whole," shouted out a verdict after intimidating any long-winded defense lawyer brave enough to lecture them about due process.

Because this trio had been promised a real jury trial to avoid a shootout back on Rattlesnake Creek, certain legal formalities that were normally ignored were followed. The next morning, an unfinished commercial building was fully furnished with tables, chairs, and even a judge's bench, witness stand, and jury box. The prior evening, A. J. Hoy, former chancellor of Washington University, was elected judge; prosecutors and defense lawyers were appointed from the local bar just before a jury was selected. Of course, because these measures had not been sanctioned at the Idaho Territorial capitol, no one had any real legal authority at all.

Since there was no lynching, the defendants didn't complain, even though they were found guilty and banished from Bannack. The whole affair was more or less forgotten when the weather turned too cold for the exiles to camp in the hills above town.[25]

There was, however, one serious consequence. Hank Crawford, a town butcher earlier appointed to be a town marshal of sorts, had been appointed sheriff during the proceedings. After Reeves, Moore, and Mitchell were found guilty, the jury directed Crawford to confiscate and sell their property for expenses.

He did so, but he also confiscated Plummer's guns. Plummer was angry but sent Crawford word that he would not be harmed. This was cold comfort to Sheriff Crawford, a fair butcher but a poor shot who was unwilling to take his chances with such an experienced shootist. Despite this difference in gun fighting experience, Plummer soon had a confrontation with Sheriff Crawford.

Crawford had his chance one morning in early March 1863. As Plummer stood surveying Main Street in downtown Bannack with a Winchester rifle crooked in his arm, Crawford tried to back-shoot him but succeeded only in hitting his right elbow with the first of two shots.

Crawford's missed opportunity to kill Plummer meant the end of his law enforcement career, but, inexplicably, he lived to tell the tale. Plummer only kept his arm, legend has it, because his associates told Dr. Jerome Glick that if Plummer did not survive the medical treatment, this would be the good doctor's last patient.[26]

Just before the shooting, Congress had created Idaho Territory, which included most of present day Idaho, Montana, and Wyoming, but appropriated no funds to form a government. Despite this, a gunfight in Bannack on May 17, which left a bystander and one shooter dead, convinced town leaders to appoint functionaries and elect a judge, a sheriff, and a coroner. The acting president of the mining district dressed these extra-judicial proceedings in as much formality as possible, right down to the appointment of polling monitors.[27]

Plummer was elected sheriff despite his still-immobile right arm and the reservations of town leaders. Two days later he left to claim his bride at the Vail farm, some two hundred miles to the north, leaving D. H. Dillingham as chief deputy in charge of three deputized town toughs, Ned Ray, Buck Stinson, and Jack Gallagher.[28]

And perhaps even earlier than this, during his recuperation from the Crawford ambush, Plummer partnered with three other San Quentin alumni in nearby mining ventures. Edward Richardson at least had a social pedigree of sorts; he was the son of a California judge. After serving his term in San Quentin, he promptly killed a man in a Bannack bar fight.[29] Charles Ridgley had been with Plummer during the Pat Ford killing outside Lewiston, Idaho Territory. Cyrus Skinner now owned a Bannack saloon.

Plummer promoted his mining ventures with these characters in a newspaper interview that appeared in the June 17 *Sacramento Union*. He made no effort to disguise or understate his past; Plummer even bragged of his ventures with Richardson, Skinner, and Ridgley.

He arrived at the Vail farm on June 2, just after another visitor arrived. Francis Thompson was a well-connected banker who had traveled with the Vail family on their steamboat journey up the Missouri. Although the Vail family had recruited Thompson to dissuade Electa Bryan from marrying Plummer, he noted in his 1913 memoirs, "When I saw him [Plummer] I could but wonder if this could be the young desperado whom people so much feared." Thompson observed that Plummer was modest, dignified, and devoid of swagger.[30] Little wonder, then, that Electa promptly reaffirmed her decision to marry Plummer despite all the family pressure to reject his suit.

Plummer initially agreed to wait at the Vail farm for an itinerant Methodist preacher to wander through the area, but he changed his mind on June 16 and insisted that a cleric—any cleric— be located and quick. Though neither Henry nor Electa were Catholic, the Jesuit missionary Father Minatre married them on June 20. After an elegant breakfast repast of buffalo hump and cornmeal, Henry and Electa began the slow journey to Bannack.[31]

Southwest Montana had become a far different place when Plummer returned to Bannack with his bride in August 1863. William Fairweather, who features later in the book, stumbled into a major strike at Alder Creek, also known as Alder Gulch, some seventy miles east of town in late May. Frederick Allen described the resulting prosperity in his definitive history of the Montana vigilantes:

> Along with prospectors, provisioners were flocking to the gulch as well, hauling boots, tents, tools whiskey, beer, flour, cloth, coffee, tobacco, and other notions and sundries all priced as high as the market would bear. The economy was fairly simple. Miners created wealth by digging it out of the ground and spending it freely. Gold dust was the sole medium of exchange.[32]

Alder Gulch followed a meandering creek that eventually hosted six major mining districts: Summit, Highland Junction,

Adobetown, Nevada City, Virginia City, and the town of Alder Gulch. The last two were scarcely a mile apart. Locals named the place Alder Creek for "the dense growth of green alders and willows on either side of the creek."[33]

Fairweather had triggered all this when he began spreading gold dust around at Bannack with his partners, Henry Edgar and Harry Rodgers. The trio spent freely on ham and eggs—rare delicacies in that time and place—and fancy new duds. Fairweather, Edgar, Rodgers, and three other argonauts left Bannack on June 2, the very day Plummer had arrived at the Vail farm, shadowed by some one hundred prospectors. They averted conflicts and perhaps even death by calling a mass meeting halfway to the gulch. Fairweather and his associates insisted on the right to claim 12,000 feet of the creek bed in locations of their choosing and required that it all be preserved in writing and signed by everyone on the venture.

Altogether, Alder Gulch comprised some fourteen miles, coursing "from its confluence with the Stinking Water Creek nearly to the top of Mount Baldy."[33] Until now, crime in that little corner of present-day Montana had largely been limited to bar fights. This was about to change.

Bannack hosted some 400 to 500 souls before the Fairweather strike almost turned the little burg into a ghost town. The reason was simple: Alder Gulch gold assayed at twice the value of dust scraped out of the Bannack area digs.[35]

As Alder Gulch began to draw people from Bannack some seventy miles away, Acting-Sheriff Dillingham began wondering about his fellow deputies. Dillingham suspected them of complicity in several area robberies in which travelers had been relieved of their hard-earned gold dust. The Montana pioneer Edward Purple journaled Dillingham's claim that he heard some of his deputies talking about their plans. "I am going after them," Dillingham vowed.[36]

The first suspicions fell on Buck Stinson and his associate Hayes Lyons, who barbered in a corner of the Buckhorn Saloon, operated by Plummer's mining partner Cyrus "Cy" Skinner. Dillingham whispered these suspicions to George W. Stapleton, a prominent Bannack attorney planning a trip to Alder Gulch with two others. For reasons that remain unclear, Stapleton told Stinson, who swore revenge.

Virginia City mining district president Dr. William L. Steele was hearing a dispute on June 29, 1863, when Stinson and Lyons loudly interrupted him to shout that Dillingham was back in town. His court reporter Charley Forbes promptly threw down his pen and hurried outside—but why? Within minutes, Lyons and Stinson had shot Dillingham to pieces. The acting sheriff died instantly or, according to some, within a few minutes, as most of the town looked on. According to some observers, Forbes helped kill him, although Forbes's pistol was still fully loaded afterwards.[37]

Steele promptly expanded the miner's court to include two physicians, Giles Gaylord Bissell and Dr. Rutar. Forbes was bound over for separate trial, perhaps because of his position and gentlemanly appearance.

Stinson and Lyons were tried, convicted, and sentenced by just about anyone in town who could yell "Hang em!" During the separate trial, which followed in short order, Forbes claimed he tried to prevent the killing; the mob now wavered. After a fourth voice vote failed to produce a clear verdict either way, Plummer's hard-case Bannack deputy Jack Gallagher simply rode into the middle of the street, waived his pistol, and declared *all three* suspects free to go. Alder Gulch sheriff Dick Todd shrugged his shoulders and let them lope away.[38]

Thirty years later, Dr. Steele speculated that Forbes and Gallagher had conspired to kill Dillingham; he theorized that Gallagher reloaded Forbes's pistol after Forbes shot Dillingham and then set up Lyons and Stinson as disposable, obvious fall guys. The duo would have been hanged then and there had the Virginia City mob not reconsidered, according to Steele.[39]

In August, Electa and Henry were back, living in a modest one-room cabin much like many others in the mining camp. Sheriff Plummer's office, such as it was, occupied a corner of George Chrisman's general store. Plummer now struggled with two disabilities: the fingers of his left hand were nearly as useless as the right arm which Hank Crawford crippled trying to back-shoot him. For the time being, Plummer avoided saloons and the hard-case characters he had slummed with before. Nathaniel Langford, a merchant later instrumental in the creation of Yellowstone Park, soon noticed his good behavior.

Despite this, Plummer soon suffered a severe career setback at the hands of a fellow Democrat. When Idaho Territorial U.S. Marshal Dolphus S. Payne asked staunchly Republican Nathaniel Langford to nominate a deputy U.S. Marshal for present-day south-west Montana, Langford consulted the local Union League, whose members unanimously endorsed Plummer for the appointment.

Although he was a prominent fellow Democrat, Samuel T. Hauser expressed violent opposition to Plummer several days later. Hauser was one of many Bannack citizens who believed Plummer was far too cozy with the saloon crowd. Some also suspected he was complicit in the Dillingham murder.[40] However, two Plummer biographers have also suggested Hauser based his opposition to Plummer on political factionalism within Democrat ranks.[41] In any event, the Union League endorsement was soon withdrawn. "From now on you're my enemy," Plummer warned Langford.[42] They never spoke again.

Later that summer, early on the morning of August 19, 1863, Peter Horen (Horan) settled a mining dispute with his partner Lawrence "Larry" Keeley by shooting him to death at their

Grasshopper Creek cabin.[43] Miner's court judge B. B. Burchette promptly sentenced Horen to death. Within six days, Plummer carried out the sentence on a makeshift hillside scaffold just outside town with little fanfare.

The very next day, Plummer's acquaintance Francis Thompson journeyed from Deer Lodge, in present-day Montana, towards Bannack in the company of a dozen men led by one "Doc" Howard. The party included James Romaine and "Red" Yeager, who served as cook. Howard and some of the others knew Plummer and spoke highly of him.

Plummer did not return the compliment when he spoke with Thompson in Bannack the next day. In fact, he described Howard and Yeager as "cutthroats and robbers." The sheriff did not explain how he knew this. Thompson later recalled this as the moment when he began to think that the unsavory rumors about Plummer around Bannack might be true.

Worse still for Plummer, his new wife announced on September 2 that she was leaving. Some have suggested that Electa left when she learned Plummer was an outlaw. He followed her stage several days, perhaps in the hope of bringing her back.[44]

Near present-day Idaho Falls on the Snake River, Plummer and his wife's stage encountered the Sidney Edgerton party plodding towards them on the way to Bannack. Edgerton had been named chief justice of the newly created Idaho Territory. He had planned to reach Lewiston before the snows but decided in early September to winter at Bannack, perhaps to do some mining.

Edgerton's daughter, although then only a child, claimed years later that a stagecoach driver her family encountered along the trail to Bannack warned her parents that pleasant, affable Henry Plummer was "a bad man . . . quick on the draw."[45] Several days later, they met another mining camp character along the same trail. George Ives showed them a "sack full of gold, dust and nuggets, apparently without saying much about how he got it."[46]

They arrived at Bannack on September 22, bought a cabin for $400 and settled in for the cold winter months ahead. The highest point in the little burg was then the scaffold on the hillside Plummer had constructed nearby. Edgerton made no effort to exercise his nominal authority, because no properly designated official was available to administer an oath of office. This proved convenient. Edgerton improved his small cabin and then tried his hand at mining. About seventy dollars in gold dust quickly extracted from creek water convinced him to begin investing in mining properties.

Plummer returned to Bannack alone, despite his best efforts to dissuade his wife from returning east. Now that she was gone, he changed his living arrangements. His brother-in-law James Vail had given up on the Sun River Indian Farm where Plummer and Electa had courted and moved to Bannack. Plummer sold him the small cabin purchased months earlier and stayed on as a boarder. Francis Thompson also lived with the Vail family.[47]

With about $12,000 in gold dust he earned by selling dry goods, Lloyd Magruder, another Plummer acquaintance from California, left Bannack on October 5, 1863, bound for Elk City, Idaho, some 400 miles away. He hired supposed Yale graduate "Doc" Howard, James Romaine, Chris Lower, and Billy Page as well as several other men to act as his bodyguards. Magruder was not just a miner; he was also a Democrat candidate for Territorial Delegate to Congress and a "copperhead" strongly sympathetic to the southern cause.

Four Tickets to Walla Walla

Whether Plummer warned Magruder about recent robberies in the area or not, one thing is clear—Magruder, his security team, and all that gold dust simply disappeared. Thirteen days later,

Magruder's friend and fellow copperhead Hill Beachy observed something highly unusual at the front desk of his Luna House Hotel in Lewiston. A stranger trying to hide his face bought four stagecoach tickets to Walla Walla, Washington: one for himself and one for each of three others; their names were obvious aliases.

Beachy and a friend watched the four heavily scarred men loading unusually heavy luggage into a stagecoach; this piqued their curiosity even further. Later, Beachy found Magruder's horse in a remote pasture outside Lewiston.

Armed with this evidence, Beachy convinced Acting-Governor William B. Daniels to issue four John Doe complaints and extradition requests to the governors of California and British Columbia. He didn't stop there.

By October 23, Beachy was a deputy sheriff in hot pursuit of Magruder's presumed killers.[48] He pursued them to Portland, Oregon, and then raced their ocean steamer over land. After telegraphing a hold order ahead to the police department, Beachy made his way to San Franscico on a bumpy stagecoach. Police Captain J. W. Lees easily rounded up the four suspects; the gold dust they exchanged for $7,000 in paper money at the San Francisco mint only confirmed Beachy's suspicions.[49]

Despite a blistering publicity campaign waged by the quartet's lawyers, Beachy convinced railroad magnate and then-California governor Leland Stanford to sign extradition papers. The *Portland Oregonian* published predictions that the prisoners would be lynched once they returned to Lewiston; despite this, Beachy successfully resisted *habeas corpus* efforts by solemnly swearing they would receive a fair trial. But who were these guys?

Two of the four men Beachy tracked down were San Quentin prison alumni; George Christopher Lower (Lowery) had served part of his sentence at the same time as Henry Plummer. "Doc" Howard was really David Renton, who left San Quentin a few months before Plummer had arrived there years earlier. And long ago, the third suspect, James Romaine, had known Magruder and Beachy himself in Marysville, California.[50]

Although Magruder was never found, the fourth suspect, a crippled Cornishman named Billy Page, promptly turned prosecution witness and solved the mystery with a gruesome tale of murder and mayhem. Beachy's suspicions back in Lewiston were fully justified.

The journey over the Bitterroot Mountains through the Nez Perce Pass almost 7,000 feet above sea level on the Idaho-Montana border would have been difficult even in the best conditions; even today, the Magruder corridor is an unimproved road. The murderers relied upon this very inaccessibility.

The Magruder Murder Plot

Doc Howard had a simple plan to bag all Magruder's valuable gold dust. His minion Lower would brain Magruder while they were standing guard duty together just outside the camp. Thus, no one in the plot was surprised on the night of October 10 when Lower returned alone; wearing Indian moccasins, he helped Howard and Romaine bludgeon their way through the camp, along the way axing Charley Allen, William Phillips, and the two Chalmers brothers who comprised the honest citizenry on the trip.

Later, Billy Page portrayed himself as an unwilling participant in all this. He was only left alive, or so he claimed, to help with the pack mules, which were later slaughtered for next to no reason at all.

Victim or not, Page pocketed an equal share of the booty before the blood-soaked quartet traveled on to Lewiston. Now, months later, the authorities in Lewiston believed their case against "Howard," Lower, and Romaine was strong; the Page testimony was corroborated by a horse saddle and gear left near Lewiston precisely where the diminutive Cornishman said these things could be found.[51]

Although the remote campsite where the murders occurred was totally inaccessible in December 1863, prosecutor Enos F. Gray started murder proceedings against the "Doc Howard Three" anyway. The trio was arraigned on January 10, applying the English common law which an Idaho statute had declared applicable six days earlier. Two weeks later, the Doc Howard gang stood convicted.

They were sentenced to be hanged; and, according to Nathaniel Langford, by then a vigilante apologist, on Friday, March 4, 1864, with "almost the entire Nez Perce tribe" looking on, hang they did. Lower and Romaine confessed their guilt, but Doc Howard "denied it to the very last." Anything they had to say about Plummer being involved in the Magruder murders remained unsaid.[52] This did little to stifle an emerging consensus in the area that Sheriff Henry Plummer was up to no good. And there was a pattern of sorts to talk about.

The Bummer Dan stagecoach robbery occurred on October 26, only three weeks after Lloyd Magruder and his gold dust left Alder Creek forever. Seventy miles away, the dwindling number of Bannackians not already suspicious of Henry Plummer began to have their own doubts.

About three months after he kept Plummer from being appointed deputy U.S. Marshal, Sam Hauser found his nemesis sitting across from him on the Virginia City-Bannack stagecoach. Hauser was traveling with Nathaniel Langford to St. Louis on Friday, November 13, 1863, with $14,000 in a buckskin pouch. During an overnight stop, Hauser handed Plummer the pouch for safekeeping in front of all the passengers.

The next day, as Hauser and Langford rode toward Salt Lake City to make travel connections for the rest of their journey, Plummer proceeded to Bunton's Rattlesnake Creek ranch, or so he claimed. Some of Sheriff Plummer's Bannack constituents suspected Plummer was reconnoitering a rumored silver strike to stake a claim. And a young lawyer named Wilbur Sanders wanted to be part of the action.

Sanders claimed in his late-life memoirs that he tried to find Plummer at the Bunton place. After asking a few questions there, the young barrister found himself looking at the working end of a pistol held by Plummer's former deputy Jack Gallagher.[53] Sanders later claimed that he drew a bead on Gallagher with a shotgun. Perhaps Gallagher then offered to buy drinks, just as Sanders later claimed.

Young Henry Tilden was then a fifteen-year-old boarder with Judge Edgerton. Tilden later claimed that on that same evening, Saturday, November 14, 1863, he was accosted by three robbers south of town but released because he had no money. One of the men, Tilden claimed, was Henry Plummer, whom he recognized by the red lining of his coat.[54] Judge Edgerton and his family were so dubious that they instructed Tilden to tell no one.

The next day, Sanders, Tilden, and Plummer had each returned to Bannack; neither Plummer nor anyone else filed any silver claims. Tilden told Plummer that he did not recognize any of the men who let him go. Perhaps this was just as well.

Thanksgiving was soon upon the small mining community. Sanders and Edgerton put their suspicions of Plummer aside long enough to accept his bountiful hospitality at the home James Vail now owned. They feasted on butter and expensive turkey shipped in from Salt Lake City, and enjoyed remarkably good conversation with Plummer himself. Harriett (Hattie) Sanders later waxed lyrically about Plummer's "pleasing manners and fine address [appearance], a fair complexion, sandy hair and blue eyes—the last person one would select as a daring highwayman and murderer."[55]

Still, how did he pay for all this?

The Southmayd Incident

Suspicions about Plummer only grew when Leroy Southmayd was robbed of $400 on a stagecoach that same Thanksgiving Day. Plummer later told Southmayd who led the robbers: the gentleman-bandit George Ives. Yet Ives was not arrested. Worse still, Plummer's two problem deputies, Buck Stinson and Ned Ray, seemed quite cozy with the men Southmayd fingered as masked robbers—"Whiskey Bill" Graves and Bob Zachary.[56]

The pace of stagecoach robberies accelerated in early December. First, a Virginia City-Salt Lake City stage and several wagons being led by freighter Milton S. Moody carrying John Bozeman, who blazed the Bozeman Trail, was stopped by two robbers in Red Rock Canyon. They found $1,500 in Treasury notes but missed $80,000 in gold dust that was hidden in canteens. (Today, this amount of gold dust would be worth about $1.3 million.) Some passengers on the stagecoach opened fire on them, chasing the duo into a nearby wood. Next, Norwegian immigrant Anton Holder was nearly killed December 8 by a man Holder later identified as George Ives.[57]

Despite, or perhaps even because of, this accelerating crime wave, leading citizens in Bannack and the greater Alder Gulch metropolitan area began to discuss two initiatives. They discussed efforts to create a new territory east of the Bitterroot Mountains, which ultimately led to the creation of Montana. They also talked about the organization of a vigilante association similar to California groups established in 1851 and 1855.

The discovery of dead and mutilated young Nicholas Tiebolt and the subsequent capture of his suspected killer, George Ives, on Friday, November 18, 1863, prompted "Clubfoot George" Lane to warn Sheriff Plummer that trouble was ahead. And indeed it was.

Tiebolt was robbed of the gold dust he was carrying to purchase some livestock for William Clark at a ranch near Alder's Gulch. The body was discovered by English saloonkeeper William Palmer while he was hunting near the place where George Ives employees "Long John" Franck and George Hilderman lived. Neither Franck nor Hilderman were willing to help Palmer deal with the discovery. The condition of the body suggested Tiebolt had been killed elsewhere and dragged for some time.[58] Ives, Franck, and Hilderman were suspected almost immediately.

The nearest duly-appointed law officer was Henry Plummer at Bannack, but he was not contacted. William Clark argued that the Alder Creek citizenry should deal with the murder themselves. And they did.

Soon, a posse of some twelve men began the hunt for the trio under the direction of James Williams, a man who features in the next chapter of the book. Williams was a twenty-seven-year-old Pennsylvanian who grew up near Gettysburg; he left home with an older brother eight years earlier for the Colorado mining camps.

The men found Ives and Franck within a few hours and extracted a confession. Franck claimed that Ives had seen Tiebolt purchase two mules with the gold dust and killed him for what was left. Soon thereafter, the posse found George Hilderman.

The trial preliminaries began on Saturday, December 19, 1863. The Alder Gulch vigilantes had to compose a jury and decide whether any lawyers would participate.[59] Idaho Territorial Supreme Court Justice Sidney Edgerton had not yet been sworn in and took no part in these proceedings, but his nephew Wilbur Sanders prosecuted the case with the assistance of Charles S. Bagg. The prosecution argued the case before two advisory juries from neighboring Junction and Nevada City as well as a "jury of the whole" (comprised of anyone in the area who could shout an opinion). Lacking any direct evidence establishing that Ives killed the young man other than Franck's testimony, prosecuters focused on a legally irrelevant subject: Ives' suspected but unproven participation in the "Bummer Dan" McFadden and Leroy Southmayd robberies.[60]

The third day of trial began with area miners insisting that Judge Byam conclude the proceedings by 3:00 p.m. so that the community could return to work. Despite this, the concluding arguments did not end until after dusk.

The two advisory juries didn't waste much time deliberating. Within a half-hour, they delivered guilty verdicts, unanimous but for one vote from William Spivey. Despite this, prosecutor Sanders quickly asked the mob acting as a "jury of the whole" for a guilty verdict and got it. Before defense counsel could shout "mistrial," the presiding judge ordered the selection of a good spot to execute Ives.[61] The condemned meekly asked the mob for a one-day reprieve, but John X. Beidler spoke for many. "Ask him [Ives] how long he gave the Dutchman," Beidler yelled, referring to the young German boy Ives had murdered.

Ives began writing a last letter to his mother, even as Sanders asked that his personal effects be sold for the expenses of the trial (including attorney's fees, of course). Within thirty minutes, Ives was standing beneath a makeshift scaffold on a box inside an unfinished building. He complained that his associate Aleck Carter was the real killer just as someone yelled, "Men, do your duty." The next day, the other two accused were released from custody. Hilderman was banished forever from Alder Gulch.[62]

This did not end the vigilante movement in Alder's Gulch. Instead, an organization led by James Williams was formally chartered. Some two dozen men, including community leaders John and Mortimer Lott, bound themselves to each other in a seventy-word oath signed Wednesday, December 23, 1863. The men devoted themselves to "arresting thieves and murderers and recovering stolen property" and pledged "to reveal no secrets." Their next target was Aleck Carter.[63]

This second vigilance committee now competed with an earlier organization led by Paris Pfouts. The Lott brothers and some others were members of both organizations. Members of the Williams vigilantes looking for Carter trudged north toward Cottonwood, near present-day Deer Lodge, Montana. Meanwhile, some members of the Pfouts crew met with John Lott in Nevada City to charter themselves in a more elaborate series of documents, notably including regulations and bylaws which stated that the only punishment they would inflict was "*Death*."[64]

The Williams posse stumbled onto "Red" Yeager on Christmas day along the trail to Deer Lodge; Yeager claimed that Carter was lying drunk in Cottonwood following a dance the night before. But he was not. As they waited out a storm in Cottonwood, the posse might have wondered whether Yeager himself, who was not originally a suspect, was part of the greater Alder Gulch criminal complement. Williams later related that, as they returned from Cottonwood, he decided to arrest Yeager.

And then they met John X. Beidler, the very man who shouted down Ives's plea for a twenty-four-hour reprieve. Beidler told the Williams posse about two things that occurred earlier that day.

First, he had encountered "Dutch John" Wagner, by then a wanted man. When Beidler treated Wagner's frostbite during that encounter, Beidler didn't know that Wagner was a prime suspect in the early December robbery of the Moody wagon train.

And after that, Beilder continued, Sheriff Plummer's two deputies, Buck Stinson and Nick Ray, appeared on the same trail. They were very curious about recent news—particularly news about the two vigilante committees operating in the area. They assured Beidler that if the vigilantes came after Stinson and Ray on the trail, Beidler would become the duo's hostage.[65]

Now Williams had to choose between chasing the new suspect, Red Yeager; the two deputies, as Beidler urged; or "Dutch John" Wagner. Williams split the posse, sending most to a ranch on the Alder Gulch road while he and eight other men galloped towards the Rattlesnake ranch in pursuit of Red Yeager, who lived there. Yeager meekly submitted to arrest on the afternoon of January 2, 1864. Stinson and Ray, who were also at the ranch, quietly mounted their horses and left, perhaps surprised that Williams did not try to bag them also.

The next day, the Williams posse traveled to the Dempsey ranch on the Alder Gulch road with Yeager in tow. Drinks were being served by George Brown, one of the witnesses for George Ives during the recent trial. While there, Yeager admitted under close questioning that he had intentionally misled the Williams posse into thinking that Aleck Carter was at Cottonwood. Brown was invited along as the second prisoner after Yeager claimed that Brown wrote a message Yeager carried to Carter warning, "Get up and dust, and lie low for black ducks," supposedly a coded vigilante warning.[66]

Yeager only avoided a lynching because of one dissenting vigilante vote. Still, his fate was uncertain as the vigilantes escorted him to Alder Gulch. The party stopped for the night at the Laurin ranch. As Williams slumbered, his posse debated the pros and cons of lynching both prisoners.

The posse woke Williams up at ten that night, demanding an immediate execution. Yeager was not surprised. And in a highly debated, controversial "confession" to Williams which was recorded *a year and a half later* by English vigilante apologist Thomas Dimsdale, Yeager pointed an accusing finger at Sheriff Henry Plummer before he died.

Yeager attributed the string of recent robberies and other crimes to Plummer, his deputies Stinson and Ray, "Doc" Howard, and more obscure characters, including one "Mexican Frank."

This supposed confession revealed certain secret vigilante signs and codes, including the password "I am innocent."[67]

Brown and Yeager were hanged on the banks of the Stinking Water River with appropriate signage attached to their shirts. "Red! Road Agent and Messenger," the first sign read, whatever that meant. There was apparently no time to obtain written confessions or a written list of Plummer gang members. This was curious, given the meticulous records the Williams vigilantes compiled to record far less important matters.

Still, Yeager confessed something, whether exaggerated by Williams or not; and with that, Plummer's real problems began. Williams used the confession to claim that Plummer was the gang leader and that Bill Bunton served as his lieutenant. The Plummer crew also supposedly included Bunton's Rattlesnake ranch partner Frank Parish, George Ives, and saloonkeeper Cyrus Skinner.

The Williams posse arrived back in Alder Gulch on Tuesday, January 5, 1864, with an incredible story that implicated Plummer in the Southmayd robbery, the Lloyd Magruder murder, the Bummer Dan McFadden robbery, and the Tiebolt murder. All the posse lacked was some solid evidence.

Three days later, vigilante emissaries from Alder Gulch began the seventy-mile trip to Bannack with a mission; the Bannackians had to be convinced of Plummer's crimes and the need to hang him. They arrived the afternoon of Saturday, January 9, even as Sheriff Plummer was dealing with another problem.

"Dutch John" Wagner had been captured by Neil Howie and some freighters on the road to Salt Lake City; Wagner had fled to escape punishment at the hands of the vigilantes for his supposed role in the Moody wagon train robbery the prior month. Howie then rode into Bannack to scout for any Wagner supporters. While Howie did this, freighter John Fetherstun guarded Wagner about twelve miles outside of town.

Plummer proposed taking Wagner into custody, but Howie declined this offer. He decided to turn the prisoner over to a "People's Court" instead, even as the Alder Gulch vigilante delegation across town was trying to convince Bannackians of Plummer's complicity without much luck. And Wagner didn't help: later, when Howie and Fetherstun allowed the Alder Gulch vigilantes to question Wagner, he apparently refused to name Plummer as an accomplice in the Moody robbery, despite later claims to the contrary.[68]

This seems to be confirmed by the actions of Wilbur Sanders, the man who had prosecuted George Ives. During the early hours of Sunday, January 10, 1864, Sanders began seeking other, more convincing evidence against Plummer. Sanders and his uncle, the designated but yet-to-be-sworn-in Chief Justice of the Idaho Territorial Supreme Court Sidney Edgerton, had concluded earlier that assassinating Plummer was out of the question.

Young Henry Tilden was trotted out to claim once again that Plummer and two other men tried to rob him the prior November, despite the fact that Judge Edgerton had not believed him earlier. Despite such doubts, this convinced the newly-minted Bannack vigilantes.[69] The Bannack vigilantes included among their number Francis Thompson, who, with Henry Plummer himself, was staying at the Vail cabin. Somehow, Thompson concealed what he knew about Plummer's fate during breakfast that morning.

Some time before noon, Stinson and Ray made a brief appearance in Bannack, perhaps trying to learn more about Yeager's rumored confession. Thompson said later that Ray and Stinson were "very nervous and anxious." Eventually, they left. In the meantime, Henry Plummer was nursing an illness at the Vail cabin that Sunday; he stayed inside and rested, even as detailed plans were being made to take his life.[70]

The sheriff was silently surrounded; as he rested, his horses and those of Stinson and Ray were removed from stables nearby. Plummer's old friend George Chrisman was among those who eliminated every possible means by which the sheriff could have escaped. That evening, vigilantes seized Stinson and then surrounded the Vail cabin; they grabbed Plummer as he tried to calm and reassure his sister-in-law. The mob collected Ned Ray at a saloon and frog-marched the prisoners toward the gallows Plummer had constructed himself for the lawful execution of Peter Horen less than five months earlier. All along the way, Plummer insisted that he was innocent.

Was he? Whether Plummer was "demonstrably . . . guilty of specific crimes" beyond mere malfeasance is a matter of great uncertainty, at least in the view of one historian who has studied the issue in detail.[71] That same modern scholar suggests that "the real issue was whether the men who executed him could have taken more time to gather evidence and conduct a proceeding more closely resembling a conventional trial than the hasty, secret tribunal that took place in confusion over a sleepless night and ended in confusion."[72]

Placing the Plummer lynching in context gives us a clearer view of the injustice done by the vigilantes. They relied largely on Yeager's verbal confession, which lacked credibility in several certain respects. For example, the Plummer gang, according to Yeager, had a password—"I am innocent," all shaved themselves in a particular way, and even shared a particular necktie knot. But why would any of this be necessary in the sparsely populated reaches of present-day Montana?

The brutal, racially-motivated killing of Joe Pizanthia the day after the Plummer lynching and the killing of William Hunter on February 3, both of which were authorized with no more concrete evidence than that against Plummer, suggest that these vigilante killings were the work of an organized mob conspiring to do murder.

The less-than-heroic conduct of designated Supreme Court Justice Sidney Edgerton has been particularly criticized by historians, and with good reason. Although he had no legal authority, Edgerton had stature and credibility; he could have at least tried to stop the mob. Instead, he did nothing.

Ned Ray wasn't talking on his trip to the gallows, but his mistress "Madam Hall" was. She wailed, yelled, and even tried to rescue him herself. Ray tried to avoid death by sticking a hand through the noose just before he was dropped from the shoulders of the vigilantes; all this did was prolong his agony.

Stinson died quickly; according to some accounts, he tried to confess, but Plummer silenced him by warning, "We've done enough already to send us all to hell." Perhaps this was so.[73] More likely, although Plummer had killed four men in fights considered fair by the standards of the time, he had little or nothing to do with the robberies and murders for which he was lynched.

As Ray and Stinson were hanged, Plummer circled among the vigilantes, pleading his case to the last. He asked someone— anyone—to save him. According to Dimsdale, he also confessed his crimes, even as the dreary regions of the dead loomed ever-closer.

Finally, the noose was placed over the sheriff's head, and Plummer took his last earthly refuge in the arms of the men killing him. He threw his necktie to a friend, murmured a short prayer, and asked for a good drop. He didn't have to ask twice; in an instant, the mob lifted him as high as they could, and then let him go.

And with that, all that Henry Plummer was or might have been—perhaps in innocence, perhaps in guilt—plunged into a world unknown.[74]

Chapter 10

Joseph Alfred Slade:
The Three Jacks

It was a place where hundreds if not thousands of pioneers chose their own destiny.

Turning south meant bold, little Denver City and dreams of fortunes in gold; to the west across the South Platte River, distant California beckoned to the more adventurous. And it was here that Joseph Alfred Slade, the first western gunfighter to capture the American imagination, first confronted the archenemy who eventually made him famous. Here, Slade and his nemesis Jules Beni started on the long road that ended in two deadly encounters.

Many travelers today would consider old Julesburg, Colorado, near the confluence of the South Platte River and Lodgepole Creek, nothing more than a spot in the middle of nowhere. Yet for others, this is a place where majestic open spaces and a big sky are everything the American West should be. A modern town of the same name thrives about five miles away from this remote locale at the confluence of the South Platte River and Lodgepole Creek, where a man named Jules started his little store to trade with the Sioux and Cheyenne.

Beni was born in about 1809 of mixed French and Indian heritage. His surname may have been Benoit as his wife later said, although one noted historiographer insisted he was born Jules Reni.[1] He was considered eccentric even in those colorful times; to begin with, his hair flowed down to the shoulders of his buckskins. He began ranching, added a few outbuildings, and eventually hosted soldiers, pioneers, trappers, prospectors, promoters, and bandits on their way to somewhere else—a pattern that had become characteristically American long before the 1850s. Some twenty miles or so up Lodgepole Creek, a ranch and rustic trading post, which even included a saloon by 1858, completed the empire that Beni controlled—until Slade came along.

Beni built a boarding house the next year for stagecoach passengers on the Central Overland California & Pikes Peak Express Company. The Central Overland had acquired this route from the nearly bankrupt Jones and Russell stagecoach line operated by William Russell and then added a lucrative mail service that offered coast-to-coast delivery in three weeks' time.[2]

Russell devised an even faster mail service for those willing to pay. His Pony Express offered delivery in eight to ten days from St. Joseph, Missouri, to Sacramento, California, using a series of relay stations located every ten miles. Julesburg would become one of the stops, but obnoxious old Beni would have to be replaced as station master. Superintendent Benjamin Franklin Fricklin had someone in mind.

A Gentleman and a Terror

Joseph Alfred Slade was born January 22, 1831, to a prosperous family in Carlyle, Illinois, on the Kaskaskia River. Although many accounts refer to him as "Jack," most of his friends called him "Alf." To this day, no one is certain what America's first famous gunfighter looked like, although Orion Clemens, the brother of Samuel Clemens (Mark Twain), described him in August of 1861 as having gray eyes, very light hair, no beard, and a hard-looking face.[3]

Slade was already a legend in the West when he had arrived in Julesburg, about two years earlier in late 1859. Some twenty or more killings had been attributed to Slade by then—including a man back in Carlyle he supposedly killed with a rock. He killed nine men during the Mexican War and sixteen others, including some Indians, in various places across the Plains, but most of his killings were unconfirmed, if not mythical.

Killer or not, Slade eventually became superintendent of a five-hundred-mile stage line stretching from Julesburg to Salt Lake City.

J. A. Slade (Rose Collection, Western History Collections, University of Oklahoma Libraries)

He had no badge, no commission, and no legal authority at all. What he did have was the solemn duty to keep his stage route free of bandits and hostile Indians. Eventually he was considered the law west of Fort Kearny. One modern biographer described Slade as "neither a lawman nor an outlaw, nor a cowboy or a farmer. He was both a gentleman and a terror. . . . There was simply nobody quite like him in the history of the West."[4]

His father, Charles Slade Jr., came west from Alexandria, Virginia, and accumulated some eight hundred acres of land, which became Carlyle, Illinois, in 1818. Eventually, he was appointed postmaster and then a Congressman representing the First District of the Prairie State. Charles Slade died from cholera near Vincennes, Indiana, while returning from Washington D.C. on July 11, 1834; he left a thirty-four-year-old widow and five children, including young Joseph.

Mary Kain Slade, Charles' widow, married Elias Smith Dennis four years later. Dennis was about thirteen years younger than Mary but mature beyond his years. He became a county court clerk, as had Charles Slade earlier, and then became a state senator.

There was trouble in the Dennis household. Legend has it that Joseph Slade killed an Illinois man while still in his teens. One recent author described the victim as a Mr. Gottlieb.[5] However, there is no contemporary documentation at all supporting this story.

More likely, Slade enlisted along with his brother Richard for service during the Mexican War in the Illinois Foot Volunteers May 4, 1847, claiming to be eighteen even though he was two years too young. About four months later, the Volunteers arrived in Santa Fe, having lost three privates to disease en route. There were local issues to be sure: Governor Charles Bent had been scalped and killed during a revolt in Taos the proceeding January. And yet despite a few legends to the contrary, Slade's service during the Mexican War was largely uneventful.

While in Santa Fe, Slade's older brother was stricken by an unknown fatal disease and died at age twenty-six on February 9, 1848, the very day their company marched towards Albuquerque. They returned to Alton, Illinois, sixty-five miles northwest of Carlyle, to be mustered out in mid-October.

The following January, Slade sold his military bounty land and joined argonauts venturing west in the "most astonishing mass movement of people since the Crusades": the Gold Rush.[6] He was among several Carlylians who westered with their former company commander, Thomas Bond.

Curiously, no one knows whether this expedition ever reached California. More than thirty years later, the sojourner Joseph W. Maddux recalled traveling with Bond and Slade "by the

Overland route to Oregon." Yet 1850 census records show Slade living in Carlyle. Whatever the outcome of this first journey, J. A. Slade—as he now signed his name after leaving his home—simply disappeared from history until September 1853, when a Carlyle neighbor won a $195 court judgment against him. His stepfather contacted him by stagecoach mail at Leavenworth, Kansas, in November 1854. This suggests that Slade might have been employed in freighting already.

In about 1857, he married a woman named Virginia, whose last name remains unknown. Slade's most recent biographer suggests that they met in some Missouri River town where she might have been a prostitute, dance hall girl, or both. She was a substantial presence, estimated by one observer to weigh in at about one hundred sixty pounds. "What a swell she cut!" one acquaintance later recalled, while Slade "was well-educated, a good conversationalist, quiet and unassuming," a man who "would be taken for a law abiding citizen in any community."[7] Yet events would prove that Slade had a rough-hewn side.

A 1908 account written by bullwhacker Hugo Koch of an 1858 freighting trip confirms that Slade was eventually employed by Russell, Majors, & Waddell, a partnership engaged in the stagecoach business.

"This is no kindergarten," Slade had warned twenty-two-year-old Koch when he applied for a bullwhacker position in July 1858, according to Koch's late-life memoirs. At that time, Koch was a lowly bartender in a second-rate hotel in Leavenworth, Kansas Territory, and was looking for a way out driving oxen teams on the road west. Slade was more encouraging several days later when Koch tried again. Slade needed good men for an expedition to Salt Lake City; he was willing to train beginners. Koch was instructed to meet Slade at Atchison, Kansas, some twenty-five miles away.

Koch later learned that the night before the supply train left for Salt Lake, Slade had single-handedly disarmed a boisterous Texan in a local restaurant. The young bullwhacker was more impressed the next day when Slade promptly supplemented rancid bacon and other second-rate vittles with "plenty of beef, hams . . . new bacon, rice, beans and lots of other things."[8]

The train consisted of twenty-four wagons, three hundred steers, and perhaps ten thousand pounds of merchandise delivered to company mail stations and trading posts along the trail. The company was the Central Overland Mail Stage, a venture of John Hockaday and George Chorpenning.[9]

They caravanned through Marysville, Kansas, and then Fort Kearney, where they encountered soldiers returning from the "Mormon War" in Utah.[10] Their next major stop was O'Fallon's Bluffs on the South Platte, four hundred miles from Leavenworth. They reached Scott's Bluffs on the North Platte in present day Nebraska mid-October of 1858. One evening over a fireside political discussion, Koch mentioned his abolitionist beliefs. "If you ever expect to take your scalp back to America never let me hear you say again you are an abolitionist," Slade warned. Koch had every reason to be worried if a story attributed to Judge Alexander Davis told years later to the *St. Louis Globe-Democrat* was true. According to Davis, his friend Slade had beaten a railroad man to death the year before, if not earlier, and then skedaddled for Texas.[11]

Koch attested to Slade's cool courage in the face of three hundred menacing Indians on the trail in Nebraska. Koch described Slade as a skilled marksman who taught an outlaw named Polk Wells "Hoosier shooting," a technique for shooting without taking aim.[12] Slade also developed "a fierce hatred for horse thieves," according to Koch, in a place and time when "murder didn't amount to anything."[13] Koch further observed that "liquor seemed to change Slade into a demon." However, Slade's wife Virginia seemed to have a great influence over him even when he was drunk. Another observer noted that Slade "stood in real and deadly fear of her."[14]

Slade spent the last month of 1858 at Horseshoe Creek about 475 miles east of Salt Lake City, then arrived there on February 12, 1859, having left his wagon train behind in the snow.

Three months later he faced some changes in the Central Overland Mail Stage operations. An unforeseen May 11, 1859, Congressional reduction in subsidies for westward bound stagecoaches forced Hockaday to sell his entire operation. The buyer was the Leavenworth & Pikes Peak Express Company operated by John Jones and William Russell.[15]

The Four Shootings of Andrew Ferrin

Slade killed wagon train driver Andrew Ferrin nine days later on the Green River in a disagreement as controversial today as it was then. The killing was reported only three days later in the *Valley Tan* at Salt Lake City. The *Tan,* bearing one of the most unusual names in American newspapers, was published for about two years. The masthead name was derived from a local leather tanning process, which came to be shorthand for anything made in Utah.

The *Tan* received a late May dispatch from William Ashton, whom Slade had replaced. The dispatch implied that Ferrin was not killed that May but was killed when Slade had parked his wagon at Horseshoe Creek the previous November en route to Salt Lake City. Ashton also implied that Ferrin and others were fortified with liquor stolen out of a shipment they were freighting west. This aspect of the Ashton dispatch to the *Tan* was confirmed in a 1907 memoir written by James Wilson.[16]

Yet another memoir, published in 1925 by frontier trader and vigilante Granville Stuart, cast Slade as the drunken culprit. Stuart told his readers that while camped at Ham's Fork:

A mule train of sixteen wagons loaded with freight for Salt Lake City camped a short distance above us on the stream. In a few minutes we heard a shot fired and as there seemed to be some excitement we walked up to the wagons, and were all shocked to see one of the drivers lying on the ground shot through the heart. The wagon boss had gotten drunk at Green River the two had argued and J. A. Slade drew his revolver and shot the man dead. Later the teamsters dug a grave by the roadside, wrapped the dead man in his blankets and buried him. The train went on to Salt Lake. Nothing was done about the murder.[17]

The third version of the Ferrin shooting emerged in 1900. A Wyoming historian wrote that while "Farrar" and Slade were drinking together, Farrar dared Slade to shoot him, and he did. Farrar died despite the efforts of a surgeon Slade had quickly summoned.

The artist Charles M. Russell popularized the fourth version by titling his painting of the incident "Laughed at for His Foolishness and Shot Dead by Slade." Russell's take on the killing was inspired by Mark Twain, who made the killing a fanciful tale of deception in his semi-autobiographical *Roughing It*, published in 1872. In chapter 10 of the book, Twain described Slade and Ferrin as feuding wagon drivers who had both drawn their weapons:

[Ferrin] was the quicker artist and had his weapon cocked first, so Slade said it was a pity to waste life on so small a matter and proposed that the pistols be thrown on the ground and the quarrel settled by a fistfight. The unsuspecting driver agreed and threw down his pistol—Slade laughed at his simplicity and shot him dead.[18]

However, the Twain-Russell version in which Slade tricked and then shot Ferrin is not consistent with the quiet, routine way in which Ferrin was buried without any contemporary notoriety, as just another drunken troublemaker.

Perhaps Slade would have been more forgiving about the liquor theft, assuming that is what happened, had he known that Hockaday sold the company. The new owners, Jones and Russell, were now forced to merge two stage lines while adding service to Denver. They created a new junction at Julesburg on the South Platte River to accomplish this, but there was a problem.

His name was Jules Beni. Like many hard-living frontiersmen, Beni became "more dangerous as he grew older."[19] And he took full advantage of the opportunities presented when a new station was completed on his property that June of 1859.

Horses and supplies sometimes simply "disappeared" from the station. Beni would "track down" the thieves and then give himself a "reward" out of the stage line cash on hand. And the stagecoach passengers could have dined at Delmonico's in New York at the prices charged for the simple, barely digestible meals Beni and his minions threw on the table.

Yet Beni was even worse at delivering the mail—which could cause Jones and Russell to lose the precious government contract. They had spent $500,000—equivalent to about $12 million today—buying equipment.

When Russell proposed to start the Pony Express and reorganized as the Central Overland & Pikes Peak Express Company, the new superintendent Fricklin decided that Slade would replace Beni.

December 2, 1859, found Slade at one of his favorite watering holes across the state line from St. Joseph, Missouri—Atchison, Kansas, which boasted a population of 2,500. Atchison was then a hotbed of pro-slavery sentiment. Future president Abraham Lincoln was in town for the state elections, which would determine whether Kansas would be a free state unencumbered by slavery.

Lincoln accomplished something that day few men could match. E. W. Howe, editor of the Atchison newspaper, recalled years later that Lincoln somehow made the normally humorless Slade laugh during a hotel reception.[20] In the months ahead, however, Slade had little to laugh about.

Slade faced an old dilemma: he had neither a badge nor any authority as a peace officer, yet as Sweetwater Division Superintendent for the Central Overland, he was responsible for maintaining law and order between Atchison and Salt Lake City. There were no sheriffs, judges, or juries once a stagecoach left Kansas Territory—the military authorities ordinarily only dealt with the Indian population. There was only Slade's law along the corridor between Julesburg and South Pass, the gateway through the Continental Divide in present day southwestern Wyoming.

Uncorroborated stories about Slade's adventures during this period abound—tales of outlaws killed and hanged from gates or tree limbs, sometimes even two to four at a time. None of this is documented in any public record any more than the claim that Slade once forced a rancher off of his own place for selling some bad hay.

However his reputation was made, Slade became known as a gunfighter who had shot down at least three men. The English author, explorer, and Orientalist Sir Richard Burton traveled west by stagecoach in August of 1860 and later recalled hearing this story.[21] The next summer, Twain, still known as Samuel Clemens at the time, met Slade on August 2, 1861. He later reported that Slade had killed as many as twenty-six men.[22]

Orphans Preferred

When the Pony Express was chartered by the territorial Kansas legislature in February of 1860, Slade's duties became even more complicated. Slade, his boss Fricklin, and several other Central Overland agents purchased hundreds of horses from the military and other sources for the new enterprise. Later, Slade helped prepared the Pony Express stations, which varied from wooden buildings to hillside dugouts. One legend had it that an advertisement for the Pony Express riders supposedly read "Wanted: Young, skinny, wiry fellows not over eighteen. Must be expert riders, willing to risk death daily. Orphans preferred."[23]

Even as preparations to open the Pony Express route were being completed, Slade faced a new challenge. Although Beni had not complained when Slade relieved him as Julesburg stationmaster about a year earlier, Central Overland horses that had disappeared from the South Platte Station were discovered at Beni's place on Lodgepole Creek.

Slade was hardly subtle about his feelings after this discovery. He ordered dinner at Beni's roadhouse and then threw it in the old man's face. Perhaps he thought this would teach Beni a lesson—if so, he was wrong. When Slade returned unarmed to Julesburg in March of 1861, Beni shot him to pieces with a revolver and a double-barreled shotgun. Slade immediately had the stage driver remove his boots, so as to avoid the classic outlaw's death.[24] And although he lived—barely—his death was reported in the March 19, 1860, issue of Missouri's *St. Joseph Journal*.

His recovery is one of the most remarkable accounts of the American West—a story of luck and pluck that gave Slade another few years to live.

Incredibly, Central Overland general superintendent Fricklin arrived at Julesburg just as Beni generously donated a box for use as Slade's coffin. One popular tale claims that Fricklin responded in kind—by hanging Jules until he promised to leave the area.

Fricklin summoned an army surgeon from Fort Laramie who

arrived within twenty-four hours and removed some of the bullets and buckshot from Slade's wounds. Two weeks later, Slade was on his way home to Horseshoe Station in present day Wyoming.[25]

Slade's modern biographer relates that Fricklin soon arranged for Slade to get the best medical attention then available in the West—at St. Louis, nearly a thousand miles away from Horseshoe Station, although noted historiographer Ramon Adams discounted a similar story placing the medical attention in Chicago.[26] Fricklin may have even accompanied Slade on part of the trip.

His concerns for Slade were not entirely humanitarian. The Central Overland had a major problem west of Julesburg—outlaws. The western part of the Central Overland line was "infested by a gang of outlaws and desperadoes who recognized no authority except violence. Murders were of frequent occurrence in broad daylight, being committed on the slightest misunderstanding."[27]

While Fricklin quarreled with the Central Overland ownership over potential Pony Express expansion, Slade continued his recovery. After surgeons in St. Louis removed more bullet lead, Slade visited his boyhood home in Carlyle, Illinois, about fifty miles east of St. Louis and then returned to Horseshoe Station in mid-June, 1860. About a month earlier, Paiute Indians had attacked a Pony Express station west of Salt Lake City, killing seven men. This was a prologue to later attacks in the same Central Overland district. Reportedly, the stage line advanced about $75,000 to subdue the attacks. These measures were critical now that the Central Overland was carrying significant gold dust shipments east from Pikes Peak, typically $15,000 and sometimes as much as $135,000 a load, including amounts carried by the passengers.[28]

Sir Richard Burton stayed at the Horseshoe Station the evening of Tuesday, August 14, 1860; he noted that Slade carried both a pistol and Bowie knife. Slade's friend Nathaniel Langford later remarked that at about this time Slade sent Beni a reminder to stay out of his district. Later accounts short on specifics suggest that Slade focused instead on organized, unidentified outlaws in the Rocky Ridge area of present day Wyoming instead of Beni:

> [O]ne by one, he picked out and killed leaders of the notorious gang. In a remarkably short space of time all depredations on the stage line ceased. A considerable [amount] of the stolen stock was recovered and several of the worst outlaws in the district were shot.[29]

The Honorable Thief

With such reports increasing, Slade's reputation as a gunfighter continued to grow. The three young Davenport brothers did not look like horse thieves, but during the winter of 1860-61, they rustled many a horse and mule from Fort Laramie in present day Wyoming. Slade was one of the many men the authorities had asked to capture the brothers. A posse captured and hanged one Davenport before Slade joined the hunt.

Slade stopped unexpectedly one day at a Pony Express station east of Fort Laramie while looking for the Davenports. The proprietor quickly hid a young man he had taken in, violating a standing Pony Express rule designed to avoid problems with suspicious characters. The young man left the next day, only to come back two days later manacled to the stagecoach in which Slade was traveling.

The young Davenport brother did nothing to betray the kind-hearted station keeper—he kept the secret to himself even as he was hanged a few hours later from a bridge on the Laramie River.

Clean Out the Sarah Place

Slade could be generous and vindictive all at the same time.

During the winter of 1860-61, one of his American employees killed a Mexican employee and escaped to the John Sarah Ranch and Saloon twelve miles east of Horseshoe Station. When Sarah refused to surrender the killer, Slade ordered at least two men, and according to some accounts an entire stagecoach full of thugs, to "clean out the Sarah place." His operatives burned the house down, killing Sarah and his wife. The four children escaped through a back window, but all but one died of exposure. Eventually, someone brought the young survivor to Horseshoe Station, where Slade and his wife took him in and named him "Jemmy Slade."[30] Young Jemmy may not have been the only child the Slades tried to adopt, at least according to one convicted outlaw.

Charles Knox Polk Wells was one of many who bragged about claimed associations with Slade to enhance his own legend. Wells' highly dubious prison memoirs related that while he was a runaway working for a freight operation near Julesburg, Virginia Slade offered to adopt him—an offer he accepted before his fellow workers warned him off.[31]

A Quiet and Affable Officer

The most notorious purveyor of pure Slade fiction was young Samuel Clemens, whose single encounter with Slade occurred on August 2, 1861, at Rocky Ridge Station, while Clemens and his brother Orion were traveling west to Nevada. The precise date was discovered more than one hundred years later. After becoming Mark Twain, Clemens called Slade "the most gentlemanly appearing, quiet and affable officer we had yet found along the road." However, Twain also related that he quaked in fear until Slade insisted on giving him the very last cup of coffee available at the station the morning they met.

Twain's *Roughing It* embellished the real-life Sarah tragedy by claiming Slade himself, rather than some overzealous employees, killed the family. Twain also wrote, perhaps with exaggeration, that Slade "was a man whose heart and hands and soul were steeped in the blood of offenders against his dignity."[32]

Of course, many such Twain stories were obvious tall tales. One such yarn claimed that as Slade spotted an adversary coming towards him, he boasted that he would "clip the third button on his coat"—and did just that. Another fabrication claimed that Slade killed a bartender for not offering him the best brandy in the house.[33] Although probably just a legend, there was more than a little truth about Slade in these tales.

When sober, Slade was usually reluctant to become personally involved in violence. When his new boss Benjamin Holladay urged him to "get that fellow Jules and let everybody know that you got him," Slade first sent Beni word to stay away from his division.[34] However, when drunk, Slade was another person altogether.

"Do you know me?" The drunk bellowed at a coach station barkeeper east of present-day Julesburg, probably in 1861. John Young Nelson, the greenhorn serving up bad whiskey that day, had to admit that he didn't. "Well," Slade allowed, "I am the man who killed the Savior." He then threw an empty bottle at Nelson's head.

Though he was young, Nelson had the presence of mind to aim a shotgun at Slade's head and pull the trigger. He only missed because one of Slade's associates knocked the barrel skyward.[35]

Two Canadians

One summer, perhaps July of 1860 or 1861, two Canadians operating a trading post near a Pony Express station about sixty miles west of Slade's place became rustlers. Even as horses and cattle belonging to emigrants began appearing in their herds, Charley Bacon and Harry Smith saw better prospects ahead.

They killed their neighbor Dr. Bartholomew in a quarrel and propositioned his widow.

Joseph Plante, a merchant who lived near the Bartholomew place, contacted Slade, because he feared that his store was the next target. Years later, Amede Bessette, another Canadian who lived nearby, recalled in his memoirs that Slade appeared one Friday, hanged Bacon and Smith, and then arranged for the widow to join her parents in Omaha.

Another Canadian Sunset

Slade warned Beni to stay away from his stagecoach district twice. Despite these warnings however, in the summer of 1861 perhaps, Slade encountered a known Beni associate retrieving some of Beni's stock from the Wagon Hound Ranch about twenty miles west of Slade's headquarters at Horseshoe Creek Station. Slade detained the stock, insisted that Beni come for the herd himself, and went into action.

The most credible of several versions of what followed indicates that Slade offered three hired men a $500 reward to capture Beni alive, but they mortally wounded the wily Frenchman in a gun-fight.[36] Late-life memoirs and other accounts compiled years after the events suggest Beni was killed in August or September of 1861.[37]

After Beni died, the trio tied him upright to a corral post at the Cold Spring coach station, hoping that Slade would not notice. "I suppose you had to kill him, and if you did you do not get any reward" Slade groused before he even saw the corpse. When the men claimed Beni was still alive, Slade cut off one ear and then the other to prove them wrong.[38]

Of course there are more lurid and dramatic versions of Beni's death, however unlikely, that later captured public attention.

A September 1899 version of Beni's death related by Central Overland station keeper James Boner claimed Slade tied the man to a corral post and slowly tortured Beni by shooting him in nonvital places.[39]

However Beni died, Slade carried at least one of the man's ears with him for the rest of his life. And Slade had other things to worry about even after Beni was gone. For one thing, the eighteen-month run of the Pony Express was just about over.

Four months before Beni was killed, the Pacific Telegraph Company began pushing the new technology westward. Five months earlier, in November of 1860, a telegraph wire was brought into Fort Kearny, Nebraska.

The telegraph reached Julesburg on July 2, 1861, and then Salt Lake City on October 22. Four days later, the Pony Express stopped operations. Slade now became the *de facto* supervisor for telegraph operators along the Central Overland from Julesburg westward. His district was reduced to a mere 490 miles as early as August 1861.[40]

Perhaps it was no coincidence that Slade's drinking problems became more visible and persistent at about this time. On one occasion, Virginia Slade sent some Central Overland employees to burn a nearby store where Slade drank and played cards. And yet other more serious troubles for Slade loomed ahead.

As Federal troops in the West began moving east in March of 1862, Indians began pouncing on Central Overland stagecoach stations. Slade's division was first attacked on March 23 by Sioux, or perhaps Snake, Indians.

A pair of heavily-armed stages were ambushed on April 17. This was followed by a series of attacks that took about three hundred miles of stage routes and telegraph lines out of operations. Some three hundred bags of mail were now stranded at Julesburg.

Audacious

Ben Holladay purchased the Central Overland outright in late March, 1862, and then promptly dealt with the crisis. He convinced Pres. Abraham Lincoln to let him move the line south. The Mormon militia provided protection.

Slade eventually moved his own operation south to the "new" route, thereafter called the Cherokee Trail simply because the earliest routing began near present day Salina, Oklahoma. Even as stations, shops, and corrals worth hundreds of thousands of dollars along the old northern route were simply abandoned, Slade built a new station in a valley one hundred miles northwest of Denver and seven hundred miles from St. Joseph, Missouri. He named it Virginia Dale in honor of his wife.

Meanwhile, Salt Lake City newspapers began to attack Slade in mid-July of 1862 as the wanton killer of twenty men and "the terror of all the settlers between Pacific Springs and Julesburg."[41] Neither Slade nor his employees challenged these stories, but one Salt Lake City observer recounted the death of Beni; he noted that "if he [Slade] never does worse then hang and shoot the crowd of blacklegs who infest the plains, we shall never vote for his dismissal from the service. . . . If there is any virtue in hoping, I should really hope to see a half dozen Slades on the eastern line."[42]

Somehow, the Holladay and Slade crews had managed to slash a newer, faster route west through the wilderness to Salt Lake City while picking up stray mail and equipment along the old line. Slade also benefited from favorable press reports and increased emigrant traffic through his Virginia Dale rest stop, which one account romanticized as a rare, picturesque "oasis of natural beauty in the desert."[43] Soon, the old Central, Overland, California & Pikes Peak Express Company simply became the Overland Stage Company.

The new route was far less challenging than the old; perhaps this was the reason Slade began to drink more, as one recent biographer has theorized.[44] Stage passengers arriving at the Virginia Dale station were now frequently invited in for drinks—and a close look at Beni's ear. Slade even let one young passenger fill an ear with pebbles as a rattle, according to an account written many years later.[45]

Local opinion about Slade slowly began to change as his behavior deteriorated. He often apologized later for his antics, but most Westerners of his time saw this as an acknowledgment of weakness rather than good manners.

One observer watched him terrorize a stage station bartender with a loaded shotgun. On two other occasions, men he was terrorizing while in his cups would have killed him had not wiser heads prevailed.

Slade was a mean drunk, and Denver, only a hundred miles away from Virginia Dale, was a perfect place to carouse. The mining camp started in 1858, but within three years became the largest settlement between St. Joseph in Missouri and California. Denver was full of saloons near the Overland depot, at least until Slade methodically began destroying them on drunken binges.

Overland employee Robert Spotswood later recalled that Slade would "shatter all the mirrors, drive everybody into the street and then shoot out the lights." Eventually he would return and pay the damages.[46] "That he lived through it all was a miracle," recalled Langford, who was sympathetic, but became a Slade critic.[47]

Slade returned with Virginia to Carlyle, Illinois, in late 1862. They discovered that Slade's once prosperous relations were bogged down in protracted litigation over the large estate that his father had left twenty-eight years earlier. There was nothing for the Slades here—and so they returned west.

That February, Slade and three stage drivers were indicted for attempting to murder stage station-keeper George R. Sanders who had disregarded Slade's warnings not to sell liquor to his stage drivers. The Denver indictment encouraged the Slades to move to a ranch near Fort Bridger, Utah Territory. While there, Slade began a freighting venture with fellow Illinoisan Jon Ely and encountered Fitz Hugh Ludlow, who chronicled his stage trip across the West seven years later. Slade promised him an account of his conflict with Beni but never sent it.[48]

A new gold strike to the north soon provided new opportunities for Slade and other freighters. By May 26, 1863, Bill Fairweather and some companions found nuggets and flakes of gold, called "placer gold," in sand and gravel near what became Virginia City, Montana.[49] The strike drew men from all over the states, including a notable contingent of Confederate deserters from Missouri who had arrived earlier in Idaho. The place was named Virginia City by a Connecticut doctor turned judge who refused to name it for Jefferson Davis' wife Varina.

The month after the Fairweather discovery, Henry Gilbert, a former Central Overland station-keeper now residing at Fort Bridger, asked Slade to deliver a wagon train of merchandise and his household goods to Virginia City. Slade began the journey that June. On the trail he fell in with James Williams of Pennsylvania who was leading a second wagon train. The two parties voted at Soda Springs to merge, but Slade ruined his chance to become captain by getting loaded during the voting.

They arrived at Virginia City in late June or early July. Slade's former station agents, George Chrisman and Amede Bessette, as well as two former Pony Express riders were already there. Slade promptly became the talk of the town; "miners dropped pack and shovel . . . to get a glimpse of the legendary new arrival."[50]

He invested some of his Gilbert expedition profits in mining operations about two miles away at Nevada City and perhaps also at Granite Gulch. However unlikely it may seem, Slade focused on starting a dairy operation about fourteen miles to the northwest of Virginia City on the Madison River. Later, Slade also constructed a toll road shortcut on the Bozeman Trail about eight miles east of Virginia City. He called the stone tollhouse located there Spring Dale. Virginia operated the toll road while Slade ran the dairy operations.[51]

Tiny, isolated Virginia City quickly became indebted to Slade. The Hardie brothers, lately of St. Joseph, Missouri, had attempted to provision the town with a steamboat load of goods, but the boat had to be unloaded due to low water at the confluence of the Missouri and Milk rivers roughly 350 miles away. Local citizens financed a September 1863 Slade expedition to the Milk River along a route unknown to this day. A wagon train carrying essential life-saving provisions returned to Virginia City on December 10, 1863. How Slade accomplished this is open to conjecture.[52]

Local hero or not, Slade soon confronted a deadly challenge.

Even before the Milk River expedition, Slade had returned to the bad habits that caused him to lose the stage line position, which had made him a legend. Twenty-three years later, Langford recalled how Slade used his largely unearned reputation as a gunslinger to filch a load of lumber. "You must of heard of Slade of the Overland," he asked, but Langford confessed, "Never before" as he watched a wagon load of his prime lumber jostle away. Langford once watched Slade pick a fight with Jack Gallagher, not long before he knocked two of his own friends to the ground in a saloon fight. Despite this, Langford dared refusing to drink with Slade but somehow avoided injury.[53]

Forces beyond Slade's control were now gathering in Virginia City and seventy miles away at a rival upstart community.

In September of 1863, Bannack City, simply called Bannack, was attracting miners by the hundreds; it was easier to find gold than to travel with it. A series of robberies beginning that month were eventually laid at the feet of mining district sheriff Henry Plummer, as detailed in a previous chapter. Back in the Alder Gulch area, because duly organized law enforcement was nowhere to be found, vigilantes began organizing. The Nevada City vigilantes were professionals and merchants, many sharing membership in the Freemasons.[54]

Their first victim was George Ives, who was tried for the murder of young Nicholas Tiebolt in an open air miner's court. The night before the Ives trial concluded, five men met in Virginia City; they decided to take control if Ives was convicted and hang him on the spot.

And so, when Ives was found guilty on December 21, he was promptly lynched from an improvised scaffold. The leader was James Williams, a non-mason who had outpolled Slade as captain when his Gilbert expedition had merged with another group of travelers the previous June.[55]

A second vigilante group eventually numbering some 250 members formed a mile away in Nevada City the next day. There was some interlocking membership: John Lott and Slade's nemesis James Williams belonged to both. Slade knew many of these men; one biographer argues quite reasonably that Slade was probably among the first fifty Virginia City recruits.[56] Their deliberations would be entirely secret and the punishments deliberately harsh in order to discourage lawbreaking in a community four hundred miles away from the nearest jail.

When Slade returned from his Milk River expedition on December 10, 1863, he found Virginia City not nearly as tolerant of his shenanigans as the place he had left three months earlier. Worse yet for Slade, the two lawyers who had defended George Ives and criticized lynch law were soon run out of the territory. This happened shortly after the Nevada City and Virginia City

Vigilance committees combined efforts. In early January of 1864, they captured Erastus "Red" Yeager, whose verbal confession before he was hanged on January 4 with George Brown led directly to the lynching of seven suspected road agents.[57] Eight more were added to the death toll by January 26.

All but five of these earlier suspects named by Yeager had been lynched; one surviving gang member, a desperado named Bill Hunter, had escaped from an improvised Virginia City hoosegow on January 13, 1864. Hunter was spotted east of Alder Gulch about two weeks later. A posse chasing him stopped at Slade's stone toll house long enough reportedly to lose $1,200 in card games with Slade's wife.[58] The next evening the posse found shelter in the same cabin unlucky Hunter had stumbled into earlier—and promptly lynched him.

None of this bothered Slade, who had earned enough drinking money to burn from the Milk River expedition in which he arguably saved Virginia City. His wife did her best to keep him out of town but tried to no avail, although she had previously had a great influence over Slade even when he was drunk.

Gone were the days he "stood in real and deadly fear of her."[59] Soon Slade was carousing with the very miner whose early discoveries had made it all happen. Fairweather was nearly always present to watch Slade's antics, some of which were also observed by young Molly Sheehan. She later recalled Slade "galloping his horse recklessly down the street . . . firing a six-shooter in the air and whooping wildly" just before he urged his horse through some saloon doors. Worse still, Slade and Fairweather loudly ridiculed two Virginia City luminaries in songs and stories they had composed. One was deputy sheriff Jeremiah M. Fox whose wife left him for an earlier paramour. The other, Henry Edgar, struck it rich in Alder Gulch and re-conquered the deputy's wife—at least temporarily—with about $9,000 in gold dust, worth about $122,000 today. Eventually Mrs. Fox dumped them both and headed east.[60]

Neither Fox nor Edgar appreciated these musical reminders of their double duping and said so, but Slade was apparently unsympathetic. He began entertaining local saloon denizens with a new song recounting that Edgar and Fox were now drowning their sorrows in the company of a suggestively named local brothel madam, Moll Featherlegs.

It's little wonder then that Virginia City soon forgot that Slade had recently saved them from possible starvation. He began getting drunk with increasing frequency, even as his old habit of begging forgiveness and paying the damages began to wear thin with the merchants, madams, and saloon keepers who were his targets.

In February, Slade was warned that he was in danger. When Slade tried to enrich a local theater performance by shooting into the ceiling from the cheap seats, local attorney Wilbur Sanders warned him once again that he must put an end to such antics.[61] Earlier that month, a "code of morals and manners" had been approved at a Virginia City miner's meeting. Fines were to be imposed for cursing, shooting guns, and endangering the lives of others.[62]

Slade was not entirely oblivious to these changes. He stayed away from a performance of *Othello* later that month and dutifully paid fines for two infractions of the new morals codes. Judge Alexander Davis, one of four apologists who tried to keep the now hopelessly alcoholic Slade alive, had imposed the fines. Vigilance committee president Paris Pfouts, prosecutor Sanders, and Sheriff Alvin Brookie saved him from the local Virginia City vigilantes, but they had little influence over the independent Nevada City Regulators nearby.

And the Virginia City conduct code did not address the punishment for a third infraction.

In late February, Slade managed to alienate himself from nearly every man, woman, and child in Virginia City. Not satisfied with that, he resorted to sadistic torture. When some Missouri travelers arrived on Tuesday, March 1, Slade won a bet by cutting off a mule's ear as the helpless animal stood waiting for its master. Sometime earlier, he had killed a sleeping dog for no reason at all. Because there was no jail in town yet, this latest cowardice was ignored—for the moment.

The Whole Shebang

Slade disappeared until Tuesday, March 8. He returned that day with a four man gang of sorts—notably including lucky Fairweather, the very miner who had stumbled into one of the first Alder Gulch discoveries that had created the place. The "Slade gang" destroyed the Shebang brothel, then went on to the wreck the bordello operated by Featherlegs who filed a lawsuit with Judge Davis that very evening.[63] Slade spent the rest of the night roaming the streets of Virginia City singing newly composed ditties about the local vigilantes.[64] Not a good idea.

The Adventures of Copperbottom

The next morning, Slade rewarded his long-suffering horse Copperbottom with a select bottle of wine, which was refused, just before his gang commandeered the Washington Billiard Parlor, as the local betting crowd skedaddled to avoid being plugged accidentally or otherwise. After a few minutes, the swells began creeping back in, but they ran back out as the bartender pointed a Colt Navy revolver at Slade's nose to get his attention.[65] Years later, several accounts related that James Williams now sent Slade word from nearby Nevada City to go home; Slade ignored this and several similar warnings during the last few hours he had remaining on this earth.[66]

Today few remember the actress Kate Harper (or Harpe) but her performance at Virginia City that evening was remembered in Montana for many years. The mining camp had many families and children in residence by now, most being present that evening. It was a pity then that Slade stood up and urged Mrs. Harper to remove her clothes, bringing the evening to a dramatic close before he staggered off to sleep in Copperbottom's stall.[67]

Virginia City children lost their milk supply early the next morning when Slade turned over the town dairy wagon, capping the prank by pouring the last can of milk in town over the driver's head.[68]

After Slade scuffled with two members of his so-called gang in a local saloon, Acting-Sheriff Fox requested an arrest warrant for Fairweather. This was a turning point for Fox, as he was among the Virginia City vigilante leadership. He now decided to rein Slade in with extralegal means.

"We will do nothing with the warrants just now," he said. And with that he dismissed his lawfully organized posse. Something had to be done about Slade, but what? The Virginia City vigilantes decided to bring in their more numerous and strident Nevada City counterparts. Mortimer Lott went to Nevada City as Fox galloped away to find Williams. Fox found him at a place called German's Bar. Fox then returned to Virginia City where he assembled the rest of the local vigilante leadership as Williams gathered the Nevada vigilantes.

Williams later assured the Virginia City crowd that if his Nevadans took charge, Slade would hang.[69]

As the clock struck three, everyone in Virginia City except the Slade gang realized that trouble was brewing. Slade's friend John X. Beidler, himself one of the vigilante officers sworn to secrecy, tried several times to get Slade mounted on Copperbottom and out of town. Finally Beidler succeeded—at least for a few minutes. Yet, Slade soon returned to drink with some friends. Perhaps he didn't know that other friends had locked Fairweather in a store to save his life.

Slade eventually realized something was wrong. He took Judge Davis—one of his few friends left—hostage with a cocked Derringer for a few minutes. After returning to Judge Davis' office two times, Slade refused one last chance to survive. Prosecutor Wilbur Sanders begged him to ride out of town, just before the Nevada City stalwarts surrounded Virginia City at about four-thirty that afternoon. The old trailblazer was standing in the Pfouts and Russell store when Williams found him and announced "Slade, you are my prisoner." Williams then told America's first gunfighter he was about to hang.[70] And within an hour he was dead.

Later, historians noted that *none* of the conditions the Virginia City vigilantes had supposedly insisted upon in previous extralegal proceedings were met. There was no unanimous vote by "the whole body" of local miners—only the resolve of Williams and Acting-Sheriff Fox.

Much as he had many times before, Slade begged Judge Davis, and anyone else who would listen, for forgiveness. "He fell upon his knees and with clasped hands shuffled . . . from one to another of those who had been his friends, begging for his life."[71] Slade's sole remaining advocate now was Davis, who resolved to address the mob from the back of a wagon, but Williams warned "you won't more than get straightened out [stand up] in the wagon before you'll be full of bullets." Instead, Davis quietly polled a few men in the crowd and concluded that Slade was done for.

But why?

After all, the mob had simply locked Fairweather in a local

store to sober up. The answer probably lies in the myth that Slade himself had so carefully created and cultivated. Davis recalled years later that nearly everyone in the crowd was afraid of Slade. "They said, too, that if Slade were sent away as others had been . . . he would come back and kill a lot more men, and that the best thing was to hang him."

And so, Slade was the last victim of the legend he so carefully cultivated himself: the mythical gunslinger who had killed time and time again. Such a man simply could not be released alive. Davis later recalled that in the end he at last had told Slade, "I could do nothing for him."[72] Perhaps this was so, but some have speculated that a substantial portion of the crowd sympathized with Slade. These citizens might have even wished that Slade could be released but were cowed by the more militant Nevada City vigilantes.

Because the few trees at the Virginia City town site had long since been used for firewood, the crowd walked towards the Elephant Corral several hundred yards away. Even as short as Slade was, there was barely enough clearance to hang him from a beam thrown across the corral gate posts. Years later, Sheehan described what she watched as a young girl. "I recognized Slade, dressed in fringe buckskin, [standing] hatless," she recalled. "'For God's sake, let me see my dear beloved wife,'" she also heard him say three times, "in a piercing, anguished voice."[73]

Roughly an hour earlier, one of Slade's friends had galloped the uphill, eight-mile trail east toward the Spring Dale toll house Slade had built for Virginia. Now, at this very moment, she was racing her blooded Kentucky horse Billy Bay towards town. Some bystanders echoed Slade's plea to wait for her arrival, but the Nevada City crowd was unmoved and eager to return home. Someone kicked the box Slade was standing on even as he begged one last time for his life. Despite the makeshift arrangements, Slade's neck snapped and he died almost instantly.

Thus, a once heroic trailblazer of the plains was hanged because of the cowardly, abusive drunk he had become, for fear of the mythical gunfighter he had created.

And perhaps, just perhaps, a cruelly abused one-eared mule on the mend brayed obliviously in the far distance.

Chapter 11

Doc Middleton: The Adventures of Gold Tooth Charley

He was never a gunfighter, only briefly served as a law officer, and died with his boots off as an old man, but his claim to fame is remembered still: the Texas cowboy who became Doc Middleton was no doubt the most accomplished horse thief the American West ever produced.

James M. Cherry

His early background is a tangled mystery despite the bundles of letters and photographs that document his early years in Leon County, Texas. He was born James M. Cherry on February 9, 1851, near Bastrop, Texas, to nineteen-year-old Nancy Cherry.[1] The man best known today as Doc Middleton may have been the offspring of J. B. Riley, a twenty-four-year-old gunsmith who lived nearby. Earlier, Nancy bore a son, John, and a daughter, Margaret, perhaps, as the most recent Middleton biographer has speculated, to her brother-in-law John G. Shepherd.[2]

James M. Cherry Becomes James M. Riley

About seventeen months after James was born, Nancy Cherry married Mexican War veteran J. B. Riley at Lockhart, Caldwell County, Texas. Eventually, young James M. Cherry took Riley as his last name. When the Civil War began, his stepfather (or perhaps father) J. B. Riley served briefly in the Confederate-allied Texas Rangers. James Riley's older brother (or half brother) John, then about fifteen, served in Company C, 33rd Regiment of the Texas Cavalry. John may have seen action at Fort Gibson, Indian Territory; he was mustered out of service south of Waco on the Brazos River at war's end.

Only a year after the war was over, fifteen-year-old James M. Riley was indicted for horse theft in Gillespie County, Texas—the first of many such charges. He was not prosecuted, perhaps because of his youth.[3] About four years later, he became the husband of Mrs. Mary E. Edwards. The young couple lived near the Cherry and Riley families some one hundred miles from Twin Sisters in Blanco County, Texas.

Rumors and traditions in the years since have attributed three murders to young James Riley; he told one such story about himself about a decade later. Riley boasted to a brother-in-law in Nebraska that he had once killed a black cowhand back in Texas. However, his principal modern biographer found no substantiation for this.[4]

A Jim Riley of similar age killed the town marshal of Newton, Kansas, on August 11, 1871, but Doc Middleton's most recent biographer argues that James Riley was most likely in Coryell County, Texas, at that time. And if so, he was busy stealing horses. A James M. Riley was indicted for such crimes on October 31, 1872; letters he sent from Denison City (now Denison), Texas, in late June 1873, intimate that he was in "a heap of trouble" and homesick.

He was indicted on March 19, 1874, for stealing a gelding worth $75 from a woman named Mary Jacobs. His stepfather (or father) J. B. Riley posted a $500 surety bond for young Riley, who promptly bolted. Later, he was charged with three counts of

Doc Middleton on far right

horse theft with his cousin Lewis Bell in Cooke County, Texas, on the Indian Territory border. After conviction, Riley escaped the penitentiary at Huntsville in mid-September 1875, but he was quickly captured.

His modern biographer has noted that Riley's brother (or half brother) Thomas Riley was charged with horse theft in November 1876. Their brother (or half brother) John Riley stayed clear of criminality and dealt in land.[5] Perhaps John Riley encouraged young James to join a cattle drive rather than returning to horse theft.

James M. Riley Becomes Doc Middleton

James M. Riley changed his name to David C. Middleton in April or May 1876. This choice of names has inspired rampant speculation but little verifiable fact. Riley had an uncle named Crockett Riley, most likely a namesake of the famous frontiersman who died at the Alamo. Perhaps this inspired James to take the fictitious given name David and initial "C." And his murky connection with a Texas Middleton family might have inspired the surname. More mysterious still is his nickname; the most plausible explanation to date has been the possibility that he served as a horse doctor of sorts while droving as a cowboy.

Capt. James H. Cook's 1923 memoirs mentioned meeting Doc Middleton on the northern plains in the summer of 1876 with John Riley, whom Cook misidentified as "Joe."

Doc Middleton cared little for dirty and difficult cattle work. According to Cook, "He preferred to spend his time gambling."[6] And yet later in Nebraska, his "cultured appearance and general bearing . . . were noted by all who knew him and did much to build his legend."[7]

This was not long before he may have served a six-month sentence for larceny as "A. Wallace" at the Fort Madison, Iowa, prison (as is discussed later in this chapter). More certainly, that fall Middleton worked on a cattle ranch near Cheyenne, Wyoming, operated by William Irvine. Middleton thanked his employer by stealing several horses from his Horse Creek Ranch and moving on.

Later that year, in December 1876, while teamed with John Baldridge, George Smith, and Texas horse thief Ed Scurry, Middleton stole more horses and galloped back towards Kansas, chased by a classic, worthy-of-fiction posse led by stock detective William C. Lykens. The men were chased some 140 miles east to Jack Slade's old haunts at Julesburg, Colorado. Scurry, Smith, and Middleton abandoned the stolen horses some twelve miles outside of town and separated.

Middleton was later captured, but only after exchanging potshots with the posse; according to one account, Lykens charged Middleton on horseback and took him into custody.

Having bagged Middleton, the posse rode towards Sidney, Nebraska, where Middleton had killed a man some eleven months earlier, on January 13, 1877.

Years later, S. D. Butcher interviewed Middleton for his *Pioneer History of Custer County*. Because Middleton threatened to kill the historian if he was named in the narrative, Butcher chose to identify Doc Middleton as "Dick Milton" while describing what happened on "soldier's night" at Joe Lane's Dance Hall in Sidney that cold winter evening. Only military men were allowed to dance with those few women available for the soiree, and:

> In a moment everything was confusion and uproar in the place . . . two men were locked in a fierce struggle. The music ceased and a stampede was made for that part of the room in which the fight was going on. Milton was getting the best of his antagonist when the other soldiers in the room took a hand in the fight and kicked and beat the herder ["Milton"] unmercifully. The sharp report of a revolver was heard in the melee and the sergeant fell back into the arms of one of his friends.[8]

Three days later, the January 16, 1877, *Cheyenne Daily Leader* provided more detail about the combatants, reporting that, "In a row between a lot of soldiers and teamsters Sunday night, Private James Keith [Keefe] of Co. C, 5th Cavalry was shot and instantly killed."

Middleton escaped by walking to a stage stop north of Sidney; he rode as far as Fort Robinson in the extreme northeast corner of Nebraska wearing a borrowed buffalo robe. He was nowhere to be found on April 7, 1877, when "Dock Middleton" was indicted for second-degree murder.[9]

Middleton was hardly the only legendary westerner to operate in Nebraska. Sixteen years earlier, Rock Creek Station, a stage depot near present-day Fairbury, became the unlikely setting for James Butler "Wild Bill" Hickok's frequently misreported July 12, 1861, confrontation with three *unarmed* men.

"Come out and fight fair," David Colbert McCanles (McCanless) supposedly said, just before "Wild Bill" Hickok shot him dead from behind a lace curtain or blanket partition inside the Rock Creek Station. There are several versions of why McCanles and his hapless "gang" of two were there, but there is no dispute as to who else was killed that day. James Woods, a McCanles cousin, was mortally shot just before station master Horace Wellman smashed his skull with a garden hoe. McCanles employee James Gordon saw all this and ran for his life. He didn't get far.

Station stock tender "Doc" Brink chased Gordon down with some help from Gordon's own blood-hound and finished him with a shotgun. Hickok, Wellman, and Brink were tried for murder in Beatrice, Nebraska, some forty miles south of Lincoln but were acquitted on grounds of self-defense. And then the legends began.

The most fantastic version of these events has Hickok single-handedly killing "ten men in an encounter that must be one of the goriest fights in Western legend."[10] In yet another version, Hickok shot McCanles at the station door, but only after offering him a drink of water.

And still another variation, supposedly based on court records, suggests that McCanles was not shot by Hickok at all. According to this theory, Horace Wellman shot McCanles in a dispute between the two over money which Wellman's employer, Russell, Majors, and Waddell, owed McCanles for purchase of the adjoining East Rock Creek Ranch.[11]

Sam Bass was yet another notorious gunfighter who operated in Nebraska. Some five months after Doc Middleton was indicted on September 18, 1877, the Sam Bass gang robbed a train at Big Springs, Nebraska of about $60,000, worth nearly $1.2 million today.[12] Railroad magnate Leland Stanford, the founder of Stanford University, was among the passengers that day.[13]

Middleton's modern biographer has speculated that Middleton's disappearance during most of 1877 is perhaps explained by the six-month stretch at the Fort Madison, Iowa, prison served by one "A. Wallace" for a theft in Henry County, Iowa.[14] "Wallace" was released in August, but Middleton was jailed in Sidney for horse theft by December. His jailers apparently did not know—or perhaps did not care—about the second-degree murder charges that had been pending since April 1877. It was no matter; Middleton promptly escaped.

Five months later, in May 1878, indictments were issued against Middleton, Scurry, and George Smith; the latter was captured, pled guilty, and was sentenced to one year in the Nebraska penitentiary. The three men had stolen thirty-four horses from three ranchers.[15]

By now, the Middleton gang was well-known in northern Nebraska and the adjoining territories. And Doc Middleton received bad news from Texas in December 1877. "Don't come here," his stepfather (or father) J. B. Riley warned, "for the Rangers and the police is a hunting [sic] down all thieves and convicts and you better stay away from here until I write you."[16]

As the years went by, press focus on the Middleton gang only increased. The May 15, 1879, Oakdale, Nebraska, *Pen and Plow* called them "the Niobrara [River] Bandits," claiming they occupied "an impenetrable fortress" where a few men could defend against many times their number. This yarn is no more believable than fables about huge underground Middleton hideouts capable of accommodating large herds of horses.[17]

Perhaps these stories emerged in Doc Middleton's own lifetime because no one could understand how he evaded capture. Middleton's biographer offers a simple, far more credible explanation: a small number of men on fast horses grazed and watered in deep, timbered canyons, using field glasses; they carefully cultivated friendships to avoid arrest.

The upper Elkhorn and adjacent Niobrara River Valleys were nearly the last prime ranching areas settled in Nebraska, even as increasing numbers of gold-seekers trekked through the state on the Black Hills Road.

According to Middleton's biographer, his gang largely preyed upon Indian herds rather than those of white settlers. Black George Holt started an "outlaw ranch" for just this purpose near the Nebraska-Dakota boundary in 1878. Doc Middleton was reportedly associated with this enterprise, as was one "Little Joe" Johnson. Some say they stole Indian horses, which they traded for other stock kept at the J. R. Poor family ranch nearby. Middleton also sold stolen herds to "F. J. Franklin," in reality a Mr. Barto, who arrived on the Niobrara as early as the fall of 1877. The relationship continued until Franklin sold some of Middleton's stolen stock and kept the money himself.[18]

Indian horses became available for theft as early as November 1877, when Oglala and Brule Sioux began gathering near the confluence of the Missouri and Niobrara rivers, a mere six months after the Lakota collaborated with the Cheyenne to slaughter Custer's Seventh Cavalry at Little Bighorn. Early that December, white horse thieves stole an entire Sioux herd but lost as much as half of the stock to the Niobrara River during their escape.[19]

Doc Middleton and his gang now developed a business plan of sorts. Their ideal customer was a rancher with the wherewithal to purchase an entire herd of Indian horses for cash. This left the Nebraska Indians "in a vicious mood. They think their horses [have been] scattered all along this [Niobrara] Valley and have been sold in Columbus," according to one observer.[20]

The Indian ponies were probably sold as far away as the Platte River country, but closer as well, among the scattered settlements along the Elkhorn River. Legends and stories of that era suggest the Middleton gang distinguished themselves from competing horse thieves mainly by targeting Indian herds, doing small favors for the white settlers, and even providing law enforcement of sorts in the river valleys. Perhaps this was so.

Still, in mid-May 1878, some seventy-five horses were stolen at the agency established for the Spotted Tail band of Sioux while neighboring white settlers lost some fifteen horses to the same thieves. Two posses, one Indian, and one white, soon merged, following the trail in a southwesterly direction. The white posse could not keep up with the daily eighty-mile pace set by the Indians and soon dropped behind.

A man named Captain Wessels joined the chase and caught up with the stragglers at the Carberry Ranch near Atkinson. This merged posse encountered some of the Sioux driving back horses recovered from the horse thieves, but they soon became discouraged about recovering more and gave up.[21]

J. D. Butcher related a similar adventure in his *Pioneer History of Custer County;* Butcher described a "Milton" [Middleton] and "Ed Smith," as leaders of the gang. One Middleton biographer believed "Ed Smith" to be a pseudonym for Texas horse thief Ed Scurry.[22] That same writer also estimates that in 1878 and 1879, the Middleton gang stole about 3,000 horses, which they sold to white settlers in present-day Nebraska, the Dakotas, Iowa, Wyoming, and Colorado. One story cites an incident in which Middleton and Scurry were trapped by Sioux warriors on a bluff and forced to jump their horses into a river ten feet below.[23]

Middleton mostly stole horses from the Sioux, but he occasionally made an exception for the stock of German-immigrant brothers Henry and Charles Tienken. On one such occasion, the gang stole a $235 span of mares from Charles during a thunderstorm. The horses were tracked to a ranch some fifteen miles west of the Snake, where a rancher named McCann was forced at the point of a gun to buy them.[24]

One effort to capture Middleton was instigated by his former associate "F. J. Franklin," who raised a posse only a few months after chiseling Middleton out of money received for stolen horses. The fifteen-man posse organized by Antelope County, Nebraska, Sheriff Jeptha Hopkins included Peter Longfoot, a son of the Yankton tribal chief War Eagle. Middleton had recently relieved Longfoot of some horses during a nighttime raid in which one Texas horse thief was shot dead.[25]

Maybe Franklin knew where to look; perhaps it was even common knowledge. Somehow the posse found part of the gang with some stolen horses on Wednesday, October 9, 1878, at the Holt ranch near the Keya Paha River on the Nebraska-Dakota territory line. Middleton's brother-in-law Tom Richardson described this incident years later. Middleton supposedly watched from a distance with binoculars as Franklin arrested John Morris, "A. Mason," and George Holt. According to Richardson, a gang member known as Joe Smith talked Middleton out of shooting Franklin from a distance with a Sharps rifle.[26]

Five days later, Sheriff Hopkins, Franklin, and the posse arrived at the town of Niobrara, where Holt, Morris, Mason, and Joe Johnson were bound over for trial. They were convicted of stealing eighty-one horses in March 1879. A Middleton biographer concluded many years later that neither Morris nor Mason was guilty of anything more than being in the wrong place when the Franklin posse arrived at the Holt ranch.[27]

That fall, the Middleton gang staged yet another robbery at the Tienken place. Henry Tienken later recalled that "Two of them kept us covered with guns, another drove in our horses and the other two ransacked our cabin and trunks." And then he learned what brought the gang to his door: "Texas Charley [alias Charles Fugate, in reality William Riley, Doc Middleton's half brother] wanted to know where we had our money hidden, saying they would [use] a few Indian tricks to make us tell."[28]

William Riley was trapped and arrested after a brawl on January 19, 1879 at North Platte, Nebraska, with Sheriff Con Groner and some railroad detectives. He somehow shot off several of his own fingers before being subdued. Riley was convicted of horse theft and shooting at the sheriff, earning ten years for each offense.[29]

And soon the authorities were also closing in on Doc Middleton himself. On Sunday, April 27, 1879, Middleton and his crew were in Sidney, Nebraska, but a posse led by Sheriff J. G. Hughes of Keith County, Nebraska, was trailing only a day behind. Another account says a Texas gambler named Charley Reed lured Middleton gang member Joe Smith into Sidney from a camp just outside town, where he was shot and killed by the posse.[30] Middleton heard the commotion and escaped, but not before the posse chased him some twenty miles. One version claims poor Reed was not shot but lynched later in Sidney. Seeing no escape, he supposedly adjusted the noose himself, said "Good day, gentleman," and jumped.[31]

Perhaps all this explains why stories about Middleton abound in Nebraska. In one, he steals a horse to avenge himself against Franklin; another tale with several variations recalls Middleton saving an immigrant family stranded in their wagon when a horse died. Yet another story may be the origin of Middleton's variant sobriquet "Gold Tooth Jack." The A. J. Leach *History of Antelope County* describes a settler named Caldwell being robbed by a young man who displayed a gold tooth "when he smiled or was engaged in conversation." Apparently, Middleton stayed the night as was customary but stole a horse and left his worn-out steed behind.[32]

The Rob Roy of the Sand Hills

Years later, tramp printer John Edward Hicks described the area surrounding O'Neill, Nebraska, as the Sand Hills. He also erroneously described horse thief Doc Middleton as a cattle rustler and noted that in that region "up to that time [the late 1870s] there had been a minimum of organization on behalf of law and order." Further, "the doctor [Middleton] though lawless was a sort of law in the land." Hicks described the Middleton gang as "the pony boys" opposed by "cowboys" who were usually in trouble themselves.[33]

Little wonder, then, that the printer described Middleton as a "tall, dark man with a natural gift of leadership and a glint in his eye for those who dared to oppose him. He was a sort of Rob Roy of the sand hills and many tales were told of his helping the wretched settlers."[34] Despite Middleton's "leadership," Curly Grimes, Black Jack Nolan, and Joe Smith sometimes operated independently. The trio once disarmed Dawson County Deputy Sheriff Valentine and stole his money, guns, and horse after Valentine tried to arrest Nolan on a murder charge. Settlers constructing a sod house nearby pretended not to see the incident.[35]

Frank Slaven, known professionally as "Black Hank," was sometimes confused with Black Jack Nolan. Slaven was one of several competing horse thieves often erroneously identified as a Middleton associate. "Black Hank" Slaven stole twenty-nine horses from the Pine Ridge Agency in May 1879, prompting the agent there to send William Kellum to retrieve them for the agency, which he did.

Of course, some white settlers benefited when hundreds of quality horses were stolen from the Sioux and other Nebraska Territory tribes. This might explain why the settlers protecting Slaven tried to mislead Kellum.[36]

Still, not everyone condoned thefts from the Sioux. The *Black Hills Journal* opined that:

the interests of this entire region demand that the agents succeed in restoring [the] ponies to their original owners. The Spotted Tail Indians have been uniformly friendly to the whites during the late war. And the Red Cloud Band nominally so . . . this nefarious practice of carrying off their ponies causes a just indignation among those Indians which may at any time lead to an outbreak, when troops would have to be sent to punish the savages for seeking to recover their own property wrongfully taken from them.[37]

A Pardon for the Pony Boy

Doc Middleton wedded Mary Richardson in May 1879, as "J. M. Sheppard." The fledgling regional press soon began speculating whether reported efforts to pardon his crimes were appropriate. The daily *Press and Dakotian* took an optimistic view of Middleton's chances on August 1, 1879:

Middleton has lived in the Niobrara Valley since last fall and during his residence there, no crime has been charged against him. He is a fine looking man six feet in height, well proportioned and with a frank and manly countenance.

A gang of desperate thieves and outlaws infest the upper Niobrara Region, but it is claimed that Middleton has no connection with them.

Twenty days earlier, the July 11, 1879, *Niobrara Pioneer* offered a somewhat more realistic view:

For the last 18 months, the upper Niobrara and Elkhorn regions have been infested with a set of bandit horse thieves keeping in danger the stock of the settlers and causing trouble with the Indians. They have been daring outlaws and have free access to the whole country. Various expeditions have started out to catch this notorious gang led by Doc Middleton, but in vain.

The *Pioneer* noted that Niobrara attorney Fred J. Fox asked the governor to pardon Middleton but was turned down. According to the newspaper, the governor observed that "We do not know much of Doc Middleton's past history except where it bears a criminal point. It is quite reasonable to suppose, however, that if he is an innocent man, he would not flee from justice and become an outlaw in the wilds of the Niobrara."

The Worst Scoundrels Yet Unhung

Perhaps as much as anything, the company Middleton kept worked against his brief efforts to obtain a pardon. The August 5, 1879, *Sioux City Journal* noted that:

> Although Middleton has such a gentlemanly and even romantic bearing, he has in his band a lot of the worst scoundrels yet unhung. One of the chief of those is Jack Nolan, who escaped from jail, where he was awaiting trial for a fiendish murder. . . . And yet with all the general charges against Middleton, there are few well-defined crimes laid positively at his doors.

None of this escaped the attention of federal authorities. Several months earlier, the Department of Justice had formulated a plan to investigate the theft of Indian livestock and other offenses against the tribes, then refer the cases to local U.S. District Attorneys. On the ground in Nebraska, the Department of Justice hired William Harrison Llewellyn of Omaha, who had served there earlier as a tax collector and jailer. Llewellyn in turn recruited Lyman P. Hazen to capture Middleton. Apparently, Hazen served time at Fort Madison with Middleton or met him earlier. Whatever the connection, Llewellyn deemed Hazen capable of capturing Middleton. Atty. Gen. Charles Devens confirmed the general arrangement with Llewellyn on May 27.

Llewellyn accepted the position on May 31 and soon contacted the respective U.S. Attorneys for the Nebraska and Dakota territories. But early that June, the gang struck again. Middleton and his pony boys (or perhaps some competitors) stole about forty-five horses from the Sioux at Fort Robinson "without alarming a single red [sic], although there were 7,000 of them at hand," the *Sidney Telegraph* reported on June 14, 1879.

Four days later, the June 18, 1879, *Cheyenne Daily Sun* falsely reported that Doc Middleton "was recently killed about twenty miles northwest of Laramie" by a detective posing as a horse thief. Special Agent Llewellyn knew better. When he returned from "Doc Middleton country" on June 24, he claimed that about 150 men were stealing and marketing Indian and government livestock, using "numerous agents at different points on the line of the Union Pacific road and as far south as the Solomon River in Kansas."

No more than thirty-five men were engaged *directly* in these thefts, according to Llewellyn. Most were "Texas outlaws who from time to time drift north to Nebraska with the great cattle drives from Texas to Nebraska." He described "Doc Middleton, alias Texas Jack, alias Jack Lyons" as "chief of the active operations." Llewellyn also reported at the time that since Middleton's arrival in Nebraska, Middleton "has committed murder." He claimed to have sufficient evidence to bring in "a dozen indictments against him" and then boasted on June 14, "I think I can turn him into the hands of a U.S. Marshall [sic] within the next four weeks."[38]

Llewellyn reported from Omaha that he was returning to the Niobrara River that very day. Four days later, even as Llewellyn plotted his capture, "Doctor Middleton, Alias Gold Tooth Charley," was indicted for the theft of a single horse from A. A. Sloan in Antelope County. Whether Llewellyn knew about this or not, he arranged to meet Middleton on the Niobrara River on June 29, with Hazen acting as an intermediary.

Llewellyn claimed to represent the governor in negotiations that would lead to a pardon, when at that time the only formal charges against Middleton in Nebraska were killing a soldier at Sidney and stealing a single horse in Antelope County. Middleton was to receive a pardon in exchange for his assistance ridding the Niobrara and Elkhorn Valleys of outlaws.

After this meeting, someone stole Llewellyn's horse at the O'Connell ranch near Atkinson, Nebraska. Some suspected Black Jack Nolan. After finding another mount, Llewellyn continued his reconnaissance of the Elkhorn and Niobrara country; he discovered illicit whiskey peddling and lumbering operations that preyed upon the Indians before he returned to Omaha on July 8 .

Even as Middleton waited for word of his pardon, three of his associates committed their last known crime as a gang. Black Jack Nolan, Little Joe Johnson, and Curly Grimes robbed a post office near present-day Ainsworth, Nebraska, on the Cook and Towar Ranch. They also threatened ranch owner Ed Cook, who had earlier fired Grimes. Nolan and Johnson were captured and convicted within a few months. Curly Grimes was blown off his feet and out of this world while trying to escape into the Black Hills.[39]

None of this reduced Middleton's media footprint. A July 19, 1879, feature in the *Sidney Telegraph* described him as "The Man with the Golden Tooth," on a par with the English road agent Dick Turpin and lesser rogues Ned Scarlett and "Sixteen-String Jack." The article disclosed that his real name was Riley, said that his father was hanged for murder, claimed that Middleton had stolen more than 2,000 horses, and closed by assuring readers that "He is one of the most remarkable and successful desperadoes of the West."

That was about to change.

An Incident at Laughing Water

On Saturday morning July 20, 1879, Doc Middleton and his sixteen-year-old gang member William Albert "Kid" Wade were ambushed in northern Nebraska about twenty-seven miles southwest of Fort Randall between two small tributaries of the Niobrara River, each called Laughing Water. The plan to capture Middleton between West Laughing Water, now called Coon Creek, and East Laughing Water was somewhat elaborate, but the premise was simple. As we have seen, Special Agent Llewellyn promised him a pardon, using Hazen as an intermediary.

First, Llewellyn had handed Doc Middleton the promised pardon, a fake of course, as Wade watched. Later, when Middleton and Wade appeared to meet Llewellyn and sign some documents related to the pardon, they spotted stock detective William C. Lykens, who had once chased Middleton to Julesburg, Colorado, hiding in the brush.

And with that, the ball began. The Middleton version of the ambush was published in the August 5, 1879, *Cheyenne Daily Leader*: "I thought I heard the click of a gun in the brush by the roadside; imagining I had been mistaken, and that it was a wild turkey . . . I passed along, but had not gone more than a few feet when it clicked again. This time I was certain it was a gun."

Middleton claimed that after he slipped down on the side of his saddle opposite Lykens's hiding place, "a shot from the brush caused my horse to jump away from me." Hazen tried to reassure Middleton but then diverted his attention: "Hazen said, 'There's a man down there, see him?' I [Middleton] turned to look, and as my head was averted he blazed away at me with his Winchester rifle, the ball hitting me about two inches below the navel. I then fired two shots at him [Hazen] which were all the shots I fired. I then looked to see how I should escape Llewellyn and I saw him going for dear life over a hill away from us."

The Lykens account in the July 27, 1879, *Cheyenne Daily Leader* seems to acknowledge that an ambush may have been in the works: "Lykens allowed him [Middleton] to approach within about twenty paces from him when he drew a bead . . . with his carbine . . . it would not go off, although he tried it ten or a dozen times." Middleton heard the snapping and turned his horse in the direction from which it came, saying "By G—there's something wrong here."

This account acknowledged that Middleton shot Hazen three times before escaping. No one was killed, but Middleton soon had rewards totaling $2,000 on his head.

The Wrong Doc Middleton

Word of this encounter soon spread throughout the Niobrara country. Six days after the gunfight, the July 26 *Yankton Daily Press* of the Dakota Territory reported that the outlaw ambushed was not even Middleton. "It is quite certain that the noted Niobrara desperado was in Yankton Saturday night [when the gunfight occurred]. It was reported in Yankton yesterday that . . . Middleton was in town. As the rumor gained currency, considerable excitement was manifested and a determination developed to capture the celebrated ranger and the reward."

The imposter was hauled before local justice Roberts. With some prompting, he identified himself as a steamboat worker named James McMullen; a witness who claimed McMullen was, in fact, Doc Middleton soon paid a three dollar fine to avoid being thrown in jail for contempt of court.[40]

That same day, Llewellyn and sixteen troopers from Fort Hartsuff arrived at the Bassett ranch south of Laughing Water. Within a day, they forced Middleton's father-in-law Henry Richardson to reveal Middleton's hideout. On July 29, Middleton himself and one gang member were on their way toward Cheyenne, Wyoming, in custody.

Some fifty days later, the authorities intercepted jailhouse correspondence indicating that Middleton and others were plotting a breakout. "Two or three men can take this [jailer] without any trouble whatsoever," the letter said. Yet Middleton was somewhat desperate, saying, "It is all that I depend on in getting out of here. If you boys don't come and get me out I will never get out."[41] And in this he was right, at least for the time being. Middleton pled guilty to stealing three horses and on September 18, 1879, was sentenced to five years in prison. During a *Cheyenne Daily Sun* interview he gave twelve days later, Middleton admitted, "It's pretty hard, but I've made up my mind to take it philosophically. I expect that five years down there will seem as long as ten years on the prairie."

Middleton had no more mentioned his acquaintance with local Judge D. C. Tracy than the jurist himself hove into view. "I never expected to see you [Middleton] in this fix," Tracy quipped. The reporter noted that "After some more chin music, the judge bade Doc goodbye and walked away."

The September 29, 1879, *Lincoln Journal* reported the difference between man and myth: "Middleton in appearance is not what we expected to see. He is neither a large nor small man, and his physique does not indicate great strength. Taken altogether, he is rather a good-looking man. He has a very high cheek bones, a piercing black eye and a mouth indicative of great firmness."

Let Him Steal a Few More Horses

Middleton was released from the Nebraska State Penitentiary on June 18, 1883; he left with one finger fewer than he went in with, due to a buzz saw accident just a few days before his release. And he was faced with other changes. While he was imprisoned, his wife, Mary, had, in the casual way of the American West, simply declared herself to be divorced and then remarried. Her father, Henry Richardson, became active in a vigilante group known as the Niobrara Protective Association. Perhaps he was even involved in the disappearance of Kid Wade's father John a few days before Middleton walked away from those prison walls. John Wade was found the following spring full of holes in a shallow grave. Kid Wade was not among the mourners, because he had been lynched a few months earlier near present-day Bassett, Nebraska on February 18, 1884.

Doc didn't pine away about his former wife Mary Richardson. Instead, he eloped with her fifteen-year-old sister Rene that June, despite their eighteen-year difference in age. The Fremont, Nebraska, *Daily Herald* welcomed the couple on July 3: "Let him steal a few more horses and they will want to send him to Congress," the *Herald* spouted, perhaps without too much exaggeration. The *Daily Herald* also reported that "A grand ball was given . . . in honor of the arrival of the distinguished couple."

Middleton and his new wife lived briefly in Stuart, Nebraska. From time to time, visitors would swing by just to see a living legend. He told one star-struck couple that they had better horses than he ever stole himself. Middleton started a shooting gallery in late October and opened a series of saloons, the last in early December 1884. He and Rene eventually settled in Gordon, Nebraska.

It was here that Middleton began reshaping his public image. The town started as a camp full of tents;when permanent construction began, Middleton built his saloon on Main Street. The *Gordon Press* published a January 1885 open letter from Middleton to his new neighbors admitting that he stole Indian ponies but denying ever stealing from cattlemen or settlers.[42] This fib likely proved useful when Middleton was first considered for a law enforcement position in newly formed Sheridan

County, Nebraska. The first sheriff, Texan John Riggs, appointed Middleton in 1885 to serve as a deputy responsible for Gordon.

Middleton also went into show business; although the timeline is murky, he appeared in the show "Buffalo Bill's Wild West" that April and again the next year.[43] His half-brother William Riley, who called himself Charley Fugate when they partnered in the horse thievery busines, also had an eventful year in 1886. According to one Middleton biographer, "Fugate" was killed at Buffalo Gap, Dakota Territory, that year trying to outdraw city marshal Archie Riordan in a local saloon. Riordan later became a South Dakota politician and civic leader.[44]

Whiskey and Chickens

A reliable observer reported that by mid-December 1890, Doc Middleton was on the wrong side of the law again. Capt. James H. Cook, who had known Middleton some fourteen years, encountered him at the Pine Ridge Agency in South Dakota just before the Battle of Wounded Knee. Middleton was selling whiskey and chickens to the Indians.[45] One old-timer told a Middleton biographer that Doc herded some forty Indian ponies and ran to the southeast. A posse led by his old boss, ex-sheriff John Riggs, intercepted him and retrieved the horses.[46]

A Lesson in Small Town Justice

Middleton now had family responsibilities; his wife Rene had born him two sons and a daughter Lulu, who died at age five in 1890. Perhaps this is why he began gambling more than ever.

Middleton gambled frequently in Covington (now Sioux City), Nebraska, then a hell-hole across the Missouri River from Sioux City, Iowa. The Wednesday, March 26, 1891, edition of the *Sioux City*

Journal reported that Tuesday-night saloonkeeper John Peyson, former mayor of Covington, Nebraska, complained that he had been cheated in craps at a gambling dive called the White House. He left the place but returned later with a crony named Brown and a pistol.

Peyson and Brown stormed into the White House at 3 a.m. looking for a man named Wilson, the man running the crap game when Peyson lost.[47] Peyson found and chased Wilson through a narrow hallway. According to the *Journal:*

> just as [Peyson] emerged from the passage, someone hit Peyson, who drew his revolver and made for Wilson, who hastened to get out of his way. *Then there was a wild time,* the particulars of which are told differently by each of the eye witnesses. In the mêlée, a shot was fired by Brown, it is believed. The ball passed through Ed Owen's coat sleeve and struck Middleton in the right side, just below the shoulder blade. A moment later, Peyson was knocked senseless by a blow to the head, but who it was struck him is not known, but Ed Owens is accused of doing it.

Neither Peyson nor Brown heard the clink of silver bracelets when Dakota sheriff William H. Ryan made arrests on Thursday, March 26. Instead, White House proprietor Ed Owens was arrested in Sioux City and placed under $2,500 bond pending extradition across the river to Covington.

Of course, Middleton had something to say about the fracas. The March 26 *Journal* reported that he persisted "in the assertion that the shooting was accidental. At one time he [Middleton] told a *Journal* reporter that the pistol fell to the floor and went off, but the nature of the wound makes the statement impossible." A *Journal* article published that Friday reported, "Doc Middleton is getting along comfortably. . . . He talked very cheerfully on every point except the question of who . . . fired the shot which hit him in the side." Doc was placed under a $500 bond for assault with intent to murder; the final disposition of charges against Owens and Middleton is simply unknown.

Although the wide-open Covington gambling community was temporarily out of business, locals such as "Beefsteak Bob" soon returned to the houses of joy and gambling dens.

GTC: Gone to Chicago

About two years later Doc Middleton became a central feature in a controversial competition when John G. Mayer, the county clerk of Dawes County, Nebraska, announced a cowboy horse race from tiny Chadron, Nebraska, to the Chicago site of the 1893 World's Fair. The race, however, was apparently a joke. City fathers soon transformed this little inside joke into a national event promoted by "Buffalo Bill" Cody himself. During a March 1893 organizational pep rally, boosters decided the race would begin June 13, 1893, from the Blaine hotel in downtown Chadron. Chadron had been founded nine years earlier by Charles Henry King, grandfather of Pres. Gerald Ford. The place was named for Louis Chartran, who started a trading post on Bordeaux Creek in about 1841.[48]

The actual race distance was controversial from the start. The promoters along the route from Chadron to Chicago touted a 1,000-mile race, although modern estimates shortened the trek by 150 miles.

Despite the long distances involved, the ground rules allowed each rider only two Western-bred horses. Animal lovers from Boston to Los Angeles condemned the event. George Thorndike Angell even offered $100 to anyone who could stop it; he promised to contact ten thousand American editors about the "scandal" and concluded "I earnestly pray the assistance of all who are able in any way to assist in saving them [the horses] from the torture and our country from disgrace."[49]

The promoters offered a $1,000 first place prize, worth about

$21,000 today. Sponsors included the Colt Firearms Company and Montgomery Ward of Chicago. The Lowenthal Brothers store in Chadron presented a handsome saddle blanket and white Stetson hat to the crowd-pleasing race favorite: America's horse thief, Doc Middleton.

Sioux warriors He Dog and Spotted Wolf joined noted equestrian Emma Hutchinson to round out the field, but all three eventually bowed out.

The race started in Chadron at 5:34 p.m. on June 13 as planned. However, yet another Doc Middleton imposter captured much of the excitement. On June 23, the *Dawes County Journal* reported that an old gentleman dressed himself in a slicker and a slouch hat and then hired a young boy to yell "Doc Middleton" just for the fun of it.

A *New York Times* article filed from Valentine, Nebraska, three days later reported, "During the heat of the day, the riders have made four miles per hour, but at night . . . are nearly doubling that pace." In several places along the route, the celebrations began before the riders had even arrived. The race coursed through Sioux City and then Covington, South Dakota, where the crowds hurrahed Doc Middleton near the place he had been arrested scarcely two years before.

Middleton was in a trouble again. His "horses played out at Sioux City and he is no longer in the race," the *O'Neill Frontier* reported on June 22. Still, he did not officially withdraw until reaching Dubuque; there he and his remaining horse quietly slipped aboard a train for Chicago. Despite this, Buffalo Bill awarded Middleton fifty dollars in prize money—perhaps for old times' sake but more likely for the publicity.

Middleton returned to little Chadron in Nebraska; he moved on to two even-more-obscure South Dakota villages: Oelrichs and finally Ardmore, where he opened a saloon in about 1900. One of his suppliers was former city marshal Archie Riordan of Hot Springs, South Dakota—the very man who had killed Middleton's half-brother William Riley fourteen years before.

His fortunes were now at such low ebb that, when his second wife died in 1911, his brother-in-law had to pay the undertaker's bill.

Within two years, Middleton was keeping bar in yet another boomtown. Douglas, Wyoming, became a bustling place when the Colorado and Southern Railroad constructed a line through nearby Orin. Although liquor was illegal in Wyoming, the law did not matter much. Middleton signed a lease on October 13, 1913, and joined the hordes of saloonkeepers breaking the law by opening a dive: a "blind pig" where alcohol was sold illegally. The *Laramie Republican* acknowledged on December 3 that "there are enough unincorporated towns in Wyoming to do all the liquor business . . . demanded."

His Life Thread Parted

Middleton's saloon was shut down when two customers got into a knife fight about ten days after the Blind Pig opened for business. He was jailed because he could not pay the $200 fine and court costs. While there, Middleton contracted erysipelas and later pneumonia, which brought his life to a close Saturday, December 27, 1913. He was sixty-three.

An anonymous old cowboy waxed lyrical upon hearing that Doc Middleton was dead, without mentioning the hundreds of horses he had stolen: "Peace to the ashes of the old range-rider; may his long sleep be as free from worry as were his sleeps [sic] on the western prairie of Nebraska."[50]

One wonders what Middleton's victims might have thought of that.

Frank Canton (Western History Collections, University of Oklahoma Libraries)

Chapter 12

Frank M. Canton:
In the Paradise of the Desperado

The controversial, ruinously expensive 1982 film *Heaven's Gate* portrayed Frank M. Canton as a villain in the notorious Johnson County, Wyoming, range war. Yet, he also spent time as a law officer in Wharton—now Perry, Oklahoma—then a roaring land-rush boomtown called Hell's Half Acre full of booze, brothels, and gamblers. In fact, Canton had six careers. During his early years, while working cattle as Joe Horner, the man who became Frank M. Canton was also a cattle rustler and bank robber. Eventually, Horner reinvented himself as a cattle "detective" who carried a list of small ranchers to kill, became a law officer, and was appointed first adjutant general of Oklahoma.

When historian Edward Everett Dale discovered Canton's handwritten autobiography among other unpublished papers that Canton's widow had donated to the University of Oklahoma in 1927, Dale immediately noticed gaping holes in Canton's account of the late 1870s. Despite assurances that Canton would tell his readers the "plain uncolored truth," Canton totally omitted much of his prior life in Texas as Joe Horner.[1]

After punching cattle with Texas legend and family friend Burk Burnett, Horner partnered with William M. "Bill" Cotnam to form the Horner-Cotnam gang, which rustled cattle and robbed a post office. After he was indicted for these crimes and released on bond, Horner and his best friend Frank Lake killed a discharged soldier during a gunfight in Jacksboro before escaping together astride a single horse.

Horner was soon arrested and thrown into the Jacksboro hoosegow, but he was rescued on September 13, 1875, most likely by the Horner-Cotnam gang. Four months later, the gang robbed a bank at Comanche, Texas. Horner was arrested again less than four months later, after trying to have a bullet-proof steel vest custom manufactured in San Antonio. After escaping the local jail, known as the "Bat Cave," Horner was recaptured, convicted, and sent to the Texas state prison at Huntsville in May 1877.

Twenty-seven months later, in early August 1879, he escaped while in an outside prisoner work gang and galloped towards a new life as "Frank M. Canton," a moniker combining his best friend's given name and middle initial with the name of a small burg 150 miles north of Huntsville. The name change was hardly a surprise. After all, Henry McCarty, known to history as Billy the Kid, had become William H. Bonney about two years earlier after killing Francis P. Cahill at Fort Grant, Arizona.

Liars, Indians, and Cattle Thieves

Horner, known as Frank M. Canton, claimed in his memoirs, "In the early summer of 1878, I [was] in charge of an outfit that was driving twenty-five hundred head of cattle from north Texas to Ogallala, Nebraska."[2] In fact, Canton was in prison at that time, but he fabricated quite a tale for the memoirs published after his death. He claimed in those memoirs that he "crossed paths" with Cheyenne Indians who had killed "a number of white settlers in a swift raid across Kansas and Nebraska." This supposedly happened near Julesburg, Colorado, when in fact he was eight hundred miles away in the Huntsville prison.

Canton did eventually work for the Wyoming Stock Raisers

Association in Cheyenne. However, his claim that he was once a deputy sheriff in Custer County, Montana, is uncorroborated.[3]

His journey to Wyoming is understandable. After all, Canton followed numerous Texans attracted to the lush grazing grasses of the northern plains. The more compelling question is why a criminal of Horner's pedigree would change sides at the then-advanced age of thirty. His principle biographer Robert K. DeArment points to some clues in his prior life: "Horner greatly respected power and those who wielded it. He had tried to exert [power] as an outlaw but had failed, because, even on the unstable frontiers of Texas, the law and its enforcers were powerful enough to strike him down." Thus, DeArment reasons, Horner decided in jail "to take a different" path, one that would serve the powerful, and "perhaps acquire some of that power himself."[4]

It worked.

However, instead of joining law enforcement on the northern plains as he later claimed, Canton first became a cowboy in Wyoming. More importantly, he began currying the favor of Powder River Cattle Company manager, Englishman Moreton Frewen; Thomas Jefferson Carr of Cheyenne, Wyoming; and three sheriffs.[5] Eventually, Canton moved to the Johnson County, Wyoming, ranges grazed by the Hackney, Holt and Williams Cattle Company.[6] Two years after Horner escaped from Huntsville prison, his alter ego Frank M. Canton was hired as a cattle inspector of the Wyoming Stock Growers Association (WSGA) headquartered in Cheyenne on August 22, 1881. The WSGA secretary later described him as follows:

> Quick and active in his movements, with light hair, blue eyes that were always looking at you and good, clean-cut features. In manners he was exceedingly quiet and unassuming with a low distinct voice that [was] never heard raised above an ordinary conversational tone. There was no limit, however to his nerve, even if his ways were modest.

Conflicts between large and small ranchers had already begun before Canton joined the WSGA. Canton made his loyalties known quite early:

> A certain cattleman of this country [region] told me that if I worked for Frewen's interests the other stock men would have nothing to do with me. I informed him that I was working under instructions of the Cheyenne Association and [I] supposed for stockmen generally and would ride as far for Frewen's cows as one else's unless ordered not do so.[7]

Canton was also appointed a deputy sheriff of Johnson County in April of 1881, registered his own cattle brand in mid-December, and eventually homesteaded a 480-acre tract southwest of Buffalo, Wyoming.

The larger ranchers urged him to run for Johnson County sheriff. Despite spirited opposition, their support provided the margin of victory on November 7, 1882. Canton had now parlayed a stellar record as a $100-per-month stock inspector into a prestigious office paying more than twice that much. The rustler and bank robber once known as Joe Horner was now entitled to be addressed as "The Honorable Frank M. Canton."

Canton was a shrewd judge of potential deputies. He picked John A. McDermott to be undersheriff for his administrative skills, despite McDermott's poor gun-fighting abilities.[8] McDermott once observed a holdup in broad daylight in front of the Occidental Hotel in Buffalo and tried to make an arrest, but soon had his hands in the air with the other victims until Canton rescued him.

Canton did well as Johnson County sheriff. Years later, he wrote that the most dangerous criminal he arrested was the obscure Alonzo Edenfield, who had stolen six horses from Hackney, Holt and Williams, Canton's first employer on the northern plains. Edenfield only surrendered when threatened with death.

Canton was easily nominated for reelection and defeated his Republican opponent. He celebrated by marrying Annie Wilkerson, who was only seventeen years old. One can only wonder what Canton's new in-laws must have thought when he, however reluctantly, told them about his earlier exploits as Joe Horner.

The Jacob Schmerer murder in late March 1885 presented two very different challenges for Sheriff Canton as he first protected and then executed a convicted murderer. A young ranch hand named Bill Booth had crushed the old man's skull, strangled him, and stolen three high-quality horses from him. He was arrested by local officers at Miles City. From there Canton returned him to Buffalo, where Booth was nearly lynched before being lawfully convicted and hanged. Canton had to obtain technical advice on conducting a hanging from his friend Tomas Jefferson Carr, who was then serving as U.S. marshal for Wyoming Territory and had appointed Canton as deputy U.S. marshal the prior October.

Notorious Desperados

Jim Cummings once rode with the James-Younger gang, but he was just a shoe cobbler in Buffalo when Canton discovered his background and arrested him for the reward money. Perhaps Canton was surprised when Missouri authorities declined to request Cummings's extradition, but a bad man named Teton Jackson was already in his sights.

Jackson Hole, Wyoming, could have been named for Teton Jackson, born Harvey Gleason, but wasn't. Canton related in his memoirs that during the Sioux war, Jackson managed a pack train for General Crook, but he also stole a number of government horses and reputedly killed two soldiers while escaping from jail.

According to Canton, Jackson and his gang adopted a system "to steal ten or fifteen head [of horses] from each herd . . . scattered over a large area of the country and drive them to Jackson Hole. The owners would probably not miss their stock for months and even then would think [they] strayed off."[9]

Jackson found a ready market for these horses in Deadwood and other Black Hills mining camps. But soon Billy Hosford, a law officer in Blackfoot, Idaho, alerted Canton to the idea that they could arrest Jackson and split the reward. Thanks to an informant's tip, Canton and two deputies arrested Jackson without incident, only to have him escape from the penitentiary at Boise, Idaho, and disappear from history a short time later. Canton soon faced other challenges.

The No Wood Creek Incident

Two grizzled trappers named George McLennan and Bill Glass had been hunting in the Big Horn Mountains for years the day they encountered two young braves skinning a freshly killed dairy cow stolen from a settler. When the Indians spotted the trappers about a hundred yards away, they bolted. They probably did not know Wyoming Territory had a standing bounty of $250—about $5,000 in modern money—for information leading to the arrest and conviction of horse and cattle thieves. Sheriff Canton had offered the trappers just such a reward about a week earlier. And so McLennan and Glass finished skinning the cow, salvaged the meat, which otherwise would be wasted, and returned to Buffalo with two clues.

Stetson hats came in many styles even then, but this one was so dirty Canton had to use a magnifying glass to identify "Samuel" as the owner.[10] This was not much of a clue, but the medicine bag found next to the hat clearly indicated that the young men were Arapaho. And soon Canton was on their trail with a posse.

The evidence pointed to the Indian agency at Fort Washakie, two hundred tough miles from Buffalo. Along the way, they stopped back at No Wood Creek for more clues. They found evidence that the hunting party was much bigger than just two braves. Canton later recounted, "As we could tell from the scaffolds for drying meat and signs of teepees, the party must have consisted of nearly one hundred . . . [Chief] Black Coal and his village were camped at the forks of the Wind River." Canton went there first to enlist Black Coal's support and from there he traveled on to the agency to deal with Black Coal's rival, Chief Sharp Nose.

And it was there that Canton found and arrested Samuel, in Sharp Nose's tent, no less. The next morning the Canton posse was confronted by five hundred Shoshone and Arapaho, many in war paint, led by Black Coal and Chief Washakie, for whom the fort had been named. Black Coal offered to surrender Beaver, the second brave who earlier had been observed by the two trappers, but Sharp Nose also warned Canton that they would kill him if he tried to remove Samuel and Beaver from the reservation.

Perhaps Sharp Nose said this just to look tough because he made little effort to stop Canton from leaving the Indian camp. Later, Canton quietly arranged for the two braves to be released early from the penitentiary at Joliet, Illinois, and returned to the reservation at his personal expense.

Despite these accomplishments, Canton declined to run for a third term as Johnson County sheriff in 1886. Instead he retired from public life and ranched "under the peaks of the Big Horn Mountains in the finest climate in the world."[11] Perhaps he didn't know that great difficulties in this part of Wyoming loomed on the horizon.

Prelude to a Range War

The Johnson County War was one of the most deadly clashes of its kind in American history. Canton's description of that conflict is self-serving yet informative, reflecting the views of large ranchers—many of them English—whose previously undisputed right to exclusive free grazing was now challenged by smaller ranchers accused of being cattle rustlers and frequently described as such in historical accounts.

The larger ranchers for whom Canton worked notably included English brothers Moreton and Richard Frewen, two United States senators, and a former Wyoming governor.[12] Canton considered his successor as Johnson County sheriff to be a "good man and a big-hearted fellow, but not sufficiently aggressive to make good as a Western Sheriff." Canton observed that "the criminal element of the County was . . . handled in a loose and easy-going way. . . . In a short time there was organized the most systematic and powerful gang of cattle thieves ever known in the United States." Canton recognized, however, that "there were hundreds of honest [small] ranchers." He blamed "much of the Johnson County trouble on foremen from Montana or Texas, who would acquire their own herds" in the winter months.[13] One of their leaders was Nate Champion.

Champion and his twin brother Dudley were born near Round Rock, Texas. Nate cowboyed on the Goodnight-Loving Trail in 1881, became a ranch foreman, and somehow accumulated about 200 head of cattle, which he grazed in a canyon that later became a hideout for Butch Cassidy's Hole-in-the-Wall gang. By November 1, 1891, Champion lost his foreman job, perhaps because some of the ranchers believed he was allied with John A. and Martin Tisdale, brothers from the same region of Texas as Champion.

Canton admired Champion's shooting ability, even when the gunfire was directed at his own posse. On November 1, 1891, according to a Champion account published on November 5 in the *Buffalo Bulletin*, three men burst into his cabin, demanded his surrender on rustling charges, and then began firing. "The first shot just missed my head," Champion recalled. "As I raised my right arm from the side of the bed, I fired at the men. They answered the shot and made a hasty exit, I firing a second shot as they went out the door."

Twenty days later the small ranchers, whose leadership included Nate Champion, formed the Northern Wyoming Farmers and Stock Growers Association. Meanwhile, Canton sent his family to visit his in-laws in Chicago. A week later, the tension between small and large ranchers turned into violence.

Canton himself was considered locally to be a suspect in the late November 1891 killings of John A. Tisdale, brother of Martin Allison Tisdale, and Orley E. "Ranger" Jones, a small rancher and locally renowned bronco buster who was about thirty-three years old. John A. Tisdale and his brother Martin had attended Texas Military Institute and followed the cattle trails north to Wyoming in 1884. Canton's friend Frank Hesse, the foreman of the Frewen brothers' ranch, had quarreled with Jones at a dance near Buffalo a few days before Jones was killed. Tisdale and Jones were friendly with small ranchers who had been blacklisted by the WSGA for supporting "maverickers" who took unbranded, stray cattle as their own, a practice formerly common in Texas, from where many of the small ranchers haled.

Canton insisted that he was innocent and demanded a trial to clear his name. On Friday, December 4, Canton and two friends confronted five "rustlers" and demanded that somebody file charges. They did.

A justice of the peace conducted a one-day hearing four days later and declined to bind Canton over for trial.[14] Canton later claimed that after he was cleared someone, encouraged by an unidentified law officer now assumed to be Sheriff Angus, followed and tried to ambush him. Tisdale's friends were also rumored to have gathered new evidence against Canton, which they intended to bring in front of another justice of the peace.

Facing that prospect, Canton and Hesse left town, pursued by cattle rustlers or, as reported by the *Buffalo Bulletin,* just ahead of a posse carrying arrest warrants issued by a different justice of the peace. Canton met with WSGA officials in Cheyenne on Christmas Eve to arrange for legal representation in the Tisdale-Jones murder charges, and then left for Chicago where his family was battling diphtheria; his youngest daughter died of that disease in mid-January, 1892.

And yet there was more bad news for Canton, although it was some time before he was fully informed. He was charged with first degree murder on March 8, 1892, but the governor of Wyoming refused to request Canton's extradition from Illinois. Wyoming cattle barons posted the $30,000 bond for his trial the following year.

By March 26, the small ranchers were conducting their own spring roundup in Johnson County. The large ranchers intended to stop this "rustler" roundup, which they believed would be little more than raids on their own herds. Their Montana counterparts had developed an effective plan of action for such situations eight years earlier. Vigilante leader Granville Stuart had solved a major rustling problem in Montana with an army-sized posse and a death list of small ranchers to eliminate.

The Johnson County list of thirty-four names was later published on April 19, 1892, by the *Chicago Herald.* Two similar lists surfaced later: one in an injunction issued against the small ranchers and another reportedly found in Canton's luggage. In his memoirs Canton claimed that arrest warrants had been issued for those listed, but this was not so.[15] Gunmen were recruited from Texas to supplement local forces for this expedition.

They assembled in Cheyenne, Wyoming, where men and horses were loaded onto a special train the evening of Tuesday,

April 5. The force was under the nominal command of New Yorker Frank E. Wolcott, a former Union army major who ceded *de facto* command of the expedition to Canton the next day. Their numbers included ranchers John N. and David Robert "Bob" Tisdale, brothers who had no relation to rustler factionists John A. and Martin Allison Tisdale.

The "invading army"—as detractors soon described the Canton forces—boarded a train at Casper early the next morning and arrived at the John N. Tisdale ranch Thursday evening. They immediately began heated discussions about where to start the campaign. Canton and Hesse unsuccessfully argued that they should begin at Buffalo to avoid losing the element of surprise.

A House Afire

Instead, they started for the KC ranch where Champion lived in a cabin. The Wolcott-Canton party left the John N. Tisdale ranch for the fourteen mile trip at about eleven o'clock that evening in bitter weather conditions. Once there, a dawn deployment around the cabin surrounded whoever slept within.

Trappers Bill Walker and Ben Jones were down on their luck when they arrived at Champion's earlier, but now their luck improved. They were intercepted outside the cabin and quietly locked in a stable instead of being added to the death list. Champion's partner, a reputed two-time murderer and cow thief from Texas named Reuben "Nick" Ray, was not so lucky.

Perhaps Ray wondered why Walker and Jones had not returned to the cabin. Whatever the reason, when Ray opened the door, D. C. Booker, the "Texas Kid," fatally wounded Ray with several rifle blasts. Champion braved the lead shower long enough to drag the bullet-riddled body back into the cabin before he began recording his last hours on earth in a pocket notebook. "I don't think they intend to let me get away this time," he wrote at about noon, three hours after Ray died.[16] He heard a commotion outside as the invaders threw a rope against the cabin door in a futile effort to lure him out. At about two-thirty that afternoon, the cattlemen lost that element of surprise that had sparked so much debate a few hours earlier when one of the "rustlers" drove by the ranch.

Oscar H. "Jack" Flagg was prominent on the death list carried by the invading army that day. But at first, no one recognized him as he drove by the KC on his way to the Democratic state convention at Douglas. Flagg saw what was happening. When Scott "Quick Shot" Davis realized that Flagg shouldn't be allowed to escape alive, he fired, but was wide of the mark allowing Flagg to escape.

The invaders now realized that Flagg would alert other small ranchers. Canton argued that the force should move immediately to Buffalo, but he was overruled again. Instead of abandoning the Champion siege, Wolcott resumed his leadership long enough to have the men fill a wagon with pitch and straw—a contraption called a go-devil—then push it seventy-five yards to burn the cabin.

Inside the cabin, Champion soon wrote in his pocket notebook that "The house is all fired. Good-bye boys, if I never see you again." Within a few minutes, Champion tried to escape from the cabin but was shot down; a note was pinned to his bullet-ridden body with the warning "cattle thieves beware," while Ray was immolated within the cabin. His notebook was found in a pocket.

The invaders now began the trip to Buffalo even as ordinary settlers began arming themselves. The invaders were warned by an ally to stay away from Buffalo and consequently diverted to the TA ranch fourteen miles south. By Monday, April 11, the invaders were surrounded by citizens. But one of them had already raced to Gillette. He telegraphed both Moreton Frewen, who was then dining at the Washington home of secretary of state James G. Blaine, and Amos W. Barber, the governor of Wyoming. The governor persuaded Pres. Benjamin Harrison to help the invaders.

Thanks to Frewen, three troops of the Sixth Cavalry hurried from Fort McKinney, near Buffalo, to the TA ranch and arrived at dawn on Wednesday, April 13, in time to avert further bloodshed. A go-devil had been inched close enough to burn the invaders out of the makeshift wooden fort that they had constructed. The cavalry commander, Col. Van Horn, disarmed the invaders and then escorted them first to Fort McKinney and later to Fort Fetterman to the south. Eventually, after months of legal maneuvering, they were all released. When the principle witness in the Tisdale murder charges against Canton disappeared, those charges were also dropped. By that time, Johnson County had spent about $30,000—equivalent to about $780,000 today—on the conflict between large and small ranchers.

From Heaven's Gate to Hell's Half Acre

Despite all this, Canton eventually found his way back into law enforcement after a brief interlude as a packinghouse manager in Nebraska. His old Texas saddle partner Frank Lake had become sheriff of "Q" County—now Pawnee County—in Oklahoma Territory, whose county seat was and is the town of the same name. In early May 1894, Canton was sworn in as undersheriff, and his brother George Horner became one of Lake's deputies. They also became deputy U.S. marshals for Indian and Oklahoma Territories and were soon chasing horse thieves.[17] In that capacity, Canton frequently found himself in Wharton, Oklahoma Territory—in those days often called Hell's Half Acre, but today known as Perry.

A few months after he became a law officer, Canton traveled

south to resolve some unfinished business. Texas governor James M. Hogg issued a July 17, 1894, pardon to Joe Horner, alias Canton, based on a plea for mercy drafted by an Amarillo judge, perhaps arranged by Canton's old friend Burnett. The document understated Canton's age when, as Joe Horner, Canton held up the Comanche, Texas, bank. All of Horner's other crimes were omitted.[18]

A host of lawmen were then chasing the remnants of the Dalton gang who were now riding with Bill Doolin. But Canton was chasing the Shelley (Shelly) brothers, two small-time criminals who lived on the "Q" county border with the Osage Nation. Canton later recalled that they were wanted for murder elsewhere.[19] After being arrested for stealing a wagon, the Shelleys overpowered a guard on August 15, 1894, and escaped. Several months later deputy sheriff Cook Horton briefly traded shots with them on the Pawnee-Tulsa road.[20]

In January of 1895, Lake and Canton learned that a large Newfoundland dog meeting the description of the Shelley's dog "Bum" was living with a woman eight miles east of Checotah, Indian Territory. Lake and Canton assembled a posse and plodded through a snowstorm in pursuit. They were joined by Dr. John C. W. Bland—destined to discover the first commercial oil well in the Tulsa area—and two lawmen.

When the sun rose the following morning, the posse had surrounded the Shelley hideout, a modest twelve-by-twelve cabin in the woods. When the lawmen called for surrender, the Shelleys said they would dress and come out, but soon invited the posse to come get them. After allowing Bum and Bill Shelley's wife safe passage, the posse filled the cabin with eight hundred rounds of ammunition. When the Shelleys returned fire, Checotah City marshal John H. McCann was only saved from death by a holstered pistol that deflected a bullet strike to the heart.[21]

Confronted by this resistance, Canton commandeered a

farmer's wagon. Within minutes, the posse pushed a flaming go-devil against the cabin door.[22] The Shelleys surrendered and soon disappeared from outlaw lore.

But extreme lawlessness in Pawnee did not end with the Shelleys. One of Canton's least favorite Pawnee merchants was Lon McCool, a stable owner suspected of dealing in stolen horses. "He was an open enemy of the officers of the county and especially bitter against me." And, Canton continued, McCool also warned criminals whom law officers were hunting.[23]

Maybe this is why Canton shot McCool in the forehead with a Derringer in late October of 1894 while trying to arrest a suspect. McCool lived to file a complaint, which was dismissed when Canton testified that the shooting was an accident. Years later, Canton admitted that McCool had slapped him and Canton had shot him in retaliation.[24] When McCool lived, Canton threw away the derringer in disgust.

Soon a cadaverous cattle rustler from Iowa named Ben Cravens caught Canton's attention. Cravens was described as "bow-legged, heavily mustached and droopy shouldered" when he became a problem in "Q" County.[25] Although there are several versions of the details, Cravens and William Crittenden were caught with about twenty stolen cattle from the Osage agency in May of 1894. They escaped from the Perry jail, but Cravens was captured again and escaped again, this time from the hoosegow at Newkirk.

Canton and two deputy U.S. marshals traced Cravens back to the Osage nation with the help of an informant.[26] At sunrise, Canton walked up to the front door, demanded surrender, and kicked the door in. Cravens gave up the pistol in his hand and meekly surrendered. He was convicted and sentenced to a term in Leavenworth penitentiary but was back in Oklahoma territory by 1896.

Snookered

That was the year Canton killed Bee Dunn. Few today have heard of the Dunn brothers, but Deputy U.S. Marshal Charles F. Colcord considered Charles T. "Dal," William T. "Bee" or "Bill," and John Dunn, the "worst men that ever infested Oklahoma."[27] They came from Winfield, Kansas, to Oklahoma Territory with two other brothers in the 1889 land run.

Bee Dunn settled near Ingalls in present day Payne County and operated a meat market there, supposedly slaughtering cattle stolen by his brothers. He partnered with G. C. "Chris" Bolton in another shop in Pawnee. Dunn was sole proprietor of other shops in Perry and Guthrie. According to one source, Bee Dunn sometimes rode with the Doolin gang, as the Dalton gang survivors were now called. Other occasional gang members may have included Bill McElhanie, known as the "Narrow Gauge Kid."[28]

Canton shared Colcord's low regard for the Dunn brothers but described Bee Dunn as "a dead shot . . . the quickest man with a revolver I ever met."[29] That would explain why Canton shot Dunn dead without a moment's hesitation on the streets of Pawnee in early November of 1896. And therein lies a tale.

Two years earlier, on June 15, 1894, the *Pawnee Times-Democrat* told its readership that Bee Dunn's partner Bolton had been arrested, and a warrant had been issued for Dunn himself. Sheriff Lake and Undersheriff Canton offered Dunn and one of his brothers a way out. "We gave [sic] the Dunn boys to understand plainly that we knew they were members of the Dalton [Doolin] gang and had committed many crimes . . . but that . . . we would not prosecute them any further . . . and use our influence with United States Marshal Nix to have him promise the same thing."

Canton claimed that a Guthrie lawyer reduced this to a written contract signed by Nix. The agreement was kept secret because

"Doolin furnished many [settlers with] grocery money when they first settled in that country" and it was "almost impossible for a party of officers to travel . . . without being seen by some friend of the outlaws."[30]

Eventually the Dunn brothers made other arrangements. On May 1, 1895, Doolin gang members Charley Pierce and Bitter Creek Newcomb were killed at the Dunn ranch. Although the Dunn boys claimed that Pierce and Newcomb were killed while dismounting their horses, some who viewed the bodies suspected they were killed while sleeping. After weeks in the bush chasing Pierce and Newcomb, Canton received some of the publicity but none of the $2,500 reward money.

After this, Nix arranged for charges Canton made against the Dunn brothers for aiding outlaws to be dropped and permitted them to be appointed as federal posse men. Worst of all, not long before that, Canton's own horse was stolen in Pawnee by Doolin groupie Jennie "Little Britches" Stevens, the same famous Little Britches who was association with Cattle Annie.

Canton was little more than a bystander as other law officers finished off the Doolin gang. Other deputy U.S. marshals killed Tulsa Jack, captured Little Bill Raidler, and later put down Doolin. Canton learned that Dynamite Dick Clifton was being held in Paris, Texas, on minor alcohol charges. Trumping those charges, Canton returned Clifton to Guthrie on federal charges only to have Clifton escape from jail with Doolin and other prisoners, ruining Canton's chances for any reward money.

When Doolin was killed near Lawson, Oklahoma Territory in late August, 1896, Bee Dunn was in the posse assembled by Deputy U.S. Marshal Heck Thomas. Despite all Canton's efforts, Dunn, not Canton, collected reward money on Doolin, Newcomb, and Pierce. However, Canton got the last word.

Bee Dunn 's business partner Bolton was convicted of receiving stolen property the morning of Friday, November 6, 1896, at Pawnee, thanks to evidence compiled by Frank M. Canton. Dunn rode into town that very day. Saloon keeper Horton spotted him at the base of a stairway next to Bolton's meat market just before the gunfire started.

And this time, Canton had something heavier than a derringer. This time, a bullet to the head meant sudden death for Bee Dunn, unlike McCool who had survived such an encounter two years earlier. Canton was nearly killed that day. "Dunn reached for his gun without saying a word," Deputy U.S. Marshal Charles Colcord remembered, "But momentarily, his gun seemed to hang on his suspenders or his belt, and in that second of delay, Frank cut Bee's right eyebrow in two with a bullet."[31]

Of course, the Dunn family claimed that Bee was ambushed, but three days later, a grand jury found that Canton had acted in self-defense. This was not Canton's last close call, but it was his last gunfight. He survived an assassination plot and an argument that almost became a shooting scrape back in Buffalo, Wyoming. Canton tried to join the search for Butch Cassidy and the Hole-in-the-Wall gang after a major robbery. He became a deputy sheriff again, this time in Lawton, Oklahoma Territory. Canton even became a prospector and deputy U.S. marshal again in the Alaska Territory, where he lived in a cabin later occupied by former lawman Wyatt Earp.

Finally, he was appointed adjutant general of the Oklahoma National Guard in 1907. The West was changing, and as adjutant general Canton of all people became an instrument of reform, canceling prizefights in Oklahoma City, Sapulpa, and Tulsa, often with little or no assistance from local authorities. In February of 1913, with moral indignation and the assistance of heavily armed national guardsmen, he climbed into a boxing ring and confronted an Oklahoma City crowd replete with state legislators and local politicos to announce that the scheduled prizefight would not be held. Canton had done this before, spoiling a scheduled match between Jack Johnson and another contender for the title of heavyweight champion near Tulsa on July 4, 1911.

Similar raids in Sapulpa, Tulsa, and elsewhere culminated in a dramatic confrontation between Canton and Tulsa impresario R. J. Allison, who had scheduled a horse race with open gambling on July 4, 1914, sponsored by the Tulsa Fair Association. The county attorney reportedly left town, leaving Adjutant General Canton to enforce an injunction obtained by Gov. Lee Cruce. Local racing touts did not take Canton seriously. To the contrary, they smirked and gave him a one finger salute for the cameras. Nevertheless, the injunction was enforced with the assistance of national guardsmen carefully selected from outside Tulsa. Canton was vindicated, despite subsequent litigious efforts of the crestfallen Tulsa gambling community.

Canton died peacefully in 1927, one of the most respected and regarded lawmen of his time. Among his many notable friends was Owen Wister, author of the once famous novel, *The Virginian.* In the flexible, easygoing Oklahoma of the 1920s, few noted that years earlier Canton had quietly obtained a full pardon from the crimes of his youth.

Yet in those last years he fondly looked back on his boyhood days in West Texas when wild cattle and wilder buffalo were free to graze unrestrained by barbed wire over the finest grass in the world, "in the natural home of the cow, the land of the cowboy, and the paradise of the desperado."[32]

Notes

Prologue

1. DeArment, *Deadly Dozen,* 127, citing Ball *Lawman In Disgrace.*

2. DeArment, 148.

Chapter 1

1. Francis Stanley, *Dave Rudabaugh, Border Ruffian* (Denver: World Press, 1961), 31.

2. *Kinsley Graphic*, June 22, 1878.

3. Stanley.

4. Stanley, 156.

5. Ibid., 151-52.

6. *Ford County Globe*, May 23, 1882, quoted in Stanley, 181.

7. Stuart N. Lake, *Wyatt Earp* (New York: Pocket Books, 1994) 343-44.

8. Bill McGaw, "Loses Head In Parral," *The Southwesterner,* August 1962.

9. Stanley, 194.

Chapter 2

1. *Chicago Times,* quoted in "Hoodoo Brown" Wikipiedia.org.

2. Asfar, *Outlaws and Lawmen of the West,* 68.

Chapter 3

1. Quoted in Miller and Snell, *Great Gunfighters of the Kansas Cowtowns,* 51.
2. Miller and Snell, 52.
3. Miller and Snell, 59.
4. Miller and Snell, 59.
5. Miller and Snell, 80.

Chapter 4

1. DeArment, *Knights of the Green Cloth,* 259.
2. Ibid., 260.
3. DeArment, *Bravo of the Brazos,* 5.
4. Sonnichsen, *I'll Die Before I Run,* 152.
5. Ibid., 157.
6. Ibid., 69.
7. Ibid., 70.
8. Ibid., 74-75.
9. Ibid., 77-78.
10. Ibid., 164.
11. Ibid., 165.

Chapter 5

1. Eyewitness, *The Dalton Brothers,* 58 ff.
2. Ibid.
3. Smith, *Daltons!*
4. Latta, *Dalton Gang Days.*
5. Summary transcript, magistrate's hearing, Fort Smith.
6. Smith, *Daltons!*, 42.
7. Summary transcript, Fort Smith.
8. Ibid.
9. Ibid.
10. Ibid.

11. Ibid.

12. Smith, *Daltons!* 51-52.

13. Ibid., 64.

14. Ibid.

15. Ibid., 129

16. Ibid., 100.

17. Ibid., 101.

18. Ibid.

19. Ibid., 150.

Chapter 6

1. *Helldorado.*

2. Ibid.

3. *The Earps Talk,* xvi.

4. *Helldorado.*

5. Authors Glenn Boyer, Alford E. Turner, Ben Traywick.

6. *The Earps Talk,* 7.

7. In the film *Tombstone,* Doc says, "you're a daisy if you do," which sounds more like Holliday.

8. Guinn, *The Last Gunfight,* 230.

9. *The Earps Talk,* 70.

10. Ibid.

11. *The Last Gunfight,* 221 ff.

12. Ibid., 257.

13. Arizona Historical Society, recorded in *The Earps Talk,* 13, note 2.

14. Turner, *The Earps Talk,* ix.

Chapter 7

1. Fisher & Dykes, *King Fisher,* 6.

2. *King Fisher,* 40.

3. *King Fisher,* 44-45.

4. *King Fisher*, 53.

5. *King Fisher*, 82.

6. *King Fisher*, 118.

7. *Ellsworth Reporter,* August 21, 1873, quoted in Miller and Snell, *Great Gunfighters of the Kansas Cowtowns,* (University of Nebraska Press, 1967) 444.

8. Encyclopedia of Western Lawmen & Outlaws

9. Erdoes, *Saloons,* 221.

Chapter 8

1. Henry F. Mason, "County Seat Controversies In Southwestern Kansas," *Kansas Historical Quarterly* 2, no. 47 (1933).

2. *State v. Commissioners of Seward County,* quoted in Mason.

3. Westlund, "The Tale of Two Cities In Kansas." (Ms, Kansas Historical Society).

4. Ibid.

5. Ibid.

6. Snell, "The Stevens County Seat Controversy," Master's Thesis, K.U., Kansas Historical Society.

7. Ibid.

8. Ibid.

9. Ibid.

10. Ibid.

11. Kelly, "A Tragedy and Trial of No Man's Land." Ms, Kansas Historical Society, and 9 *Green Bag* (1897).

12. Rister, *No Man's Land,* 134-35.

13. *Green Bag,* 496.

14. H. B. Kelly, "A Tragedy and Trial of No Man's Land." 9 *Green Bag* (1897) 494 ff.

15. *Green Bag,* 497.

16. Ibid.

17. *Green Bag,* 498.

Chapter 9

1. Allen, 137-40.

2. Plummer is used here for consistency.

3. Allen, 17-19. But see Mather and Boswell, *Hanging the Sheriff,* 197-99, contending Plummer's father was Jeremiah.

4. Mather, 122.

5. Mather, 124.

6. Mather, 125.

7. Allen, 28-29.

8. O'Neal, *Encyclopedia of Western Gunfighters,* 255.

9. Pauley, 93-95.

10. *Nevada Democrat,* October 29, 1861.

11. *Nevada Democrat,* October 29, 1861.

12. *Sacramento Daily Union,* November 1, 1862.

13. Mather, 177 citing Defenbach, Volume I, 324.

14. Pauley, 106-7.

15. Stuart, *Frontier,* 223.

16. Allen, 62.

17. Thompson, *Massachusetts Magazine* (1913), 159.

18. Dimsdale, *Vigilantes of Montana,* 27.

19. Dimsdale, 28. Dimsdale identifies the victim as George Evans.

20. Langford, *Vigilante Days and Ways,* 80.

21. Allen, 73.

22. Langford, 82.

23. Allen, 78-79.

24. Langford, 84.

25. Allen, 80.

26. Langford, 97.

27. Allen, 88.

28. Dimsdale, 74.

29. Mather and Boswell, *Gold Camp Desperadoes,* 22-35.

30. Thompson (October 1913), 161.

31. Thompson (July 1913), 117.

32. Allen, 100.

33. Rottenberg, *Death of a Gunfighter,* 280; Stuart, 262.

34. Allen, 94.

35. Stuart, 266.

36. Purple, *Perilous Passage,* 188, as quoted in Allen, 101.

37. Dimsdale, 75.

38. Langford, 133-34.

39. Allen, 107.

40. Allen, 116.

41. Mather and Boswell, *Hanging the Sheriff,* 74.

42. Langford, 139.

43. Pauley, 170-71.

44. Thompson, "Reminiscences" (July 1913), 122-23.

45. Plassman "Daughter," 118.

46. Allen, 128.

47. Allen, 133.

48. Allen, 136.

49. Welch, 55, citing Joe Bailey, "The Magruder Murder," *The Pacific Northwesterner,* (Spring 1962).

50. Mather and Boswell, *Vigilante Victims,* 108-21.

51. Allen, 239.

52. Langford, 348.

53. Allen, 148-49.

54. Dimsdale, 58.

55. Allen, 154, quoting Mather, 72.

56. Langford, 150.

57. Dimsdale, 93.

58. Allen, 9.

59. Allen, 173; Dimsdale, 104.

60. Dimsdale, 106.

61. Sanders, *Beidler,* 71.

62. Allen, 195; Sanders, *Beidler,* 78.

63. *Madison County Monitor,* March 2, 1900. The oath can still be seen at the Montana Historical Society.

64. Allen, 197.

65. Allen, 210.

66. Dimsdale, 129.

67. Allen, 215; Dimsdale, 132-33.

68. Allen, 224.

69. Allen, 224.

70. Allen, 226; Thompson (1913), 181.

71. Allen, 229-30.

72. Ibid.

73. Allen, 228.

74. References to the dreary regions of the dead and a world unknown are from the 1783 Charles Wesley hymn "Am I born to die?" performed during the opening scene of the film *Cold Mountain.*

Chapter 10

1. Adams, *Burs Under the Saddle,* 49.

2. Rottenberg, *Death of a Gunfighter,* 5-7.

3. Morris, *Lighting Out for the Territory,* 59.

4. Rottenberg, xii. This chapter is largely drawn from the Rottenberg account.

5. Turner, 109-10.

6. Rottenberg, 40-42, 53; Brands, *Age of Gold,* 16.

7. Rottenberg, 59-60, 83.

8. Koch, Part 4.

9. Rottenberg, 107; 56 U.S. Congress, Senate, *Report of the Postmaster,* 35th Cong., 2nd Sess., S. Ex. Doc 1, 722.

10. Koch, Part 10.

11. Reprinted in the *Helena (Montana) Weekly Herald*, July 25, 1878.

12. Wells, 42.

13. Alderson, "Some New Slade Stories: Beatty and the Horse Thieves."

14. Rottenberg, 79, 81.

15. Gray, "The Salt Lake Hockaday Mail, Part II."

16. Wilson, "Reminiscences," 4.

17. Stuart, 150-51.

18. Twain, *Roughing It,* 80-97.

19. Rottenberg, 154.

20. *Atchison Globe,* May 26, 1927.

21. Burton, *City of the Saints*, 114.

22. Twain, *Roughing It*, 84-97.

23. Corbett, *Orphans Preferred*, 84

24. Rottenberg, 181.

25. Boner, "He Nursed Jim Slade."

26. Adams, *Burs Under the Saddle*, 55.

27. Root and Connelly, 480.

28. Root and Hickman, 74.

29. Root and Connelly, 480.

30. Rottenberg, 213-14.

31. Wells, 42-43.

32. Rottenberg, 216, quoting *Rouging It,* 217-18.

33. Ibid, 216.

34. Callaway, *Two True Tales,* 113.

35. Rottenberg, 220-22.

36. Bessette, 4-6.

37. Rottenberg, 441, note 46.

38. Callaway, 110-11.

39. Boner Interview, "He Nursed Jim Slade."

40. Rottenberg, 235. Julesburg was now called Overland City.

41. *Salt Lake City Desert News,* July 16, 1862.

42. Rottenberg, 256.

43. *Sacramento Daily Union,* August 15, 1862.

44. Rottenberg, 260.

45. *Rocky Mountain News,* August 19, 1932.

46. Chapman, 191.

47. Langford, 362.

48. Ludlow, 295-96.

49. Rottenberg, 280.

50. Rottenberg, 287.

51. Callaway, *Montana's Righteous Hangmen,* 53.

52. Callaway, *Montana's,* 122.

53. Langford, 369.

54. Rottenberg, 309.

55. Langford, 224-41.

56. Rottenberg 312; *See* Dimsdale, 168; Langford, 373.

57. Callaway, 56-57.

58. Callaway, *Montana's,* 52.

59. Rottenberg, 81.

60. Rottenberg, 320.

61. W. F. Sanders, 28.

62. Allen, 271.

63. Odell and Jessen, 77-78.

64. Rottenberg, 328.

65. Sander, *Beidler: Vigilante,* 97-98.

66. Toponce, 123-24.

67. Sanders, *Beidler,* 98.

68. Rottenberg, 331.

69. Dismdale, 109.

70. Langford, 374.

71. Rottenberg, 342; Langford, 374.

72. Rottenberg, 343.

73. Ronan, *Frontier Woman,* 24.

Chapter 11

1. Hutton, *Doc Middleton,* 9. The most recent Middleton biography was published in 1976.

2. Hutton, 9. Hutton reported that Margaret later married a gunfighter named Zach Light. This proved erroneous. Hutton, 197; DeArment, *Deadly Dozen,* 300, note 27.

3. Office of the Clerk, District Court Courthouse, Fredericksburg, Texas.

4. Hutton, 13.

5. Hutton, 18.

6. Cook, *Fifty Years on the Old Frontier,* 81-82; Cook, "Early Days in Ogallala," *Nebraska History,* 14, no. 2: 89.

7. Hutton, 7.

8. Butcher, 121-23; Hutton, 5-6.

9. Hutton, 7.

10. Rosa, *Wild Bill Hickock: The Man and His Myth,* 113-16. The version of the McCanles shooting most favorable to Hickok appears in *Bad Men and Bad Towns* by Wayne C. Lee, 113-16.

11. Faulkner, *Round Up,* 27-33.

12. Yadon, *Ten Deadly Texans,* 191-92; Gillett, *Six Years with the Texas Rangers,* 109.

13. And three years later "Texas Billy" Thompson of Knottingley, England, the brother of deadly gunfighter Ben Thompson, shot it out with Lone Star native Jim Tucker in Ogallala, Nebraska on June 26, 1880. Bat Masterson rescued Billy from the authorities and probably a date with the gallows.

14. Hutton, 30.

15. Hutton, 36.

16. Tom Richardson Interview, as cited in Hutton, 36, spelling but not grammar corrected.

17. Hutton, 44.

18. Hutton, 46.

19. Hutton, 47.

20. *Oakdale Pen and Plow,* April 27, 1878.

21. Hutton, 50.

22. Hutton, 51.

23. Butcher, 123-26.

24. Tienken Memoirs.

25. Hutton, 42, 46.

26. Hutton, 59-60; Tom Richardson interview.

27. Leach, *History of Antelope County,* 87-88.

28. Tienken Memoirs.

29. Hutton, 68.

30. Butcher, 132.

31. Ibid.

32. Leach, 82-83.

33. Hicks, *Adventures of a Tramp Printer,* 85-86.

34. Hicks, 68-71.

35. Butcher, 107.

36. *Sidney Telegraph,* July 5, 1879; *Chicago Times,* June 10, 1879.

37. As quoted in Hutton, 93-94.

38. Hutton, 107.

39. *Omaha Daily Bee,* October 20, 1879.

40. Hutton, 132.

41. *Omaha Daily Bee,* September 23, 1879. The spelling has been modernized and corrected.

42. Hutton, 160-61.

43. Hutton, 164-65.

44. Kinsbury, *History of Dakota Territory,* 468.

45. Cook, James H. "Early Days in Ogallala," *Nebraska History* 14, no. 2, 91-92.

46. Hutton, 166-67.

47. Emphasis supplied.

48. Today, Chadron has a population of 5,000 and hosts the American Museum of the Fur Trade.

49. *O'Neill, Frontier,* June 22, 1893 (italics in original).

50. Hutton, 221.

Chapter 12

1. Dale edited the Canton memoirs initially published in 1930, three years after Canton's death.

2. Canton, *Frontier Trails,* 26.

3. DeArment, *Alias Frank Canton,* 50.

4. DeArment, *Alias Frank Canton,* 49, Ch. 3 note 1. However, information Canton's wife provided for Canton's death certificate listed his middle name as Melvin.

5. DeArment, *Alias Frank Canton* 45.

6. Bard, *Horse Wrangler,* 4.

7. DeArment, *Alias Frank Canton,* 51-52.

8. Canton, *Frontier Trails,* 35.

9. Canton, *Frontier Trails,* 36-37.

10. Canton, *Frontier Trails,* 56.

11. Canton, *Frontier Trails,* 77.

12. O'Neal, *Johnson County War,* 9-10.

13. Canton, *Frontier Trails,* 79-81.

14. DeArment, *Alias Frank Canton,* 112.

15. Canton, *Frontier Trails,* 87-88; DeArment, *Alias Frank Canton,* 121.

16. DeArment, *Alias Frank Canton,* 125.

17. *Pawnee Democrat,* May 18, 1894.

18. *Ex Parte Horner,* July 14, 1894, Governor's Pardon Papers.

19. Canton, *Frontier Trails,* 122.

20. DeArment, *Alias Frank Canton,* 160.

21. Canton, *Frontier Trails,* 124; *Pawnee Times-Democrat,* February 8, 1895.

22. Canton, *Frontier Trails,* 122-31.

23. Canton, *Frontier Trails,* 116-17.

24. *Pawnee Times-Democrat,* November 2, 1894.

25. Shirley, *West of Hell's Fringe,* 366-67.

26. Shirley, "Killer with Two Faces," 14. U.S. Marshal E. D. Nix recalled that a woman opened the door, revealing Cravens inside. Nix, *Oklahombres,* 137-41.

27. Colcord, *Autobiography,* 170.

28. Hanes, *Bill Doolin, Outlaw, O.T.,* 64-65. McElhanie was supposedly as tall as an iron rail.

29. Canton, *Frontier Trails,* 111.

30. Canton, *Frontier Trails,* 111.

31. Colcord, *Autobiography,* 171.

32. Paraphrased from Canton, *Frontier Trails,* xviii.

Bibliography

Articles

Baily, Joe. "The Magruder Murder." *The Pacific Northwesterner* 7, no. 2 (Spring 1962).

Cook, James H. "Early Days in Ogalalla." *Nebraska History* 14, no. 2.

DeArment, Robert K. "Another Wyatt Earp Tale: Myth or Fact." *Wild West History Association* 3, no. 6 (December 2010).

DeArment, Robert K. "Wyatt Whoppers." *Wild West History Association* 2, no. 5 (October 2010).

"Early Days in Ogallala." *Nebraska History* 14, no. 2: 89.

Evans, Bill. "Gunfight in the Whetstone Mountains." *Wild West History Association* I, no. 6 (December 2008).

Mason, Henry F. "County Seat Controversies in Southwestern Kansas," *Kansas Historical Quarterly,* no. 47 (1933).

Root, George and Russell K. Hickman. "Pike's Peak Express Companies, Part III: The Platte Route." *Kansas Historical Quarterly* 13, no. 8 (November 1945).

Shirley, Glenn. "Killer with Two Faces." *True West* 36, no. 6 (June 1989).

Smith, Robert Barr. "King Fisher." *Wild West* (1996).

———. "Murder By Moonlight." *Wild West* (June 2003).

———. "No God West of Fort Smith." *Wild West* (October 1991).

———. "The Short, Nasty Life of Dave Rudabaugh." *Wild West* (June 1996).

————. "The Worst Man I Ever Met," printed as "Killer In Deacon's Clothing." *Wild West* (August 1992), reprinted in *The Best of Wild West*. Cowles History Group, 1996.

Thompson, Francis. "Reminiscences of Four Score Years." *Massachusetts Magazine* 5, Supplement (January 1912) 1:141-67; 6 (July 1913) 3; (October 1913) 4:114-90; 7 (January 1914) 1:11-29.

Wilson, James W. "Reminiscences of Overland Days." *Sons of Colorado* 1, no. 12 (May 1907).

Young, Roy. "Wyatt Earp, Outlaw of the Cherokee Nation." *Wild West History Association* 2, no. 5 (December 2008).

Books

Adams, Ramon F. *Burs Under the Saddle: A Second Look at Books and Histories of the West*. Norman: University of Oklahoma Press, 1964.

Allen, Frederick. *A Decent Orderly Lynching: the Montana Vigilantes*. Norman: University of Oklahoma Press, 2009.

Asfar, Dan, II. *Outlaws and Lawmen of the West*. Renton, WA: Lone Pine Publishing, 2001.

Bard, Floyd C, as told to Agnes Wright Spring. *Horse Wrangler: Sixty Years in the Saddle in Wyoming and Montana*. Norman: University of Oklahoma Press.

Brands, H. W. *The Age of Gold: the California Gold Rush and the New American Dream*. New York: Doubleday, 2005.

Breakenridge, William M. *Helldorado*. Lincoln: University of Nebraska Press, 1992.

Burns, Walter Noble. *Tombstone*. New York: Grosset and Dunlap, 1929.

Burton, Sir Richard F. *The City of the Saints and Across the Rocky Mountains to California*. London: Longman, Green, Longman, and Roberts, 1862.

Butcher, S. D. *Pioneer History of Custer County.* Chicago: Sage Books, 1965.

Butler, Ken. *More Oklahoma Renegades.* Gretna, LA: Pelican Publishing Company, 2007.

Cain, Del. *Lawmen of the Old West, the Bad Guys.* Plano, TX: Republic of Texas Press, 2001.

Corbett, Christopher. *Orphans Preferred: the Twisted Truth and Lasting Legend of the Pony Express.* New York: Broadway Books, 2003.

Cunningham, Eugene. *Triggernometry.* Caldwell, ID: Caxton Printers, 1989.

Callaway, Lew L. *Montana's Righteous Hangman: The Vigilantes in Action.* Norman: University of Oklahoma Press, 1982.

Callaway, Lew L. *Two True Tales of the Wild West.* Oakland, CA: Maud Gonne Press, 1973.

Chapman, Arthur. *The Pony Express: The Record of a Romantic Adventure in Business.* New York: G. P. Putnam's Sons, 1932.

Canton, Frank M. *Frontier Trails: The Autobiography of Frank M. Canton.* Edited by Edward Everett Dale. Norman: University of Oklahoma Press, 1966.

Colcord, Charles Francis. *The Autobiography of Charles Francis Colcord,* 1859-1934. Tulsa: Privately Printed, 1970.

Cook, James H. *Fifty Years on the Old Frontier as Cowboy, Hunter, Guide, Scout and Ranchman.* Norman: University of Oklahoma Press, 1954.

Dalton, Emmett. *Beyond the Law.* Coffeyville, KS: Coffeyville Historical Society, n.d.

DeArment, Robert K. *Alias Frank Canton.* Norman: University of Oklahoma Press, 1996.

DeArment, Robert K. *Deadly Dozen: Twelve Forgotten Gunfighters of the Old West.* Norman: University of Oklahoma Press, 2007.

DeArment, Robert. *Bravo of the Brazos*, Norman, OK: University of Oklahoma Press, 2002.

DeArment, Robert. *Forgotten Gunfighters of Old West*. Vol. 2. Norman, OK: University of Oklahoma Press, 2007.

DeArment, Robert. *Twelve Forgotten Gunfighters of the Old West*. Norman, OK: University of Oklahoma Press, 2003.

Defenbach, Bryon. *Idaho: the Place and Its People*. 2 vols. Chicago: American Historical Society, 1933.

Dimsdale, Thomas J. *The Vigilantes of Montana*. Norman: University of Oklahoma Press, 1953.

Erdoes, Richard. *Saloons of the Old West*. New York, NY: Gramercy Press, 1979.

Elman, Robert. *Badmen of the West*. The Ridge Press, 1974.

Eyewitness. *The Dalton Brothers*. New York: Frederick Fell, 1954.

Faulkner, Virginia. *Round Up*. Lincoln: Bison Books, University of Nebraska Press, 1957.

Fisher, O. C. and J. C. Dykes. *King Fisher, His Life and Times*. Norman, OK: University of Oklahoma Press, 1966.

Fulton, Maurice G. *History of the Lincoln County War*. Tucson, AZ: University of Arizona Press, 2008.

Garrett, Pat F. *The Authentic Life of Billy the Kid*. New York: Indian Head Books, 1994.

Gillett, James B. *Six Years with the Texas Rangers, 1875 to 1881*. New Haven: Yale University Press, 1925.

Guinn, Jeff. *The Last Gunfight: The Real Story of the Shootout at the O.K. Corral and How It Changed the American West*. New York: Simon & Schuster, 2011.

Hanes, Co. Bailey C. *Bill Doolin, Outlaw, O.T.* Norman: University of Oklahoma Press, 1968.

Hicks, John Edward. *Adventures of a Tramp Printer, 1880-1890*. Kansas City: Midamericana Press, 1950.

Hutton, Harold. *Doc Middleton: Life and Legends of the Notorious Plains Outlaw.* Chicago: Sage Books, 1974.

Kinsbury, George Washington. *History of Dakota Territory,* Vol. 5.

Langford, Nathaniel. *Vigilante Days and Ways.* Missoula: Montana State University Press, 1957.

Lake, Stuart N. *Wyatt Earp.* New York: Pocket Books, 1994.

Latta, Frank. *Dalton Gang Days.* Santa Cruz, CA: Bear State Books, 1976.

Leach, A. J. *A History of Antelope County, Nebraska from its First Settlement in 1868 to the Close of the Year 1883.* Chicago: R. R. Donnelly & Sons, 1909.

Lee, Wayne C. *Bad Men and Bad Towns.* Caldwell, ID: The Caxton Printers, Ltd., 1993.

Ludlow, Fitz Hugh. *The Heart of the Continent: A Record of Travel across the Plains and in Oregon.* New York: Hurd and Houghton, 1870.

Masterson, W. B. (Bat), *Great Gunfighters of the Western Frontier.* Mineola, NY: Dover Publication, 2009.

Mather, R. E. and F. E. Boswell. *Gold Camp Desperadoes: Violence, Crime and Punishment on the Mining Frontier.* San Jose: History West Publishing, 1990.

Mather, R. E. and F. E. Boswell. *Hanging the Sheriff: a Biography of Henry Plummer.* Salt Lake City: University of Utah Press, 1987.

Mather, R. E. and F. E. Boswell. *Vigilante Victims: Montana's 1864 Hanging Spree.* San Jose: History West Publishing, 1991.

McPherson, M. A. and Eli McLaren. *Outlaws and Lawmen of the Old West.* Vol. 1. Renton, WA: Lone Pine Publishing, 2000.

Metz, Leon Claire. *Pat Garrett.* Norman, OK: University of Oklahoma Press, 1974.

Metz, Leon Claire. *The Shooters.* El Paso, TX: Mangan Books, 1976.

Miller, Nyle H. and Joseph W. Snell. *Great Gunfighters of the Kansas Cowtowns.* Lincoln: University of Nebraska Press, 1967.

Morris, Roy. *Lighting out for the Territory: How Samuel Clemens Headed West and Became Mark Twain.* New York: Simon & Schuster, 2010.

Nash, Jay Robert. *Encyclopedia of Western Lawmen and Outlaws.* New York: DaCapo Press, 1994.

Neal, Bill. *Getting Away With Murder on the Texas Frontier.* Lubbock, TX: Texas Tech University Press, 2006.

Nix, E. D. *Oklahombres.* Lincoln: The University of Nebraska Press, 1993.

Nolan, Frederick. *The Lincoln County War.* Norman, OK: University of Oklahoma Press, 1992.

O'Dell, Roy P., and Kenneth C. Jessen. *An Ear in His Pocket: the Life of Jack Slade.* Loveland, CO: J. V. Publications, 1996.

O'Neal, Bill. *Encyclopedia of Western Gunfighters.* Norman: University of Oklahoma Press, 1979.

O'Neal, Bill. *Henry Brown, the Outlaw-Marshal.* College Station, Texas: Creative Publishing Co., 1980.

O'Neal, Bill. *The Johnson County War.* Austin, TX: Eakin Press, 2004.

Parsons, Chuck and Marianne E. Hall Little. *Captain L.H. McNelly.* Austin, TX: State House Press, 2001.

Pauley, Art. *Henry Plummer: Lawman and Outlaw.* White Sulphur Springs, MT: The Meagher County News, 1980.

Purple, Edwin Ruthven. *Perilous Passage: a Narrative of the Montana Gold Rush, 1862-1863.* Helena: Montana Historical Press, 1995.

Rasch, Phillip K. *Warriors of Lincoln County.* Stillwater, OK: National Association for Outlaw and Lawman History, 1998.

Rister, Carl C. *No Man's Land.* Norman: The University of Oklahoma Press, 1948.

Rosa, Joseph G. *The Gunfighter: Man or Myth?* Norman: University of Oklahoma Press, 1969.

Rosa, Joseph G. *Wild Bill Hickock: the Man and His Myth.* Lawrence: University of Kansas Press, 1996.

Rottenberg, Dan. *Death of a Gunfighter: The Quest for Jack Slade, the West's Most Elusive Legend.* Yardley, PA: Westholme Publishing, LLC, 2008.

Ronan, Margaret. *Frontier Woman: the Story of Mary Ronan as Told to Margaret Ronan.* Edited by H. G. Merriam. Missoula: University of Montana, 1973.

Root, Frank A. with William E. Connelly. *The Overland Stage to California.* Topeka, KS: 1901. Reprint, Glorietta, NM: Rio Grande Press, 1970.

Sanders, Helen F. *A History of Montana.* Chicago: Lewis Publishing, 1913.

Sanders, Helen F., ed. *X. Beidler: Vigilante.* Norman: University of Oklahoma Press, 1957.

Sanders, Wilbur F. "The Story of George Ives." In *X. Beidler: Vigilante,* edited by Helen Sanders. Norman: University of Oklahoma Press, 1957.

Sanders, W. F. and Robert T. Taylor. *Biscuits and Badmen: the Sanders Story in Their Own Words.* Butte, MT: Editorial Press, 1982.

Shirley, Glenn. *Red Yesterdays.* Wichita Falls, TX: Nortex Press, 1997.

Shirley, Glenn. *West of Hell's Fringe.* Norman, OK: University of Oklahoma Press, 1978.

Smith, Robert Barr. *Daltons!* Norman, OK: University of Oklahoma Press, 1996.

Smith, Robert Barr. *Last Hurrah of the James Younger Gang.* Norman, OK: University of Oklahoma Press, 2001.

Smith, Robert Barr. *Outlaw Tales of Oklahoma.* Guilford, CT: Globe Pequot Press, 2008.

Smith, Robert Barr. *Tough Towns.* Guilford, CT: Globe Pequot Press, 2007.

Sonnichsen, C. L. *Billy King's Tombstone*. Caldwell, ID: Caxton Printers, 1942.

———. *I'll Die Before I Run*. Lincoln: The University of Nebraska Press, 1988.

Stanley, Francis. *Dave Rudabaugh, Border Ruffian*. Denver: World Press, 1961.

Stuart, Granville. *Forty Years on the Frontier*. Vol. 1. Edited by Paul C. Phillips. Cleveland: Arthur H. Clark, 1925.

Toponce, Alexander. *Reminiscences of Alexander Toponce*. Norman: University of Oklahoma Press, 1971.

Traywick, Ben T. *The Chronicles of Tombstone*. Tombstone: Red Marie's Bookshop, 1990.

Turner, Alford E. *The Earps Talk*. College Station, TX: The Early West, 1992.

Turner, Erin H., ed. *Badasses of the Old West: True Stories of Outlaws on the Edge*. Guilford, CT: Globe Pequot Press, 2010.

Twain, Mark. *Roughing It*. Pleasantville, NY: The Readers Digest Association, Inc., 1994.

Wells, Polk. *Life and Adventures of Polk Wells, the Notorious Outlaw*. Halls, MO: G. A. Warnica, 1907.

Wilson, R. Michael. *Encyclopedia of Stagecoach Robbery in Arizona*. Las Vegas: Rama Press, 2003.

Yadon, Laurence J. and Dan Anderson. *Arizona Gunfighters*. Gretna, LA: Pelican Publishing Company, 2010.

Yadon, Laurence J. and Dan Anderson. *Ten Deadly Texans*. Gretna, LA: Pelican Publishing Company, 2009.

Yadon, Laurence J. and Robert Barr Smith. *Old West Swindlers*. Gretna, LA: Pelican Publishing Company, 2011.

Government Publications
56 U.S. Congress, *Report of the Postmaster*. 35th Cong., 2nd Sess., S. Ex. Doc 1, 722.

Office of the Clerk, District Court Courthouse, Fredericksburg, Texas.

Newspapers
Atchison (KS) Globe
Salt Lake City Desert News
Helena (MT) Weekly Herald
Madison County (MT) Monitor
Nevada Democrat
Oakdale (NE) Pen and Plow
Oklahoma State Capital
Omaha Daily Bee
O'Neill (NE) Frontier
Pawnee (OK) Democrat
Rocky Mountain News
Sacramento Daily Union

Other Sources
Kansas Historical Society papers.
Plassman, Martha Edgerton. "Judge Edgerton's Daughter," MS. 78, Montana Historical Society Archives (undated).
Snell, Joseph W. "The Stevens County Seat Controversy." Master's Thesis, University of Kansas, Kansas Historical Society.
Tienken Memoirs (Private Collection of Harold Hutton).

Acknowledgments

Research for this project was conducted as part of our studies for previous works. A number of organizations have assisted the authors in the research for these projects over the past seven years. These institutions included but were not limited to: the Flying Fingers Typing Service, Sand Springs, Oklahoma; Texas Ranger Museum, Waco, Texas; the Haley Library; Harris County Public Library; Dallas Public Library; El Paso Public Library; Fort Bend County Public Library; Houston City Public Library; Young County Historical Commission; Tulsa City-County Library; Oklahoma Historical Society; Western History Collection; University of Oklahoma Library; Oklahoma Heritage Association; Oklahoma Centennial Commission; Woolaroc Museum, Bartlesville, Oklahoma; Texas Jack Association; Oklahombres, Inc.; Oklahoma Outlaws; Lawmen History Association; Tulsa Police Department; Public Library, Enid, Oklahoma; Beryl Ford Collection, Tulsa; Oklahoma Publishing Company; Lenapah Historical Society; the University of Tulsa; Kansas State Historical Society; Will Rogers Museum; National Cowboy Hall of Fame; Gilcrease Museum; Enid Public Library; Boone County Heritage Museum, Harrison, Arkansas; and the Lincoln Heritage Trust, Lincoln, New Mexico.

Individuals who have assisted us in these projects have included Bill O'Neal, Nancy Samuelson, Bob Ernst, Bob Alexander,

Robert K. DeArment, David Johnson, Chuck Parsons, Rick Miller, Phil Sanger, Ron Trekell, Armand DeGregoris, John R. Lovett, Mike Tower, Michael and Suzanne Wallis, Rod Dent, Gary Youell, Phil Edwards, Terry Zinn, Michael Koch, Diron Ahlquist, Willie Jones, Clyda Franks, Emily Lovick, Lisa Keys, Harvey Schell, Joseph Calloway Yadon—ardent researcher and author's son, Danielle Williams, Irene and Larry Chance, Glendon Floyd, Curt Johnson, Dee Cordry, Rik Helmerich, and Herman Kirkwood. Thanks are also due Helen J. Gaines, Jim Bradshaw, Adrienne Grimmett, Beth Andreson, Jim Hamilton, Dana Harrison MacMoy, Mary Phillips, Stacy M. Rogers, Rand McKinney, Jana Swartwood, Gini Moore Campbell, and Phillip W. Steele, Dorman Holub, Sgt. Kevin F. Foster, Jane Soutner, Brian Burns, Jim Bradshaw, Ashley Schmidt and Dana Brittain, Roy Young, and Marshall Trimble, the official state historian of Arizona.

Lastly, without the patience of our families, this book would not have been possible.

Index